Friedrich Dürrenmatt

PLAYS AND ESSAYS

The German Library : Volume 89

Volkmar Sander, General Editor

Friedrich Dürrenmatt

PLAYS
AND ESSAYS

Edited by Volkmar Sander
Foreword by Martin Esslin

CONTINUUM · NEW YORK

1982

The Continuum Publishing Company
575 Lexington Avenue, New York, NY 10022

Copyright © 1982 by The Continuum Publishing Company

Foreword © 1982 by Martin Esslin
Introduction © 1982 by Volkmar Sander

Printed in the United States of America

Library of Congress Cataloging in Publication Data

Dürrenmatt, Friedrich.
Plays and essays.

(The German library ; v. 89)
Contents: Romulus the great—The visit—21 points
to The physicists—[etc.]
I. Sander, Volkmar. II. Title.
PT2607.U493A6   1982   832'.914   81-22184
ISBN 0-8264-0257-7   AACR2
ISBN 0-8264-0267-4 pbk

For acknowledgments of previously published material, see page 313,
which constitutes an extension of the copyright page.

Contents

Foreword

A t the outbreak of World War II Friedrich Dürrenmatt was eighteen years old. The German-speaking Swiss of his generation were the only inhabitants of the German cultural sphere of Central Europe not to be dragged into the vortex of desctruction and hardship, bombing, frontline fighting, starvation, and omnipresent death that engulfed their contemporaries. Switzerland remained a haven of peace and affluence throughout the entire period. And, what is even more significant, the young Swiss of that generation were the only ones in the German-speaking world to remain entirely free from the pressures of Nazi indoctrination, relentless propaganda, and brainwashing, and thus in continuing contact with the mainstream of the German cultural tradition, which—with Goethe, Schiller, Fontane, or Thomas Mann—had always retained a strongly humanistic bias.

Hence it is not surprising that after the war ended—when Dürrenmatt was twenty-four—the cultural vacuum that was left on the German stage by the intellectual collapse and artistic bankruptcy brought about by the Hitler regime should have been filled, above all, by playwrights from the area where traditional German culture had maintained its continuity; and where, indeed, the theaters of Zürich, Basle, and Berne had offered refuge to some of the best actors and directors who had fled from Nazi Germany and occupied Austria.

Max Frisch, some ten years older, and Dürrenmatt dominated the German theater of the late forties and fifties, or at least that part of it devoted to the production of new original work. (There was, of course, a flood of efforts to catch up with translations of foreign writers and productions of the output of emigrés like Brecht.)

Frisch and Dürrenmatt are thus frequently grouped together. They are in fact vastly different writers. While Frisch is always dignified and highminded, Dürrenmatt, at least on the surface, is inclined to frivolity, black humor, the grotesque; he uses the forms of popular fiction and theater (the detective novel and the musical comedy) and has, at times, plunged into the world of the theater as an active director and manager.

Dürrenmatt believes in the duty of artists to communicate their vision to the maximal audience, hence his use of what in the German world of cultured intellectuals is dismissed as "Trivialliteratur." In this respect he adheres to the English and French view that allows writers like Conan Doyle of the Sherlock Holmes cycle, P. G. Wodehouse, or Simenon to be prized as major authors in spite of the fact that they used these popular genres. Yet, unlike those writers, Dürrenmatt's basic purpose is always deeply serious, even philosophical. And above all, his basic impulse has always been to use his writing to come to terms with himself, with his own vision of the world in all its complexity. Behind all his writing—in however popular a form it may be couched—there lies a deeply serious thought process:

> Writing is a dialectical movement [he has said]. Writing is a continuous progression within itself, a process of deepening; writing is a form of thought, a very particular form of thinking, thinking that works with parables. Why does one write? Because one is continuously stimulated to new images. Images are answers we give to reality. Attempts to master reality by producing a counter-reality . . .

The problem of the relationship between reality and fiction is one that has preoccupied Dürrenmatt throughout his career. The real event happens, he has argued, and thus occurs in the sphere of "ontology," fiction in that of logic. In this respect his attitude as a playwright is akin to that of Georg Kaiser's famous dictum: "To write a play is: to think a thought to its ultimate conclusion." Dürrenmatt has illustrated his version of this concept by describing the sequence of chance decisions that led him to become involved in a car accident in May 1959. Each spontaneous, completely fortuitous decision that led to his being on the spot of the disaster was completely arbitrary, yet, seen from the moment of the accident, they formed a chain of inevitable and unbreakable causality. The further back you go in the chain of causality, the less probable the accident will appear; the nearer to it you come, the more inevitable it will become. This leads Dürrenmatt to formulate his dramaturgy of "the worst possible turn of events":

> An accident is at first improbable, but becomes, as time goes on, more probable, until it becomes reality; the chain of situations, accidents, etc., has taken its worst possible turn. Admittedly, I might get no more than a scratch in an accident; nevertheless this scratch constitutes the worst possible turn of events for me, because the worst possible turn of events represents reality, i.e., the accident is actually happened, and not as it might potentially have happened. But when I create a fiction I am not representing reality. Reality happens, it takes place in the "ontological" sphere, fiction in the logical sphere. Hence in thinking it out I must give my fiction the worst possible turn, I must describe the fatal accident. Only thus does my fictional thought acquire an "existential" justification. As human beings we too are existentially menaced by the worst possible turn of events, not only by the atomic bomb, but also by the worst possible form of social structure or the worst possible marriage, etc. By giving a dramatic fiction the worst possible turn I can, by a paradoxical detour through the negative, ultimately reach the sphere of ethics: the confrontation of fictional thought with the "existential."

In other words, in his fiction—both dramatic and narrative—Dürrenmatt strives to invent situations and events that will be paradigmatic and will fully exploit their inherent logical potential, which will thus always lead finally to the worst possible turn of events that situation can take.

And such is the impenetrable nature of the universe and the human condition, Dürrenmatt feels, that if any concatenation of circumstances is thought out to its complete logical conclusion, at the end of that process we shall always be confronted with a paradox, an antinomy, an irreconcilable contradiction. In a universe without a discernible purpose or plan (discernible, that is to say, for human beings with their short life span and limited intelligence) all events must of necessity appear random, fortuitous, and accidental. In discussing one of his earliest successes, the play *An*

Angel Comes to Babylon, Dürrenmatt, talking about himself in the third person in a fictitious interview with himself, maintains:

> If Leibniz saw the justification for the imperfection of creation in the fact that although our world was the best of all possible worlds, it must still, of necessity, be imperfect because only God could be perfect, F. D. justifies the imperfection of the world by pointing out that for God it must be the most unknown of all worlds: he juxtaposes to the perfect creator the absentminded creator, who is obviously inclined, again and again, to forget his own creations. The Angel who is bringing the girl Kurrubi to the earth as a gift for the poorest of the poor, only knows matter—inevitably—in a gaseous state, nor does he have any idea what God is intending with the girl; and, alas, we must come to the conclusion that God himself does not know it either. God's grace is incomprehensible not only to ourselves, but to God as well. The earth appears to the Angel as what, according to astronomy, it actually is: as a miracle, a special case (even if there existed billions of such special cases; in the universe, in the sphere of very large numbers, even a billion might constitute a special case).

In Dürrenmatt's universe we thus encounter a dialectical tension between the utter randomness of the basic situations and events at the outset on one hand, and on the other the rigid logic with which the potential of these initial situations is worked out from one worst possible turn of events to the next, until, at the end, a situation of complete paradox is reached. To remain with *The Angel Comes to Babylon:* the Angel is to give the divine girl Kurrubi to the poorest of the poor, the only remaining beggar in Nebukadnezar's Babylon, Akki. But Nebukadnezar, the King of Babylon, has disguised himself as a beggar in order to spy out Akki. The Angel thus, by mistake, gives the girl to the King. And in the end, when after a sequence of bizarre and surprising twists and turns of events Kurrubi is with Akki, and God's purpose seems to have been fulfilled, Nebukadnezar realizes that the divine girl represents complete happiness and God's grace and that thus, in fact, God's purpose has not been fulfilled because the beggar is now the richest of men, and the King, in his wretchedness and love for Kurrubi, the poorest of the poor.

Nevertheless, such a vision of a world must have its basic theological aspect. And Dürrenmatt is the son of a Protestant clergyman. His earliest plays, *The Anabaptists* and *The Blind Man,* deal with the paradoxes of faith. In the first of these, "those who believe in the faith are exploited by the man who merely uses faith and, after a senseless resistance, defeated by one who administers the faith, but who secretly admires those who were able to have faith"; while in the second a blind man who has lost his dukedom is kept by those around him in the belief that he still possesses it. In *The Physicists* Möbius's attempt to prevent his discovery of the secret of the most destructive form of energy from falling into the hands of unscrupulous politicians leads, directly, to that very thing happening. In *The Visit,* Claire Zachanassian's resolve to procure justice for herself plunges a whole town into collective guilt and the perpetration of a terrible crime. In *The Deadline* [*Die Frist,* 1977], the dissident scientist who resolutely refuses to obtain political power is, by the logic of his own decisions, irretrievably driven to assume the post of a ruler who will *have* to exercise ruthless power. Most of Dürrenmatt's plays—and novels—follow that pattern.

Basically, thus, Dürrenmatt's oeuvre is concerned with the exploration of philosophical, indeed, existential *ideas* through the use of popular forms of literature like the detective novel, the farce, or the musical. His fictions are *parables.* But he insists, again and again, that such parables are not to be taken for allegories. Allegories can be translated into a single meaning, parables—or metaphors—are multivalent. They are images open to an infinite number of interpretations that vary from individual to individual, from epoch to epoch.

> I believe that every explanation—even a psychoanalytical one—destroys the meaning of a parable, because that meaning is one with the parable itself, or to be more precise, can only mirror itself in the parable without being split, and that therefore all explanations are multivalent, refracted light; or, what amounts to the same thing: not one explanation is the meaning of the parable, but all its possible explanations put together.

Dürrenmatt's oeuvre is thus an attempt to think in *images,* to create multivalent images that can comprehend more of the real nature of the world than the unidimensional and reductionist activity of discursive thought or speech. From his infancy Dürrenmatt was fascinated by the world of Greek myth and its archetypal, universally valid truths, embodied in such powerful images. The myth of Oedipus, the man who turned himself into a detective to find that the murderer he was seeking was himself, can be seen as underlying the basic structure of most of Dürrenmatt's plays. In one of his most fascinating essayistic and theoretical works, the massive commentary to his favorite but perhaps least successful play, *The Fellow Traveler* [*Der Mitmacher,* 1973], Dürrenmatt devotes some forty pages of his "Postscript to the Postscript" to a brilliantly witty retelling of the Oedipus myth as it might have appeared to the Delphic Pythia, whose oracles, from the very beginning, were the cause of all the tragedies that followed. This amounts to an almost Offenbachian burlesque of the ancient story, embodying as it does an accumulation of wilful and accidental circumstances, misunderstandings and mistaken identifications. Yet it is also a typically Dürrenmattian attempt to rethink the ancient myth that fascinated him from the outset and to extract as many possible meanings from the parable and image of that myth.

Another basic mythical image that lies behind much of Dürrenmatt's writings is that of the labyrinth and the Minotaur. The Minotaur, half man, half bull, has been imprisoned in a structure—built by Minos, an embodiment of Justice—and yet the Minotaur is not guilty of anything, merely of being the son of Minos's wife, Pasiphae, and a supernatural bull whom she seduced.

> The guilt of the Minotaur consists in being the Minotaur, a monster, an innocently guilty being; and that is why the labyrinth is more than a prison, it is something incomprehensible that keeps us prisoner precisely by being incomprehensible; that is why it needs no locked doors; the innumerable doors of the labyrinth stand open, anyone can lose his way in it. In thinking out a labyrinth, however, I unconsciously identified myself with the Minotaur, the inhabitant of the labyrinth . . . and in doing so I made the primeval protest, I protested against having been born; for the world into which I have been born was my labyrinth, the expression of the enigma of a mythic world that I did not understand, that pronounces innocent people guilty and whose law is unknown. More than that: I also identified myself with those who were banished into the labyrinth to be mauled by the Minotaur . . . and finally I identified with Theseus himself who killed the Minotaur: every attempt to come to grips with

the world in which we live, to give it artistic shape, is a fight
with the Minotaur; that one is fighting with oneself in this
struggle only occurs to one later; at the same time this fight
also represents the Minotaur's own impotent attempt to understand the labyrinth in his own way.

Dürrenmatt's world thus can be seen as an attempt to create his
own myth, a myth adequate to the complexity, absurdity, corruption, greed, and perplexity of the world of the late twentieth century. Throughout the great diversity of Dürrenmatt's oeuvre—he
is surely the most inventive of contemporary writers of fiction,
almost inexhaustible in the bizarre richness of his imagination—a
certain number of archetypal images, therefore, tend to recur in
the most varied forms: people who are made up of artificial spare
parts like Claire Zachanassian in *The Visit* or the dying dictator
in *The Deadline;* immensely powerful characters who believe
themselves well-nigh omnipotent, but whose manipulations inevitably turn against themselves (as those of Oedipus); great con-
frontations of men of power and/or great intellectual brilliance
that result in epic battles of words and ideas.

Clearly Dürrenmatt's concerns and preoccupations, and the archetypal magnitude of his themes—faith, power, justice, the workings of fate, man's place in a Godless universe—indicate the ambition of his enterprise, as a playwright and inventor of fictions,
and also as a copious and wide-ranging essayist and aesthetician
of drama. To what extent can he be regarded as having reached
his objectives?

I, for one, am convinced that the richness and variety of his
oeuvre—its intellectual brilliance, inventiveness, black humor, sense
of the grotesque, and mastery of a variety of literary techniques,
and depth of thought in works conspicuous by their lightness of
touch and elegance of construction—establish him as one of the
most important literary personalities of the German-speaking world
in the second half of this century. He has been compared to Brecht,
even reproached with having tried to copy Brecht (without Brecht's
Marxist commitment). He himself may have been responsible for
evoking this kind of comment by having engaged in a fascinating
and long-lasting polemic with Brecht and his ideas.

Yet the attempt to place him in this line of literary genealogy
seems to me to be mistaken. Dürrenmatt belongs to a somewhat

different line of descent in the history of German literature: his intellectualism and almost mathematical sense of structure seems to me to be akin to that of Hebbel; his sense of the grotesque has features of Grabbe (notably in *Scherz, Satire, Ironie und Tiefere Bedeutung* [*Jest, Satire, Irony and Deeper Meaning*] which might almost be a definition of Dürrenmatt's whole enterprise); there is much in Dürrenmatt also that is reminiscent of Kleist (who, after all, wrote his own burlesqued Oedipus in *The Broken Pitcher,* created a synthetic, spare-parts beauty in the Kunigunde of *Das Käthchen von Heilbronn,* and created a comic Jupiter and Mercury in *Amphitryon*); but above all he has his roots in the work of that other transmuter of Greek myth and *"Denkspieler"* (thought-player) Georg Kaiser, the most original and successful of the German expressionist playwrights. Dürrenmatt himself made that point when he said, in an interview with Heinz Ludwig Arnold, *"Ganz extrem gesagt: ich bin ein Expressionist* [To put it most bluntly: I am an expressionist]."

Drama as an exercise in philosophical thought, as a laboratory of ideas, is far from the tastes and traditions of the English-speaking theater. That is why neither Kaiser nor Dürrenmatt—nor indeed Max Frisch—have ever succeeded in making more than a marginal impact on the British or American stage. The ludicrous travesty of *The Visit* by Hollywood (with Ingrid Bergman cast in the role of the hideous old lady, Claire Zachanassian, and with a happy ending to boot) is proof of the gulf that separates the tradition Dürrenmatt represents with what was regarded as bearable by American audiences; the greatly attenuated and prettified version of the play the Lunts presented on Broadway in 1964 merely confirms that observation, as does the fact that the film version of *The Judge and his Hangman,* very much more faithful to Dürrenmatt's own concept in *The End of the Game,* hardly made any impact at all in America in spite of brilliant performances by Martin Ritt as Commissar Barlach and by Jon Voigt as his quarry Tschanz.

Here, then, we have another typically Dürrenmattian paradox: that a writer who set out to conquer the minds of a mass audience by adopting the most popular forms of literary genres should—at least in the English-speaking world, but also to quite a large extent in his own linguistic sphere—remain appreciated only by the more sophisticated strata among theatergoers and readers. The high intellectualism of his basic conception and the depth of his ultimate concerns inevitably makes itself felt. Or rather: to those who are not capable of penetrating to the underlying philosophical and ethical concerns behind the surface of the plays or narratives, the story lines themselves will appear not particularly remarkable. This may be the reason for Dürrenmatt's deep disappointment with the reception of what he regards as some of his most profound works, notably *The Fellow Traveler* (which takes the form of an American gangster play) and *The Deadline* (which mixes broad satire on the world of television with the blackest of black comedy). Yet the first of these failures has stimulated him to write, in reply and justification, what must be regarded as his hitherto most brilliant prose essay, the massive *Postscript,* which includes a Preface to the Postscript as well as a Postscript to the Postscript and runs to more than 230 pages. This exercise must have given Dürrenmatt the taste for extended works of polemical prose, mingling essayistic passages with autobiographical narrative and satirical stories. He is now writing an even more massive work of this type, *Stoffe* ("Materials," or perhaps "Subjects"), which has the subtitle: "Contributions to the History of My Writing Career."

Thus, at the end of his career as a writer, Dürrenmatt's basic philosophical and essayistic impulse has come to the surface. In this respect he is akin to Bernard Shaw, who also used popular forms of theater mainly to express his philosophical and social concerns, but also resorted to more and more explicit prefaces and postscripts to make himself clear.

Both Shaw and Dürrenmatt are masters of paradox. But where Shaw's vision was essentially optimistic, Dürrenmatt's is much darker. Yet his pessimism is always tempered by a substratum of hope, however faint, however tenuous its rational justification. The very fact that he continues to write and to struggle to express his vision is to him proof that deep down he does not consider that all is lost. By always confronting himself, and us, with the worst possible turn of events, he might shock us into taking evasive action in time.

Dürrenmatt's vision was shaped by his experience as a Swiss, sitting, during the Second World War, snugly and comfortably on the sidelines of the bloodiest and most brutal holocaust of history.

To a man of his intelligence and deep moral sensibility that was an experience that not only gave him an all-pervading horror at the folly and baseness humankind is capable of perpetrating; it also gave him, and others of like mind among his generation in neutral Switzerland, an abiding sense of guilt at having—unwittingly and by a horrendous lucky chance—been spared from having to participate in all that slaughter, crime, and suffering. That is the basic impulse behind all his work. And it is this combination of intellectual detachment and passionate ethical involvement that makes Dürrenmatt the ideal spokesperson for the concerns and sensibilities of our world—the world of the atom bomb, concentration camps and Gulags, totalitarian tyrannies and mindless affluent societies hypnotized by half-witted mass media, vivisection and the destruction of the earth's natural resources, zombielike conformity and moronic pseudocults. There is hardly another writer of our time who has given as penetrating and as concerned a diagnosis of its staggering problems and paradoxes as Friedrich Dürrenmatt.

MARTIN ESSLIN

Introduction

Friedrich Dürrenmatt, born in Konolfingen near Berne in 1921, son of a Protestant pastor and grandson of a Swiss *Nationalrat*, originally wanted to become a painter. But after studying theology and philosophy in Zurich for a while, he eventually turned to writing and, at age 26, created his first theatrical scandal with *Es steht geschrieben* [*It is Written*]. There were many more plays to follow, many of which were to have considerable impact. In fact the theatrical scene after World War II in the German-speaking countries is unthinkable without them. In 1956, when he was thirty-five, Dürrenmatt achieved international fame with *The Visit*. The play was performed in over forty countries. It was made into a film starring Ingrid Bergman and into an opera by Gottfried von Einem. In 1981, on the occasion of Dürrenmatt's sixtieth birthday, his Swiss publisher brought out a thirty-volume edition of his collected works to that date. Over half of these are devoted to the twenty-six plays, including adaptations and plays for radio and television. Novels, stories, and essays on theater, politics, and philosophy fill thirteen volumes, and the bibliography lists more than a thousand critical articles on Dürrenmatt. Unquestionably we are dealing here with the work of one of the great men of contemporary letters.

Dürrenmatt began his career as an author in the forties, during the war, with short prose, literary criticism, and scripts for the radio. His early short stories (*Der Sohn, Der Alte, Die Falle, Die Stadt*) are reminiscent of those of Franz Kafka, in both their haunted obsession with unattainable justice and their lapidary brevity. Many of them were rewritten several times and remained quarries from which ideas and motives could be taken and reworked. Thus *Die Stadt* (1947) became *Aus den Papieren eines Wärters* (1952) and *Stoffe* (still unfinished). Or, to give another example, *Die Panne* (1955) with the subtitle "a barely possible story," was rewritten the same year as a radio play and again more than twenty years later as a comedy (1979).

Dürrenmatt's major success with fiction came in 1950 with the publication of the first of his detective stories, written on commission for a Swiss newspaper. While his earlier stories were under the influence of Kafka, the novels, like his plays, show his preoccupation with Bertolt Brecht and his opposition to the traditional genre. What irritated him about Brecht, in his opinion the great theoretician of epic theater, was also the flaw of the traditional detective story. *"Brecht denkt so unerbittlich, weil er an vieles so unerbittlich nicht denkt* [Brecht thinks so categorically because he categorically banishes so much from his thinking]," he said. If, unlike abstract theory, reality holds no irrefutable logic, then "things don't happen the way they are supposed to." This insight obviously undermines the well-known pattern of the detective story. If single-track logic is suspended and replaced by many-layered diversity, only chance, random and unpredictable, decides the outcome. The application of the uncertainty principle of physics and biology to literature results in a parody of the genre, in "a requiem for the detective story," as the subtitle to one of his novels reads.

The first of Dürrenmatt's anti-detective novels was *Der Richter und sein Henker* in 1950 (*The Judge and his Hangman,* 1954), followed by *Der Verdacht,* 1951 (*The Quarry,* 1961) and *Das Versprechen,* 1957 (title of the film version *"Es geschah am hellichten Tag,"* 1958; *The Pledge,* 1959). All three were made into movies, went through many reprints, and are frequently read in German schools. Close to two million copies of *The Judge* have been sold so far. In all three novels Dürrenmatt wants to show that the ordinary detective story's belief in rationality is itself irrational. Human planning is futile because reality is unfathomable and defies calculation. "The more human beings proceed by plan," he later formulates in the "21 points" to his play *The Physicists,* "the more effectively they may be hit by accident." Tschanz [Chance] is the name of the helpless policeman in *The Judge* whom Inspector Barlach uses as his instrument. By pure chance, a giant and a dwarf rescue the same inspector in *The Quarry*. After correctly solving the crime, the protagonist in *The Pledge* has prepared a trap. The murderer is about to fall into it, but on his way there he gets killed in an automobile accident; pure chance foils the clever plan. Thus in all three novels chance has only one function: to demonstrate man's powerlessness and the futility of reasoning. They offer no less suspense than the traditional detective story, yet it is a startling and uncanny world with which we are confronted, and the "justice" meted out is in a normal sense quite illegal. The quest for justice acts as substitute for religion and the reader is shocked by the conclusion.

Most commentaries count *Die Panne*, 1956 (*Traps*, 1960), among this group as well. In its introduction the narrator again formulates the dilemma: "no gods threaten us, no justice, no fate as in the Fifth Symphony, but traffic accidents, the breaking of dikes because of faulty construction, explosions of nuclear reactors caused by absent-minded lab assistants, incorrectly programmed breeders. Our course leads ever deeper into this world of snafus. Maybe, he concludes, some stories are still possible, just barely, "stories in which judgment and justice become visible, perhaps even grace, haphazardly caught, mirrored in the monocle of a drunk."

Dürrenmatt's refutation of causality, his denunciation of the basis of traditional storytelling, leads to parody, not only of the detective story, but of romance (*Griache sucht Griechin*, 1955; *Once a Greek*, 1965), and of historical drama. After some early plays on the struggle between atheism and faith (*Es steht geschrieben*, 1946 [*It is Written*], later version *Die Wiedertäufer*, 1967 [*The Anabaptists*], and *Der Blinde*, 1948 [*The Blind Man*], his third play bears the subtitle "an ahistorical historical comedy." In this play, *Romulus der Grosse*, 1949 (*Romulus the Great*, 1964), the dual role of judge and executioner rests with the last Roman emperor, who consciously furthers the decline of his empire to save mankind. First staged on Broadway in an adaptation by Gore Vidal, it proved to be Dürrenmatt's first international success and remains one of his most important plays.

Romulus was followed by *Die Ehe des Herrn Mississippi,* 1952 (*The Marriage of Mr. Mississippi,* 1964), a play about three would-be world reformers who fail in their missionary zeal because "everything can be changed except man." The morality play *Ein Engel kommt nach Babylon,* 1953 (*An Angel Comes to Babylon,* 1964), shows the incompatibility of power and grace. In 1977 Rudolf Kelterborn wrote an opera based on this most poetic and fairytale-like of Dürrenmatt's plays.

In between these major stage plays Dürrenmatt wrote a number of radio plays (*Der Doppelgänger,* 1946; *Der Prozess um des Esels Schatten,* 1951; *Stranitzky und der Nationalheld,* 1952; *Nächtliches Gespräch mit einem verachteten Menschen,* 1952; *Herkules und der Stall des Augias,* 1954; *Das Unternehmen der Wega,* 1954; *Die Panne,* 1956; *Abendstunde im Spätherbst,* 1956), which were rebroadcast many times and received wide attention and many prizes; some were also later rewritten for the stage.

The year 1956 saw the emergence of *Der Besuch der alten Dame* (*The Visit,* 1958), Dürrenmatt's most successful play. This parable about the corruptibility of human nature, taking place at Güllen (Swiss-German for "manure"), grotesquely demonstrates how "justice" can be bought, for "nothing is more monstrous than poverty." Within a year it was staged in all the major cities of Europe. In 1958 it reached Broadway in a production by Peter Brook, starring Alfred Lunt and Lynn Fontanne, which received the New York Theater Critics Award. The 1964 film version with Ingrid Bergman and Anthony Quinn was but a travesty of the original and was deservedly soon forgotten. Gottfried von Einem's opera version, on the other hand, (Vienna, 1971; San Francisco, 1972, staged by Francis Ford Coppola; Glyndebourne, 1973) proved a congenial creation. It is mainly on the vast and continuing popularity of this play that Dürrenmatt's fame as a modern classic rests.

Three years later *Frank V.* followed, "the comedy of a private bank," often compared to Brecht's *Threepenny Opera,* and caused yet another scandal at its Munich opening. Of far greater weight and of comparable stature to *The Visit,* though not quite so popular because of its grim content and pessimistic hopelessness, is *Die Physiker,* written in 1962 (*The Physicists,* 1963, see p. 153).

After another ill-deserved failure, a play called *Der Meteor,* 1966 (*The Meteor,* 1973) about a nihilistic Nobel-prize laureate who wants to die but cannot, Dürrenmatt, who had always taken an active part in the staging of his plays, for a while became a theater director. During the following years he tried out his ideas with his own adaptations of plays by Shakespeare (*König Johann,* 1968; *Titus Andronicus,* 1970), Strindberg (*Play Strindberg,* 1969), Goethe (*Urfaust,* 1970), Büchner (*Woyzek,* 1972), and Lessing (*Emilia Galotti,* 1974). In between he wrote *Porträt eines Planeten,* 1970 [*Portrait of a Planet*], an "improbable but plausible" sequence of scenes about disaster on a gigantic scale, a final portrait of the world before the solar explosion; and *Der Mitmacher,* 1973 [*The Conformist*], a play on total corruption under the dictatorship of organized capital. His last play to date is *Die Frist,* 1977 [*The Deadline*], the story of yet another scientist and his relation to power.

As mentioned earlier, most of Dürrenmatt's plays exist in several versions. Some originated as short stories or radio plays, and at least six were made into films and two into operas. For virtually every version Dürrenmatt supplied commentaries, either written for particular performances or taking the specific play as an example to elaborate on his theory of "tragic comedy." As with George Bernard Shaw and Bertolt Brecht before him, his critical comments often had a greater and longer lasting impact than the plays themselves. Their novel perspectives and provocative conclusions have had the most profound effect on the theory of drama in the German-speaking countries than anything else since the critical writings of Brecht. Apart from comments on particular plays, the most notable ones being his "21 Points" to *The Physicists* and the postscripts to *Der Mitmacher,* which run to over two hundred pages, there are a number of major essays, such as "Problems of the Theater," 1954, *"Aspekte des dramaturgischen Denkens,"* 1964 ["Aspects of Theatrical Thinking"], "Friedrich Schiller," 1959, *"Sätze über das Theater,"* 1970 ["Theses on Theater"]. In addition Dürrenmatt's speeches, theater reviews, and essays on literature and philosophy fill six volumes. One essay, which started as an acceptance speech delivered on the occasion of receiving an honorary degree at the Ben Gurion University, first grew into a one-hundred-fifty-page *"Konzeption"* about Israel (1975), then into a treatise twice as long on "freedom, equality, and fraternity in Judaism, Christianity, Islam, and Marxism, as well as on two old myths" (1980).

Over the years Dürrenmatt has received a great number of prizes, including some of the most prestigious ones that Austria, West Germany, and Italy, as well as his native Switzerland have to bestow. He was awarded honorary doctoral degrees by Temple University (1969) and the Universities of Nice (1977) and Jerusalem (1977). At age 61 he continues to live and write at Neuchâtel near Berne.

Of Dürrenmatt's voluminous output the present selection includes but two of his plays, *Romulus the Great* and *The Visit,* and the outline and critical commentary to a third, *The Physicists.* His prose writings are represented by his first and most popular detective story, *The Judge and His Hangman;* of his theoretical writings, for lack of space only *Problems of the Theater* and *A Monster Lecture on Justice and Law* could be included. All translations were revised by Susan H. Ray; the *Monster Lecture,* translated by John E. Woods, appears here for the first time in English.

V.S.

ROMULUS
THE GREAT

An Unhistorical Comedy in Four Acts

SECOND VERSION 1957

The great artistic trick of taking small deviations from the truth for truth itself upon which the entire system of differential equations is built, is also the basis for our wittiest thinking which might all collapse if the deviations were taken with philosophical strictness.

Lichtenberg

CHARACTERS

ROMULUS AUGUSTUS, *Emperor of the Western Roman Empire*
JULIA, *His wife*
REA, *His daughter*
ZENO, THE ISAURIAN, *Emperor of the Eastern Roman Empire*
EMILIAN, *Roman patrician*
MARS, *Minister of War*
TULLIUS ROTUNDUS, *Minister of State*
SPURIUS TITUS MAMMA, *Captain of Cavalry*
ACHILLES, *Chamberlain to Romulus*
PYRAMUS, *Chamberlain to Romulus*
APOLLONIUS, *Art dealer*
CAESAR RUPF, *Industrialist*
PHYLAX, *Actor*
ODOAKER, *Ruler of the Teutons*
THEODORIC, *His nephew*
PHOSPHORIDOS, *Chamberlain to Zeno*
SULPHURIDES, *Chamberlain to Zeno*
COOK, SERVANTS, TEUTONS

The Time: The morning of March 15 to the morning of March 16, A.D. 476.

The Place: The Villa of Emperor Romulus in Campania.

Act One

It is the year four hundred and seventy-six. One early March morning the Cavalry Officer, Spurius Titus Mamma, arrives on his dying horse in Campania at the imperial summer residence in which the Emperor of Rome lives the whole year round. The Captain, dirty, tired, and with his left arm in a bloody bandage, dismounts, moving with difficulty; he stumbles, stirring up a huge flock of cackling chickens; finding no one, he hurries through the villa and finally enters the Emperor's study. Here, too, everything seems to him at first empty and deserted. There are a few wobbly, half-broken chairs and up on the walls the venerable busts of Rome's statesmen, thinkers, and poets, all of a somewhat exaggeratedly solemn expression . . .

SPURIUS TITUS MAMMA: Hallo, hallo, anybody here?

> *(Silence. At last the Cavalry Officer notices two ancient, gray and immovable chamberlains, standing like statues, at each side of a door in the middle of the background. Pyramus and Achilles have been in the service of the Emperor for years. The Cavalry Officer stares at them in amazement and, fascinated by their dignified appearance, becomes quite timid.)*

Hallo!

PYRAMUS: Silence, young man.

SPURIUS TITUS MAMMA: It's about time. I was beginning to think this place was dead to the world. I'm dog-tired.

> *(Gasping for breath, he throws himself into a chair.)*

ACHILLES: And who are you?

SPURIUS TITUS MAMMA: Spurius Titus Mamma, Captain of Cavalry.

PYRAMUS: And what do you want?

SPURIUS TITUS MAMMA: I have to speak to the Emperor.

ACHILLES: Have you an appointment?

SPURIUS TITUS MAMMA: No time for formalities. I bring urgent news.

PYRAMUS: Nothing is urgent at the Court of a Roman Emperor, Spurius Titus Mamma.

(*The Captain jumps up angrily.*)

SPURIUS TITUS MAMMA: But I come from Pavia, from the Imperial Commander, Orestes, with bad news!

(*The two chamberlains look at each other thoughtfully.*)

PYRAMUS: Bad news from Pavia?

ACHILLES (*shakes his head*): News from Pavia cannot really be bad. Pavia is too insignificant for that!

SPURIUS TITUS MAMMA: But the Roman Empire is collapsing!

(*He is simply speechless at the composure of the two chamberlains.*)

PYRAMUS: Impossible.

ACHILLES: An organization as immense as the Roman Empire simply cannot totally collapse.

SPURIUS TITUS MAMMA: But the Teutons are coming.

ACHILLES: They've been coming for the past five hundred years, Spurius Titus Mamma.

(*The Cavalry Officer grabs Achilles by the shoulders and shakes him as if he were a rotten column.*)

SPURIUS TITUS MAMMA: It is my patriotic duty to speak to the Emperor! At once!

ACHILLES: We do not consider as desirable a patriotism that conflicts with cultivated behavior.

SPURIUS TITUS MAMMA: O God!

(*Discouraged, he lets go of Achilles and now Pyramus tries to appease him.*)

PYRAMUS: Let me give you some good advice, young man. Take it and you will gain your objective swiftly. First go to the Lord High Steward, at ten o'clock sharp, two hours from now. He will hold audience. Add your name to the list of new arrivals. Request permission from the Minister of State to deliver an important message to the Imperial Court and perhaps then, in the course of the next few days, you may be able to deliver your news personally to the Emperor.

(*The Cavalry Officer no longer knows what to think.*)

SPURIUS TITUS MAMMA: To the Lord High Steward!

PYRAMUS: Right round the corner, third door on the left.

SPURIUS TITUS MAMMA: To the Minister of State!

PYRAMUS: Seventh door on the right.

SPURIUS TITUS MAMMA (*still speechless*): To deliver my news in the course of the next few days!

ACHILLES: In the course of the next few weeks.

SPURIUS TITUS MAMMA: Unhappy Rome! Two chamberlains are your downfall! (*Desperately he runs out to the left. The two chamberlains again freeze into immobility.*)

ACHILLES: I note most regrettably that as our century progresses, its manners decline.

PYRAMUS: He who misjudges our worth digs Rome's grave.

(*The Emperor, Romulus Augustus, appears in the door between the two chamberlains. He is wearing a purple toga and a golden laurel wreath. His Majesty is past fifty, calm, at ease and sure of himself.*)

PYRAMUS AND ACHILLES: Hail, Caesar.

ROMULUS: Hail. Are today the Ides of March?

ACHILLES: Yes, my Emperor, the Ides of March. (*He bows.*)

ROMULUS: An historic date. According to Roman Law all officials and civil servants of my empire are to be paid today. An ancient superstition to keep emperors from being assassinated. Get me the Minister of Finance.

ACHILLES: The Minister of Finance has fled, Majesty.

ROMULUS: Fled?

PYRAMUS: With the imperial cashbox, my Emperor.

ROMULUS: Why? There was nothing in it.

ACHILLES: He did it in the hope of covering up the general bankruptcy of the imperial finances.

ROMULUS: Clever, that man. If you want to hide a great scandal, it's best to stage a little one. Let him henceforth be called "The Saviour of his Country." Where is he now?

ACHILLES: He's taken a position—as head clerk of a wine export business in Syracuse.

ROMULUS: Let's hope that in private business this loyal official will succeed in recovering the losses he incurred serving the state. There! (*He takes the laurel wreath off his head, breaks off two golden leaves and hands one to each of the chamberlains.*) Let each of you turn his golden leaf into sesterces. But after deducting what I owe you, give me back any money left. I still have to pay my cook; he's the most important man in my empire.

PYRAMUS AND ACHILLES: Yes, Your Majesty.

ROMULUS: When I began my reign there were thirty-six leaves in this golden wreath, this symbol of imperial power. Now there are only five. (*He looks at the wreath thoughtfully before putting it back on.*) My morning repast.

PYRAMUS: Your breakfast.

ROMULUS: My morning repast. In my house I decide what is classical Latin.

(*The old man brings in a small table; on it stands the Emperor's breakfast. There is ham, bread, asparagus wine, a small bowl of milk, an egg in its cup. Achilles brings in a chair. The Emperor sits down and cracks the egg.*)

ROMULUS: Didn't Augustus lay anything?

PYRAMUS: Nothing, my Emperor.

ROMULUS: Tiberius?

PYRAMUS: All of the Julians, nothing.

ROMULUS: The Flavians?

PYRAMUS: Domitian did, but Your Majesty expressly did not wish to eat even one of Domitian's eggs.

ROMULUS: Domitian was a bad emperor. He can lay as many eggs as he wants, I won't eat them.

PYRAMUS: Yes, my Emperor.

(*The Emperor eats up the egg.*)

ROMULUS: And who laid this egg?

PYRAMUS: Marcus Aurelius, as usual.

ROMULUS: A fine bird. Compared to him, the other emperors are worthless. Did anybody else lay anything?

PYRAMUS: Odoaker. (*He is somewhat embarrassed.*)

ROMULUS: What do you know!

PYRAMUS: Two eggs.

ROMULUS: Marvelous. And Orestes, my Commander-in-Chief, who is supposed to conquer this Teutonic chieftain?

PYRAMUS: Nothing.

ROMULUS: Nothing? I never did think much of him. I'd like to see him on my table tonight, stuffed with chestnuts.

PYRAMUS: Yes, Your Majesty.

(The Emperor eats ham and bread.)

ROMULUS: And what news of the bird bearing my name?

PYRAMUS: She is the noblest, most gifted fowl we possess, the blue-ribbon product of Roman poultry raising.

ROMULUS: Did she lay, this noble bird?

(Pyramus looks at Achilles, pleading for help.)

ACHILLES: Almost, my Emperor.

ROMULUS: Almost? What does that mean? A hen either lays or she doesn't.

ACHILLES: Not yet, my Emperor.

(The Emperor makes a decisive gesture.)

ROMULUS: Not at all. If a hen's good for nothing, it's still good for the pot. Let the cook prepare my namesake along with Orestes and Caligula.

PYRAMUS: But, Your Majesty, the day before yesterday you ate Caligula together with Philippus Arabus, served with asparagus.

ROMULUS: Then let him take my predecessor, Julius Nepos. He wasn't good for anything either. And in the future, I want to find Odoaker's eggs on my breakfast table. This fine animal has my fullest admiration. What enormous talent. Let us take from the Teutons whatever good they produce; they seem to be coming anyhow.

(The Minister of State, Tullius Rotundus, pale as death, rushes in from the left.)

TULLIUS ROTUNDUS: My Emperor!

ROMULUS: What do you wish of your Emperor, Tullius Rotundus?

TULLIUS ROTUNDUS: It's terrible, it's frightful.

ROMULUS: I know, my dear Minister. I haven't paid you for two years now, and today, when I meant to do it, the Minister of Finance made off with the imperial cashbox.

TULLIUS ROTUNDUS: Our position is so catastrophic that nobody, but nobody, thinks of money any more, my Emperor.

(The Emperor drinks his bowl of milk.)

ROMULUS: Well, I'm in luck again.

TULLIUS ROTUNDUS: A cavalry captain, Spurius Titus Mamma, galloped two days and two nights to bring Your Majesty news from Pavia.

ROMULUS: Two days and two nights! No kidding? He shall be made a Centurion for his athletic prowess.

TULLIUS ROTUNDUS: I will lead the Centurion, Spurius Titus Mamma, to Your Majesty right away.

ROMULUS: But, my dear Minister of State, isn't he tired?

TULLIUS ROTUNDUS: Of course, he's close to a physical and mental breakdown.

ROMULUS: In that case, my dear Tullius Rotundus, you had better lead him to the quietest guest chamber in my house. Even athletes have to sleep.

> (*The Minister of State is taken aback.*)

TULLIUS ROTUNDUS: But his news, Your Majesty.

ROMULUS: Precisely. Even the worst news sounds quite acceptable from the mouth of a person who is well rested, freshly bathed, shaved, and well fed. Let him come tomorrow.

> (*The Minister of State is speechless.*)

TULLIUS ROTUNDUS: Your Majesty! But this is world-shaking news.

ROMULUS: News never shakes the world. Only events do that, and once we get news of them, they're over and done and past altering. News only agitates the world: it's best to get used to as little news as possible.

> (*Tullius Rotundus bows in confusion and exits left. Pyramus sets a large roast beef before Romulus.*)

ACHILLES: The art dealer, Apollonius.

> (*Apollonius, the art dealer, enters from the left. He is dressed elegantly in the Greek manner. He bows.*)

APOLLONIUS: Your Majesty.

ROMULUS: I've been waiting for you for three weeks, Apollonius.

APOLLONIUS: I beg your forgiveness, Emperor. I've been at an auction in Alexandria.

ROMULUS: You prefer a business deal in Alexandria to the bankruptcy of the Roman Empire?

APOLLONIUS: Business is business, my Emperor.

ROMULUS: Well, weren't you delighted with the busts I sold you? Cicero, especially, was a valuable piece.

APOLLONIUS: An exceptional item, my Emperor. I was able to send off five hundred plaster casts to the academies which are now being built all over the ancient Teutonic forests.

ROMULUS: For heaven's sake, Apollonius, is Germania being civilized?

APOLLONIUS: The light of reason cannot be stopped. When the Teutons become civilized at home, they will no longer invade the Roman Empire.

(The Emperor carves the beef.)

ROMULUS: When the Teutons come to Italy or Gaul, we will civilize them. But if they remain in Germania, they will civilize themselves and that will be ghastly. Do you want to buy the remaining busts or not?

(The art dealer looks around.)

APOLLONIUS: I'd better take another closer look at them. There's not much call for busts these days; as a matter of fact, the only ones that sell are those of famous boxers and buxom courtesans. Besides, some of these busts seem of rather dubious style.

ROMULUS: Each bust has the style it deserves. Achilles, get Apollonius a ladder.

(Achilles hands a ladder to the art dealer. The Greek climbs the ladder and keeps himself occupied examining the busts, sometimes on the ladder, sometimes off, moving it from place to place. The Empress Julia enters from the right.)

JULIA: Romulus.

ROMULUS: My dear wife.

JULIA: How can you eat at a time like this?

(The Emperor puts down his knife and fork.)

ROMULUS: As you wish, my dear Julia.

JULIA: I'm deeply troubled, Romulus. The Lord High Steward, Ebius, gave me to understand that we have had terrible news. Now I don't quite always believe Ebius, since he is a Teuton and his real name is Ebi—

ROMULUS: Ebius is the only man fluent in all five world-languages: Latin, Greek, Hebrew, German, and Chinese, though I must admit that German and Chinese sound alike to me. But no matter, Ebius is better educated than any Roman will ever be.

JULIA: You are a real Germanophile, Romulus.

ROMULUS: Nonsense. I do not like them half as much as I like my chickens.

JULIA: Romulus!

ROMULUS: Pyramus, set a place for the Empress and bring Odoaker's first egg.

JULIA: Remember my weak heart!

ROMULUS: Precisely. Sit down and eat.

(*The Empress sits down at the left of the table with a sigh.*)

JULIA: Now will you finally tell me what terrible news came this morning?

ROMULUS: I don't know. The courier who brought it is sleeping.

JULIA: Then have him awakened, Romulus!

ROMULUS: Think of your heart, my dear wife.

JULIA: As the mother of my country . . .

ROMULUS: As the father of my country, I am probably Rome's last emperor. For that reason alone, I occupy a rather forlorn position in world history. No matter what happens I shall end up with a bad reputation. But there is one bit of fame no one shall take from me: no one shall ever say that I had wilfully disturbed the sleep of any man unnecessarily.

(*The Princess Rea enters from the right.*)

REA: Good morning, Father.

ROMULUS: Good morning, dear daughter.

REA: Did you sleep well?

ROMULUS: Since I've been the Emperor I've always slept well.

(*Rea sits down at the right of the table.*)

ROMULUS: Pyramus, set a place for the Princess, too, and bring Odoaker's second egg.

REA: Oh, did Odaker lay two eggs today?

ROMULUS: These Teutons always lay eggs. Would you like some ham?

REA: No, thank you.

ROMULUS: Cold roast beef?

REA: No, thank you.

ROMULUS: A little fish?

REA: No, thank you.

ROMULUS: Some asparagus wine?

(*He frowns.*)

REA: No, thank you, Father.

ROMULUS: Ever since you've been taking dramatic lessons from that actor, Phylax, you have no appetite any more. Just exactly what are you studying?

REA: Antigone's elegy before her death.

ROMULUS: Why study that old tragic text? Why not comedy? It's more fitting for our time.

(*The Empress is enraged.*)

JULIA: Romulus, you know very well this would not be fitting for a young maiden whose betrothed has been languishing for more than three years in a Teutonic dungeon.

ROMULUS: Calm yourself, my dear wife; the only thing that's left for people whose number is up, like us, is comedy.

ACHILLES: His Excellency, the Minister of War, wishes to speak to His Majesty. He says it is urgent.

ROMULUS: Strange, but the Minister of War always comes when I'm discussing literature. Let him come after my morning repast.

JULIA: Will you tell the Minister that the Emperor's family will be delighted to see him, Achilles.

(*Achilles bows and exits left. The Emperor wipes his mouth with his napkin.*)

ROMULUS: You are being excessively martial again, my dear wife.

(*The Minister of War enters, bowing, from the left.*)

MARS: My Emperor.

ROMULUS: Odd, how pale all my officials are today. I noticed it earlier in the Minister of State. What do you wish, Mars?

MARS: As the Minister responsible for the conduct of the war against the Teutons, I must demand that Your Majesty receive at once the Captain of Cavalry, Spurius Titus Mamma.

ROMULUS: But isn't our athlete asleep yet?

MARS: It is unworthy of a soldier to sleep when he knows his Emperor is in need.

ROMULUS: My officers' sense of duty is beginning to annoy me.

(*The Empress rises.*)

JULIA: Romulus!

ROMULUS: My dearest Julia?

JULIA: You will receive Spurius Titus Mamma immediately.

(*Pyramus whispers something into the Emperor's ear.*)

ROMULUS: That is quite unnecessary, my dear wife. Pyramus has just announced that Odoaker has laid a third egg.

JULIA: Romulus, your empire is tottering, your soldiers are sacrificing themselves, and you do nothing but speak of your feathered flock!

ROMULUS: And it is entirely legitimate ever since the geese saved the Capitol. I don't need Spurius Titus Mamma any longer. Odoaker, the ruler of the Teutons, has conquered Pavia. I know this because the hen bearing his name has just laid three eggs, and all things come in threes. You see how it all fits; without this natural harmony, there would be no order in the world.

(*Great consternation.*)

REA: My dear Father!

JULIA: That cannot be true.

MARS: Unfortunately, it is the truth, Your Majesty. Pavia has fallen. Rome has suffered the bitterest defeat of its history. The captain brought us the last words of the Commander, Orestes. He and his entire army fell into the hands of the Teutons.

ROMULUS: I know the last words of my generals even before they fall into Teutonic hands: As long as there is a drop of blood in our veins, no one will give up. Every one of them said that. Now, my dear Minister of War, will you please go and tell the Centurion of Cavalry that he is finally to go to bed.

(*Mars bows in silence and exits left.*)

JULIA: You have to do something, Romulus. You must do something immediately or else we shall be lost!

ROMULUS: I'll issue a proclamation to my soldiers this afternoon.

JULIA: Your legions, to the very last man, have deserted to the Teutons.

ROMULUS: In that case I'll proclaim Mars the Imperial Marshal.

JULIA: Mars is an idiot.

ROMULUS: True, but there is not a sensible man left today who would become Minister of War of the Roman Empire. I'll issue a communiqué that I'm in good health.

JULIA: What good will that do?

ROMULUS: All I can do is reign, my dear. You can't possibly ask more of me than that.

(*Apollonius, who has been busy looking at busts, descends from his ladder, approaches the Emperor and shows him a bust.*)

APOLLONIUS: Three gold pieces for this Ovid, Your Majesty.

ROMULUS: Four. Ovid was a great poet.

JULIA: Who in the world is he?

ROMULUS: The art dealer Apollonius, from Syracuse. I'm selling him my busts.

JULIA: But you cannot possibly squander the famous poets, thinkers, and statesmen of Rome's great past!

ROMULUS: We're having a clearance sale.

JULIA: Do bear in mind that these busts are the only things my father, Valentinian, left you.

ROMULUS: But I still have you, my dear wife.

REA: I simply cannot stand it any more.

> (*She rises.*)

JULIA: Rea!

REA: I'm going to study Antigone.

> (*She exits right.*)

JULIA: You see, even your daughter doesn't understand you any more.

ROMULUS: That's only because of her drama lessons.

APOLLONIUS: Three gold pieces and six sesterces. My final offer, Your Majesty.

ROMULUS: Why don't you take a few more busts? Then we will settle the whole thing in a lump sum.

> (*Apollonius climbs up his ladder again. The Minister of State rushes in from the left.*)

TULLIUS ROTUNDUS: My Emperor!

ROMULUS: Now what do you want, Tullius Rotundus?

TULLIUS ROTUNDUS: Zeno the Isaurian, Emperor of East Rome, begs for asylum.

ROMULUS: Zeno the Isaurian? But is he not safe in Constantinople?

TULLIUS ROTUNDUS: No one is safe in this world any more.

ROMULUS: Well, where is he?

TULLIUS ROTUNDUS: In the anteroom.

ROMULUS: Did he bring his chamberlains, Sulphurides and Phosphoridos, along?

TULLIUS ROTUNDUS: They were the only ones who could flee with him.

ROMULUS: If he will leave Sulphurides and Phosphoridos outside, then Zeno may come in. Byzantine chamberlains are too strict for my taste.

TULLIUS ROTUNDUS: Very well, Your Majesty.

(*The Emperor Zeno, the Isaurian, rushes in from the left. He is dressed considerably more expensively and more elegantly than his West Roman colleague.*)

ZENO: Hail to you, my exalted Imperial Brother!

ROMULUS: Hail to you.

ZENO: Hail to you, exalted Imperial Sister!

JULIA: Hail to you, exalted Imperial Brother!

(*They all embrace. Zeno strikes the attitude of an East Roman emperor seeking political asylum.*)

ZENO: I plead for help.

ROMULUS: I won't insist on your reciting all the numerous verses the Byzantine ceremonial demands of an emperor seeking asylum, my dear Zeno.

ZENO: I don't want to cheat my chamberlains.

ROMULUS: But if I won't let them in?

ZENO: Well, in that case, I won't recite the prescribed formalities this time, that is, as long as my chamberlains don't see. I'm exhausted. Ever since we left Constantinople they've made me recite the innumerable verses of 'I plead for help' at least three times a day in front of all sorts of political personalities. My voice is ruined.

ROMULUS: Sit down.

ZENO: Thank you.

(*Relieved, he sits down at the table, but at this very moment his two Chamberlains rush in, both dressed in severe black robes.*)

THE TWO CHAMBERLAINS: Your Majesty!

ZENO: By Zeus! How did my chamberlains manage to get in?

SULPHURIDES: Your elegiac verses, Your Majesty.

ZENO: I have already recited them, my dear Sulphurides and Phosphoridos.

SULPHURIDES: Impossible, Your Majesty. I appeal to your pride. You are not some private person running away. You are the East Roman Emperor in emigration and as such you must gladly submit to all the ceremonial rules of the Byzantine Court, no matter how incomprehensible they may be. Now, if you please?

ZENO: If it is absolutely necessary.

PHOSPHORIDES: It is, Your Majesty. The Byzantine Court ceremonial is not only a symbol of world order, it is this world
order itself. You should have understood that a long time ago.
Get on with it, Your Majesty. Do not shame your chamberlains
any longer.

ZENO: But I'm going to.

SULPHURIDES: Step back three paces, Your Majesty.

PHOSPHORIDOS: On your knees, with head bent, Your Majesty.

ZENO: Pleading mercy, I approach you. May the moon . . .

PHOSPHORIDOS: The sun.

ROMULUS: Achilles! Pyramus!

PYRAMUS: Yes, Majesty?

ACHILLES: Your Majesty?

ROMULUS: Throw these two Byzantine chamberlains out and lock
them up in the chicken coop.

ACHILLES: Very well, my Emperor.

SULPHURIDES: We protest!

PHOSPHORIDOS: Respectfully but emphatically!

(*At last the two are pushed out of the door by Achilles
and Pyramus; they disappear with Achilles. Pyramus ex-
haustedly wipes the sweat off his brow.*)

ZENO: The gods be thanked, my chamberlains are gone. They bury
me alive under their mountain of formalities and rules. I must
walk according to style, speak according to style, even eat and
drink according to style. I cannot stand all that style. But the
moment they're gone I feel the ancient strength of my Isaurian
forefathers rise in me. The old faith, firm as a rock—is the fence
around your chicken coop good and firm?

ROMULUS: You can depend on it. Pyramus, set a place for Zeno
and bring an egg.

PYRAMUS: We only have Domitian's egg left.

ROMULUS: In this case it will do.

ZENO (*embarrassed*): As a matter of fact, you know, you and I
have been at war these past seven years. Only the common Teutonic menace kept our armies from any major engagements.

ROMULUS: We? At war? I didn't know anything about that.

ZENO: But I took Dalmatia from you.

ROMULUS: Did it ever belong to me?

ZENO: It was assigned to you, at the last division of the empire.

ROMULUS: Just between us emperors, it has been quite some time since I've had a comprehensive view of world politics. Why did you have to leave Constantinople?

ZENO: Verina, my mother-in-law, formed an alliance with the Teutons and drove me out.

ROMULUS: Odd. And you had such excellent relations with the Teutons.

ZENO: Romulus! (*His feelings are hurt.*)

ROMULUS: You entered an alliance with them in order to depose your own son as emperor—if my information about the complicated situation at the Byzantine Court is correct.

JULIA: Romulus!

ZENO: The Teutons are overrunning our empires. All our defenses have been more or less breached. We can no longer march separately. We cannot afford the luxury of petty suspicions between our two empires. We have to save our culture.

ROMULUS: Why? Is culture something anyone can save?

JULIA: Romulus!

(*In the meantime the art dealer has approached the Emperor with several busts.*)

APOLLONIUS: For the two Gracchi, Pompeius, Scipio, and Cato, two gold pieces and eight sesterces.

ROMULUS: Three gold pieces.

APOLLONIUS: All right, but in that case I'll take Marius and Scilla too.

(*He climbs back up the ladder.*)

JULIA: Romulus, I demand that you send this antique dealer away immediately.

ROMULUS: We cannot possibly afford that, dear Julia. We haven't paid for the chicken feed yet.

ZENO: Amazing. A world goes up in flames and you make silly jokes. Every day thousands of human beings are dying and here you just muddle along. What does chicken feed have to do with the approach of the Barbarians?

ROMULUS: I have my worries, too, after all.

ZENO: It seems you have not nearly recognized the full extent of the Teutonic threat to the world. (*He taps his fingers on the table.*)

JULIA: That's exactly what I've been saying, over and over again.

ZENO: The success of the Teutons cannot be explained merely on material grounds. We have to look deeper than that. Our cities are surrendering, our soldiers are defecting, our peoples no longer believe in us because we doubt ourselves. We have to pull ourselves together, Romulus, we have to remember our ancient greatness, we have to recall Caesar, Augustus, Trajan, and Constantine. There is no other way; without belief in ourselves and in our political mission, we're lost.

ROMULUS: All right then, let us believe.

(Silence. Everyone sits in an attitude of devotion.)

ZENO: Are you believing? (*He seems somewhat unsure.*)

ROMULUS: Firm as a rock.

ZENO: In our ancient greatness?

ROMULUS: In our ancient greatness.

ZENO: In our historic mission?

ROMULUS: In our historic mission.

ZENO: And you, Empress Julia?

JULIA: I have always believed in it.

(Zeno feels easier.)

ZENO: A marvelous feeling, isn't it? One can positively feel the positive power charging through these rooms. High time, too.

(All three continue in an attitude of great belief.)

ROMULUS: And now?

ZENO: What do you mean by that?

ROMULUS: Well, now that we believe?

ZENO: That's the main thing.

ROMULUS: What's supposed to happen now?

ZENO: Unimportant.

ROMULUS: But we have to do something now that we're thinking positively.

ZENO: That'll come by itself. All we have to do is find an idea to set against the slogan of the Teutons: 'For freedom and serfdom.' I propose 'For slavery and God.'

ROMULUS: I'm not so sure whether God is on our side. Information on that is rather vague.

ZENO: 'For order against anarchy.'

ROMULUS: No good either. Personally, I'm more in favor of a practical slogan, a proposition that can be realized. For example: 'For agriculture and chicken farming.'

JULIA: Romulus!

(*Mars rushes in from the left. He is beside himself.*)

MARS: The Teutons are marching on Rome!

(*Zeno and Julia jump up horrified.*)

ZENO: When is the next boat for Alexandria?

ROMULUS: Tomorrow morning, half past eight. What do you want there?

ZENO: To plead for asylum from the Emperor of Abyssinia. I've decided to continue my indefatigable fight against the Teutonic menace from Abyssinia. Even though at times it seems it might be better to fall into the hands of the Teutons than into the clutches of my chamberlains.

(*The Empress slowly gathers her composure.*)

JULIA: Romulus, the Teutons are marching on Rome and you're still eating your breakfast.

(*The Emperor rises with dignity.*)

ROMULUS: A politician's prerogative. Mars, I appoint you Field-Marshal of the Empire.

MARS: I will save Rome, my Emperor! (*He falls upon his knees and swings his sword about.*)

ROMULUS: That is just what I needed! (*He sits down again.*)

MARS: Only one thing can save us now: total mobilization. (*He rises determinedly.*)

ROMULUS: And what kind of a word is that?

MARS: I just made it up. Total mobilization means the most absolute and complete deployment of all the forces of a nation for military purposes.

ROMULUS: I don't like it even from a stylistic point of view.

MARS: Total mobilization has to encompass all those parts of the empire not yet occupied by the enemy.

ZENO: The Field-Marshal is right. Only total mobilization can save us now. That is the very idea we were looking for. 'Total mobilization' is something everyone will understand.

ROMULUS: War has been a crime ever since the invention of the stick; total mobilization will make it lunacy. I put the fifty members of my personal guard at your disposal, Marshal.

MARS: Your Majesty! Odoaker has an army of one hundred thousand Teutons, all well armed.

ROMULUS: The greater the general, the fewer troops he needs.

MARS: Never in history has a Roman general been so insulted.

(He salutes and exits left. In the meantime Apollonius has taken down all the busts, except the one in the center.)

APOLLONIUS: Ten gold pieces for the lot.

ROMULUS: I wish you'd speak in more respectful tones of Rome's great past, Apollonius.

APOLLONIUS: The expression "lot" refers only to your legacy's worth as an antique and has nothing to do with an historical judgment.

ROMULUS: You'd have to give me the ten gold pieces immediately.

APOLLONIUS: Haven't I always, Your Majesty? I will leave one bust: that of King Romulus. *(He counts out ten gold pieces.)*

ROMULUS: But my namesake was the founder of Rome!

APOLLONIUS: A beginner's effort. That's why it's already falling apart.

(The Emperor of the Eastern Roman Empire is growing increasingly impatient.)

ZENO: You failed to introduce me to this gentleman, Romulus.

ROMULUS: The Emperor of the Eastern Roman Empire, Zeno the Isaurian—Apollonius.

APOLLONIUS: Your Majesty. *(He bows coolly.)*

ZENO: You really should visit the Island of Patmos some time. It has remained loyal to me, my dear Apollonius, and I have many unique pieces of Greek antiquity there.

APOLLONIUS: I can arrange a visit some day, Your Majesty.

ZENO: Since I shall be embarking for Alexandria tomorrow, perhaps you would grant me a small advance . . .

APOLLONIUS: Sorry. On principle I never pay imperial houses in advance. The times are too turbulent, political institutions too unstable, and lately, my clients' interests have turned from antiquity towards Teutonic handicraft. Primitive art is all the rage now. A horror, but then, who can account for taste? May I take my leave of Your Majesties?

ROMULUS: I am sorry, Apollonius, that you were caught in the midst of the dissolution of my empire.

APOLLONIUS: I don't mind, Your Majesty. After all, as an art dealer, that is what I live off. As far as the busts are concerned, I'll send some of my servants to collect the ones I've lined up.

(*He bows once more and exits to the left. The Emperor of the Eastern Empire shakes his head thoughtfully.*)

ZENO: I cannot understand it, Romulus. For years I've been unable to get any credit. It's becoming clearer every day: ours is not a profitable occupation.

(*The Minister of State, Tullius Rotundus, enters from the left.*)

TULLIUS ROTUNDUS: Majesty!

ROMULUS: Is our athlete finally asleep, Tullius Rotundus?

TULLIUS ROTUNDUS: I didn't come to speak to you about Spurius Titus Mamma, but about Caesar Rupf.

ROMULUS: I don't think I know him.

TULLIUS ROTUNDUS: A very important person. He wrote Your Majesty a letter.

ROMULUS: Since I was inaugurated as emperor I haven't read any letters. Who is he?

TULLIUS ROTUNDUS: A manufacturer of trousers. The producer of those Teutonic garments pulled up over one's legs. They have become rather fashionable here.

ROMULUS: Is he rich?

TULLIUS ROTUNDUS: Incredibly rich.

ROMULUS: At last, a man who makes sense.

JULIA: You ought to receive him immediately, Romulus.

ZENO: I have an infallible instinct that he will save us.

ROMULUS: We await the manufacturer of trousers with pleasure.

(*Caesar Rupf enters from the left. He is powerfully built, and richly dressed. He heads directly for Zeno, thinking him the Emperor, but Zeno, embarrassed, directs him towards Romulus. Caesar Rupf is holding a broad-rimmed travel hat of ancient design in his hand. He nods briefly.*)

CAESAR RUPF: Emperor Romulus.

ROMULUS: Welcome. This is my wife, the Empress Julia, and this, the Emperor of the Eastern Roman Empire, Zeno the Isaurian.

(*Caesar Rupf nods very briefly.*)

ROMULUS: What do you want from me, Caesar Rupf?

CAESAR RUPF: Although my forefathers came from Germania, they settled in Rome at the time of the Emperor Augustus. Ever since that first century, we have been the leaders in the garment industry.

ROMULUS: I am pleased to hear that. (*He hands Caesar's hat to a surprised Zeno.*)

CAESAR RUPF: When it comes to manufacturing trousers, Your Majesty, I go all out.

ROMULUS: Of course.

CAESAR RUPF: And I am, of course, also perfectly aware that Rome's conservative circles are against trousers, just as they are against everything else that dawns new on the horizon.

ROMULUS: Where trousers commence, culture ends.

CAESAR RUPF: As Emperor you can, of course, afford this jest. But as a man of unclouded realism, I can quite soberly say: the future belongs to trousers. A modern state whose citizens do not wear trousers will go to pot as sure as you are standing there. There is a profound inner connection between the fact that the Teutons wear trousers and that they are making such incredible progress. This inner connection may seem a Sphinxian puzzle to men who are first, last, and always statesmen, but who never think in depth. For a man of business, however, it is as clear as daylight. Only a Rome that wears trousers will be equipped to meet the onslaught of the Germanic hordes.

ROMULUS: If I could share your optimism, my dear Caesar Rupf, I would slip into one of your fabled garments myself.

CAESAR RUPF: I have sworn, by all that is holy, to wear trousers only when it has dawned on the very simplest of souls that without trousers humanity might just as well crawl in a hole. Professional honor, Your Majesty, I'm not just spinning tales. Either all men wear trousers or Caesar Rupf abdicates.

ROMULUS: And what do you propose?

CAESAR RUPF: Your Majesty, on one hand we have the international firm of Caesar Rupf and on the other, the Roman Empire. Right?

ROMULUS: Right.

CAESAR RUPF: Let's call a spade a spade, not tarnished by any sentimentalities. Behind me stand a few million sesterces; behind you, the final abyss.

ROMULUS: The difference cannot be put better.

CAESAR RUPF: First I thought I'd buy up the whole Roman Empire.

(*The Emperor can hardly suppress his joyful excitement.*)

ROMULUS: Let's talk about this in all seriousness, Caesar Rupf. In any event, let me make you a Knight. Achilles, a sword!

CAESAR RUPF: Thank you, Your Majesty, I have already bought myself every possible title. You see, to be quite blunt about it, I decided against buying. The Roman Empire is so run-down that to put it back on its feet would be too expensive, even for an international firm like mine. And no one could know if it would turn out to be a profitable deal. We might end up with a state colossus and that wouldn't be any good either. One is either an international firm or an empire and I must say, quite frankly, an international firm is preferable—it's much more profitable. I've decided against the purchase, Emperor Romulus, but I am not against an alliance.

ROMULUS: And just how do you imagine an alliance between the empire and your firm?

CAESAR RUPF: A purely organic one. As a businessman I'm always for the organic. Think "organic" or go broke, is my motto. First we have to show the Teutons the door.

ROMULUS: That is going to be a bit difficult.

CAESAR RUPF: A businessman of international stature does not know the word "difficult," especially if he has the necessary pocket money at his disposal. Odoaker, in answer to my direct inquiry, has declared himself in writing ready to evacuate Italy for the sum of ten million.

ROMULUS: Odoaker?

CAESAR RUPF: The Teutonic Chief.

ROMULUS: Odd. Of all people I never thought he could be bought.

CAESAR RUPF: Every man has his price, Your Majesty.

ROMULUS: And what do you ask of me in return for this help, Caesar Rupf?

CAESAR RUPF: I will pay the ten million and subsidize the empire with a few more so that it might just keep its head above water like every other sound and healthy state, on one condition, and that is—aside from the fact, of course, that trousers will become obligatory dress—that you give me your daughter, Rea, for my wife. It's as clear as day that this is the only way the alliance can be cemented organically.

ROMULUS: My daughter is engaged to an impoverished patrician who for these past three years has been languishing as a prisoner of the Teutons.

CAESAR RUPF: You see, Your Majesty, I'm as cold as ice. You have to admit, without even as much as batting an eye, that the Roman Empire can only be saved by an unshakeable alliance with an experienced business firm; otherwise the Teutons who lie in wait before Rome will advance upon us in leaps and bounds. You'll give me your answer this very afternoon. If it is no, I'll marry Odoaker's daughter. The firm of Rupf must have an heir. I am in the best years of my life and the storms and stresses of business life, compared to which your battles are mere child's play, have made it impossible for me till now to seek my happiness in the arms of a beloved spouse. It is not easy to choose between these two possibilities, even though it would seem politically more natural to take the Teutonic princess without hesitation. However, my sense of gratitude towards my adopted homeland has swayed me to make this proposal to you. For I do not wish that the firm of Rupf should be suspected of partiality in the forum of history.

(*He bows briefly, tears his hat out of Zeno's hand and exits to left. The other three remain silently sitting at the table.*)

JULIA: Romulus, you must speak to Rea immediately.

ROMULUS: And what am I to say to our daughter, my dear wife?

JULIA: Simply that she will have to marry Caesar Rupf immediately.

ROMULUS: I'll sell the Roman Empire for a handful of sesterces right here and now, but I have not the faintest intention of bargaining away my daughter.

JULIA: Rea will voluntarily sacrifice herself for the empire.

ROMULUS: We have sacrificed so much to the state for hundreds of years that it's now high time for the state to sacrifice itself for us.

JULIA: Romulus!

ZENO: If your daughter does not marry him now, the world will come to an end.

ROMULUS: We will come to an end. That's quite a difference.

ZENO: We are the world.

ROMULUS: We are provincials for whom the world has grown too large, and we can no longer comprehend it.

ZENO: A man like you should never have been Emperor of Rome. (*He beats his fist on the table and exits to the right. Five pot-bellied servants enter from the left.*)

FIRST PORTER: We came to get the busts.

ROMULUS: Help yourselves, please. They are all lined up against the walls.

FIRST PORTER: They're all emperors. Don't drop them, they break like eggs.

(*The room is filled with servants who are carrying busts out.*)

JULIA: Romulus. They call me Julia, the mother of our country, and I am proud of this title. Now I want to speak to you as the mother of my country. You sit the whole day over your break-fast. You're only interested in your chickens. You do not receive your courier. You refuse total mobilization. You do not advance against your enemy. You will not give your daughter to the one man who can save us. Just what *do* you want?

ROMULUS: I don't want to interfere with the course of history, my dear Julia.

JULIA: Then I'm ashamed to be your wife! (*She exits right.*)

ROMULUS: You may clear the table, Pyramus. I have finished my morning repast. (*He wipes his mouth with a napkin. Pyramus carries the table out.*)

My finger bowl, Achilles.

(*Achilles brings a bowl filled with water. Romulus washes his hands. Spurius Titus Mamma rushes in from the left.*)

SPURIUS TITUS MAMMA: My Emperor. (*He kneels before Romulus.*)

ROMULUS: Who are you?

SPURIUS TITUS MAMMA: Spurius Titus Mamma, Captain of Cavalry.

ROMULUS: What do you want?

SPURIUS TITUS MAMMA: It took me two days and two nights, to ride here from Pavia. Seven horses collapsed under me. Three arrows wounded me and when I arrived they would not let me come to you. Here, my Emperor, is the final message from Orestes, your last general, before he fell into the enemy's hands. (*He hands a roll to the Emperor. The Emperor remains unmoved.*)

ROMULUS: You are exhausted and wounded. Why this extraordinary effort, Spurius Titus Mamma?

SPURIUS TITUS MAMMA: That Rome may live.

ROMULUS: Rome died long ago. You are sacrificing yourself for a corpse. You're fighting for a shadow. The country you live for is no more than a grave. Go to sleep, Captain, our times have turned your heroism into a pose.

(*He rises majestically and goes out through the door in the center. Spurius Titus Mamma rises very disturbed, then suddenly throws the message of Orestes on the floor, stamps upon it, and screams.*)

SPURIUS TITUS MAMMA: Emperor, you're a disgrace to Rome!

Act Two

The afternoon of the fateful day in March in the year 476. A park, with the Emperor's villa in the rear. Moss, ivy, and weeds all over. Chickens are clucking, cocks are crowing and now and again a fowl flies across the stage, especially whenever someone comes in. In the background the porch of the dilapidated villa is covered with chicken dirt. A door opens on to the porch, and some steps lead from the porch into the park. On the walls of the villa someone has smeared in chalk: "Long Live Serfdom, Long Live Freedom!" The impression of the scene is that of a chicken yard, even though in the right foreground there are a few rather elegant garden chairs that have seen better days. From time to time thick dark smoke rises from a low building in the rear. The chancery lies slightly to the left of stage at right angles to the villa. All in all the mood is one of brooding despair, of the sense of the end of the world, 'après nous le déluge.'

Characters: Tullius Rotundus sits on one chair; on another the Minister of War, Mars, now Imperial Marshal, sits asleep in full armor, a map of Italy spread across his knees, his helmet and baton lying next to him on the ground. His shield is leaning against the wall of the house. It, too, has the Teutonic slogan

*smeared upon it. Spurius Titus Mamma, who is still very dirty
and bandaged, drags himself along the wall, leans against it,
then drags himself on.*

SPURIUS TITUS MAMMA: I am tired, so tired, I am dead tired.
(*A cook wearing a white apron and a tall cook's hat appears in the door of the villa.*)

COOK: I have the honor to announce the menu for tonight's dinner. Tonight, on the Ides of March anno 476, the company shall
dine on soup Julienne and three fine hens stuffed with roasted
chestnuts à la Campania.
(*Clucking and enticing the chickens, he strides off onto
the porch toward the rear. He holds a knife hidden behind his back. The chickens scatter in all directions.*)

COOK: Julius Nepos, Orestes, Romulus, chick, chick, chick . . .
(*Zeno the Isaurian appears from the left. He stops to scrape
his sandals on the ground.*)

ZENO: I just stepped on another egg! Isn't there anything here but
chickens? My sandals are all sticky and yellow.

TULLIUS ROTUNDUS: Raising chickens is the Emperor's sole passion.
(*A courier runs into the palace from the right.*)

COURIER: The Teutons are in Rome! The Teutons are in Rome!

TULLIUS ROTUNDUS: More bad tidings. Nothing but bad news all
day long.

ZENO: And all on account of this mania for chickens. Let's hope
the Emperor is at least now in the chapel praying for his people.

TULLIUS ROTUNDUS: The Emperor is sleeping.

ZENO: We're trying feverishly to save civilization and the Emperor
is asleep—do you smell smoke?

TULLIUS ROTUNDUS: We are burning the Emperor's archives.
(*Zeno is thunderstruck.*)

ZENO: You—are—burning the archives! Why, for heaven's sake?

TULLIUS ROTUNDUS: Under no circumstances must the invaluable
documents of the Roman art of government fall into the hands
of the Teutons. To take them to safety costs money—and we
lack the financial means.

ZENO: And so you just burn the archives? With a smile on your
lips as if you did not believe in the final triumph of right. Your
whole western empire is beyond all help—it is rotten to the core.
No spirit, no courage . . .

(*The two chamberlains appear from the right.*)

CHAMBERLAINS: Your Majesty.

ZENO: My chamberlains have escaped from the chicken coop.
(*He is frightened to death. The two take him by the hand.*)

SULPHURIDES: Your Majesty, we must repeat our verses of lamentations. It is of the utmost urgency.

PHOSPHORIDOS: If you please, Zeno the Isaurian.

ZENO: I plead for help, O Sun . . .

SULPHURIDES: O Moon.

ZENO: O Moon in the dark night of the universe. Pleading mercy, I approach you. May the moon . . .

PHOSPHORIDOS: The sun.

ZENO: The sun— ouch, another egg!
(*He scrapes the egg off his sandals. Then he is led off by his chamberlains.*)

SPURIUS TITUS MAMMA: I haven't slept for a hundred hours, a hundred hours.
(*Chickens cackle fearfully. The Cook appears on the right, then disappears into the villa. He has a chicken in each hand and another under his right arm. His apron is covered with blood.*)

COOK: Call these things chickens! And I'm supposed to serve birds like this! What good is it to be named after an emperor if they're so skinny they'll hardly make a soup? Fortunately, we'll stuff them with chestnuts. That way at least their lordships will have something to fill their stomachs, even if it's only good for dogs.

SPURIUS TITUS MAMMA: This eternal cackling is driving me crazy. I'm so tired, just plain tired. Galloping all the way from Pavia, and almost bleeding to death besides.

TULLIUS ROTUNDUS: Go and rest behind the villa, the cackling isn't as loud there.

SPURIUS TITUS MAMMA: Tried that already. But the princess is having her drama lessons there, and next to the pond the Emperor of the Eastern Roman Empire is practicing . . .

MARS: Quiet! (*He goes back to sleep.*)

TULLIUS ROTUNDUS: You really shouldn't speak so loud or the Imperial Marshal will wake up.

SPURIUS TITUS MAMMA: I'm unspeakably tired. And then there's all this smoke, this stinking burning smoke!

TULLIUS ROTUNDUS: Why don't you at least sit down?

SPURIUS TITUS MAMMA: If I sit down I'll fall asleep.

TULLIUS ROTUNDUS: That would be the most natural thing for you to do, considering your condition.

SPURIUS TITUS MAMMA: I don't want sleep, I want revenge.

(*The Imperial Marshal rises in despair.*)

MARS: Who can think and plan with all this noise going on? Strategy is a matter of intuition. Before making the bloody incision it is necessary, as in surgery, to attain a certain inner composure. Nothing is worse than wanton noisemaking at headquarters.

(*Angrily, he rolls up his map, takes his helmet, and starts towards the house. Picking up his shield he looks at it, startled.*)

Someone scribbled the enemy's slogan on my shield. Even the walls of the palace have been defaced.

TULLIUS ROTUNDUS: The maid from Helvetia.

MARS: That calls for a courtmartial.

TULLIUS ROTUNDUS: We really don't have any time for such things, Marshal.

MARS: Sabotage.

TULLIUS ROTUNDUS: Lack of personnel. After all, somebody has to help the Lord High Steward pack.

MARS: But you can help. As Minister of State, what else is left for you to do now?

TULLIUS ROTUNDUS: I have to prepare the legal basis upon which the Emperor's residence may be moved to Sicily.

MARS: I shall not be led astray by your defeatism. Our strategic position grows more favorable by the hour. It improves from defeat to defeat. The farther the Teutons dare to advance into our peninsula, the sooner they end up in a dead end. Then we'll be able to squash them with ease from our bases in Sicily and Corsica.

SPURIUS TITUS MAMMA: First squash the Emperor.

MARS: We simply *cannot* lose. The Teutons have no fleet. That makes us unassailable in our islands.

SPURIUS TITUS MAMMA: But we have no fleet either! So what good are the islands to us? The Teutons will sit unassailable in Italy.

MARS: Then we'll just have to build one.

SPURIUS TITUS MAMMA: Build one! The empire is bankrupt.

TULLIUS ROTUNDUS: We'll worry about that later. Right now the main problem is how to get to Sicily.

MARS: I'll order a three-masted schooner.

TULLIUS ROTUNDUS: A three-master! We can't possibly afford one. They're as expensive as sin. Just try to find a galley.

MARS: Now I've been demoted to a shipping agent.

(*He ambles off into the villa.*)

TULLIUS ROTUNDUS: You see, now you've woken the Imperial Marshal.

SPURIUS TITUS MAMMA: I'm so tired.

TULLIUS ROTUNDUS: I only hope we'll find a villa in Sicily we can afford to rent.

(*Fearful cackling. From the left appears the ragged figure of Emilian. He is gaunt and pale. He looks around.*)

EMILIAN: Is this the Emperor's villa in Campania?

(*The Minister of State looks astonished at the eerie figure.*)

TULLIUS ROTUNDUS: Who are you?

EMILIAN: A ghost.

TULLIUS ROTUNDUS: What do you want?

EMILIAN: The Emperor is father to us all. Isn't that true?

TULLIUS ROTUNDUS: To all patriots.

EMILIAN: I am a patriot. I've come to visit the house of my father. (*He looks around again.*) A filthy chicken coop. A dilapidated villa. Call this a chancery? Look at that weatherbeaten Venus by the pond, ivy and moss everywhere, eggs hidden in the weeds—some of them have got under my feet already—and somewhere, I'm sure, a snoring Emperor.

TULLIUS ROTUNDUS: Better take off or I'll summon the guards. They're exercising on the lawn in the park.

EMILIAN: They're sleeping on the lawn in the park, lulled by the cackling of the chickens. No need to disturb their peaceful slumber.

(*The Empress appears in the doorway.*)

JULIA: Ebius! Ebius! Has anyone seen the Lord High Steward, Ebi?

EMILIAN: The mother of her country.

TULLIUS ROTUNDUS: Isn't he helping with the packing, Your Majesty?

JULIA: He hasn't been seen since this morning.

TULLIUS ROTUNDUS: Then he must have fled already.

JULIA: Typically Teuton.

(*The Empress exits.*)

SPURIUS TITUS MAMMA: When you come right down to it, it is the Romans who are fleeing!

(*For a moment he has grown extremely angry, but then his anger collapses. However, in order not to fall asleep he walks back and forth desperately. Emilian sits down in the Marshal's seat.*)

EMILIAN: Are you Tullius Rotundus, Minister of State?

TULLIUS ROTUNDUS: You know me?

EMILIAN: In the past, Tullius Rotundus, you and I often sat together. On many summer evenings.

TULLIUS ROTUNDUS: I don't remember.

EMILIAN: How should you? An empire has fallen in the meantime.

TULLIUS ROTUNDUS: At least tell me where you come from.

EMILIAN: I've come from the world of reality, straight into this farce of an imperial residence.

SPURIUS TITUS MAMMA: I'm tired, simply dog-tired.

(*More cackling of chickens. Mars comes out of the villa.*)

MARS: I forgot my marshal's baton.

EMILIAN: Here it is, Sir.

(*He gives the general the baton that was lying next to him on the ground. Mars waddles back into the villa.*)

TULLIUS ROTUNDUS: I understand: you've come from the front. You're a brave man. You've spilled your heart's blood for your country. What can I do for you?

EMILIAN: What can you do against the Teutons?

TULLIUS ROTUNDUS: Nobody can do anything against them right now. Our resistance is calculated on a long-range basis. The mills of God grind slowly.

EMILIAN: Then you cannot do anything for me.

(*Several servants bearing trunks come out of the villa.*)

ONE OF THE SERVANTS: Where are we supposed to take the Empress's trunks?

TULLIUS ROTUNDUS: To Naples.

(*The servants carry the trunks away, one by one. They dilly-dally. During the remainder of the scene one or other of the servants reappears now and again.*)

TULLIUS ROTUNDUS: These are bitter times, a tragic epoch. But still: such a highly and perfectly organized legal system as the Roman Empire will survive even the worst crises. Our superior culture, our higher standards will win out against the Teutons.

SPURIUS TITUS MAMMA: I'm so incredibly tired.

EMILIAN: Tell me, do you like Horace? Do you write in our finest classical style?

TULLIUS ROTUNDUS: I am a jurist.

EMILIAN: I loved Horace; I used to write the finest classical style.

TULLIUS ROTUNDUS: Are you a poet?

EMILIAN: I was a creature of the higher culture.

TULLIUS ROTUNDUS: Then write again, create anew! Spirit conquers brute matter.

EMILIAN: Where I just came from, the brutes conquered the spirit.
  (*Renewed cackling; more chickens flying about. From the right along the villa appears Rea with Phylax, an actor.*)

REA: Do you, citizens of my father's land,
  See me now go upon my last journey
  And see me look upon
  The last light of the sun.
  And then nevermore?

SPURIUS TITUS MAMMA: If I listen to any classical poetry now I'll fall asleep on the spot!
  (*He staggers off to the left.*)

PHYLAX: Continue, dear Princess, more forcefully, more dramatically!

REA: The god of death who silences all
  Leads me alive
  To the shores of hell. Not for me was
  The marriage hymn. Nor does a bridegroom
  Sing to me, no, not one song, for see
  I am betrothed to Acheron.

PHYLAX: For see, I am betrothed to Acheron.

REA: For see, I am betrothed to Acheron.

PHYLAX: More tragically, Princess, more rhythmically. More of a cry from within, more soul, or no one will buy these immortal verses. One feels that you do not have any real conception of Acheron, the god of death. You talk as if he were something abstract. You still haven't experienced him deep inside. He has remained literature for you, not reality. Sad, terribly sad. Listen carefully: For see, I am betrothed to Acheron.

REA: For see, I am betrothed to Acheron.

PHYLAX: Woe, a fool . . .

REA: Woe, a fool you make of me, O my father's land!
   Why do you mock me
   Though I have not yet perished,
   And while I still see the light of day, and why
   Do you force me
   With your shameful law
   Unwept by loved ones into this monstrous grave!
   Not one of the living, not one of the dead.

PHYLAX: Not one of the living, not one of the dead. Where's the tragedy, Princess? Where the feeling of immeasurable grief? Once again now: Not one of the living . . .

REA: Not one of the living, not one of the dead!
   (*Emilian has risen and is now standing in front of the reciting Princess. She stares at him in amazement.*)
   What do you want?

EMILIAN: Who are you?

REA: I should think I have a better right to ask you who you are.

EMILIAN: I am what comes back when one has gone where I have been. Who are you?

REA: I am Rea, the Emperor's daughter.

EMILIAN: Rea, the Emperor's daughter? I didn't recognize you. You are beautiful, but I had forgotten your face.

REA: Did we know each other?

EMILIAN: I have a feeling we once did.

REA: Do you come from Ravenna? Did we play together as children?

EMILIAN: We played together when I was a man.

REA: Won't you tell me who you are?

EMILIAN: My name is written in my left hand.

REA: Let me see your left hand then.
                    (*He shows his left hand.*)

REA: Oh, how terrible!

EMILIAN: Shall I take it back?

REA: I cannot bear to look at it any more.
                    (*She turns away.*)

EMILIAN: Then you will never know who I am.
(*He hides his hand.*)
REA: Give me your hand! (*She offers her right hand. Emilian puts his left into hers.*) This ring! Emilian's ring!
EMILIAN: Your bridegroom's ring, yes.
REA: But he is dead.
EMILIAN: Croaked.
REA: The ring's partly embedded in the flesh.
(*She stares at the hand lying in hers.*)
EMILIAN: This branded flesh and ring are one.
REA: Emilian! You are Emilian!
EMILIAN: I was.
REA: I no longer recognize you, Emilian.
(*She stares at him again.*)
EMILIAN: You will never recognize me again. I've just returned from a Teutonic prison, Daughter of the Emperor.
(*They stand and stare at each other.*)
REA: I waited for you for three years.
EMILIAN: In a Teutonic dungeon three years are an eternity, Daughter of the Emperor. No one should wait as long as that for anybody.
REA: But now you are here. Come, come with me into my father's house.
EMILIAN: The Teutons are coming.
REA: We know.
EMILIAN: Then go and get a knife.
(*The Princess looks at him, frightened.*)
REA: What do you mean, Emilian?
EMILIAN: I mean, even a woman can fight with a knife.
REA: We must not fight any more. The Roman armies are beaten. We have no more soldiers.
EMILIAN: Soldiers are just human beings and any human being can fight. There are still a lot of people here. Women, slaves, old folks, cripples, children, ministers. Go, get a knife.
REA: That doesn't make any sense, Emilian. We have to surrender to the Teutons.
EMILIAN: I had to surrender to the Teutons three years ago. Look what they made of me, Daughter of the Emperor. Go, get a knife.

REA: I waited three years for you. Day after day, hour after hour. And now I'm frightened of you.

EMILIAN: "For see, I am betrothed to Acheron." Didn't you just recite those verses? They've turned into reality, your verses. Go, get a knife. Hurry! Hurry!

(Rea flees into the house.)

PHYLAX: But Princess! Your lesson isn't over yet. The climax is still to come. A particularly elevated passage about Hades, the most beautiful in all classical literature.

REA: I have no need of literature any more. Now I know what the god of death is like.

(She disappears into the villa. The actor rushes after her.)

TULLIUS ROTUNDUS: Marcus Junius Emilian, returned from Teutonic prison. I am devastated.

EMILIAN: Then hurry to the front. Before your devastation becomes a luxury.

TULLIUS ROTUNDUS: My dear friend, surely you suffered much and deserve our respect. But you mustn't just assume that *we* here at the Emperor's residence have not suffered as well. To sit here and receive one frightful message after another, without being able to do anything about it all, that, no doubt, is the worst that can happen to a man of politics.

(A courier runs into the palace from the left.)

COURIER: The Teutons are marching along the Via Appia toward the south. The Teutons are marching along the Via Appia toward the south.

TULLIUS ROTUNDUS: You see! Toward the south. They're marching directly toward us. We hardly finished mentioning one bad tiding when a new one comes.

(Mars appears in the door of the villa.)

MARS: No galley to be had far and wide.

TULLIUS ROTUNDUS: But there is one anchored in the harbor at Naples.

MARS: It floated over to the Teutons.

TULLIUS ROTUNDUS: For heaven's sake, Marshal, we have to have a ship.

MARS: I'll try to get a fisherman's boat.

(He disappears again. The Minister of State is angry.)

TULLIUS ROTUNDUS: You see, here I was all prepared to reorganize the Empire from Sicily. I have plans for social reforms, including disability insurance for the dock workers. But, of course, I can only put these plans into effect if we find a vessel!

SPURIUS TITUS MAMMA: This smoke, this eternal acrid smoke.

(*Cackling of hens. Caesar Rupf enters from the left.*)

CAESAR RUPF: Gentlemen, I hope it is crystal clear to you that after the fall of Rome the empire won't be worth a hill of beans. A military defeat has been added to your bankruptcy. The Roman Empire will never be able to pull itself out of this quagmire.

EMILIAN: Who are you?

CAESAR RUPF: Caesar Rupf, owner of the international firm of Rupf, coats and trousers.

EMILIAN: What do you want?

CAESAR RUPF: It must be as clear as daylight to even a partially informed politician that there is but one way to save Rome: that is, for me to put up a few millions. I demand that, in return for the honest offer I've made, I receive a decent answer. Yes or No. Wedding feast or world defeat. Either I return home with a bride or the Empire can go to the birds.

EMILIAN: What's going on here, Minister of State?

TULLIUS ROTUNDUS: Odoaker agreed to evacuate Italy for the sum of ten million. This—manufacturer of trousers—is willing to pay that sum.

EMILIAN: His conditions?

TULLIUS ROTUNDUS: That Princess Rea marry him.

EMILIAN: Get the Princess.

TULLIUS ROTUNDUS: You mean . . .

EMILIAN: And call the entire court together.

(*The Minister of State goes into the villa.*)

EMILIAN: You shall have your answer, trouser-maker.

(*The Captain of Cavalry staggers from the right to the left of the stage.*)

SPURIUS TITUS MAMMA: I haven't slept for a hundred hours. A hundred hours. I'm so tired, I could drop.

(*In the door of the villa there appear Rea, Tullius Rotundus, Zeno, Mars, Phosphoridos, Sulphurides, the Cook and the guards.*)

REA: You called me, Emilian?

EMILIAN: Yes, I called you. Come to me.
> (*Rea slowly approaches Emilian.*)

EMILIAN: You waited three years for me, Daughter of the Emperor?

REA: Three years, day after day, night after night, hour after hour.

EMILIAN: You love me?

REA: I love you.

EMILIAN: With all your heart?

REA: With all my heart.

EMILIAN: And would do anything I ask you?

REA: I'll do anything.

EMILIAN: Even take a knife?

REA: I'll take a knife, if you wish it.

EMILIAN: So great is your love, Daughter of the Emperor?

REA: My love for you is beyond all measure. I no longer recognize you, but I love you. I am afraid of you, but I love you.

EMILIAN: Then marry this splendid pot-belly and bear him children.
> (*He points to Caesar Rupf.*)

ZENO: At last, a reasonable Westerner.

THE COURT: Marry, Princess, marry!

TULLIUS ROTUNDUS: Make this sacrifice for your beloved country, my girl!
> (*All stare at Rea, full of hope.*)

REA: And leave you?

EMILIAN: You must leave me.

REA: And love another?

EMILIAN: Yes, love him who alone can save your country.

REA: But I love you.

EMILIAN: I cast you off so that Rome may live.

REA: You want to disgrace me as you have been disgraced, Emilian?

EMILIAN: We have to do what we have to do. Our shame will nourish Italy; our dishonor will renew its strength.

REA: You couldn't ask this of me if you really loved me.

EMILIAN: I can ask it of you only because you love me.
> (*She looks at him in fright.*)

EMILIAN: You will obey, Daughter of the Emperor. Your love is beyond all measure.

REA: I will obey.

EMILIAN: You will be his wife?

REA: I shall be his wife.

EMILIAN: Then give your hand to this clearheaded trouser-maker.
(Rea obeys.)
Now, Caesar Rupf, the Emperor's only daughter has given you her hand, and a golden calf has been crowned with an imperial bridal wreath, for in our day, when mankind is being outraged as never before, coupling is a virtue.
(Caesar Rupf is deeply moved.)

CAESAR RUPF: Princess, you must believe me, the tears in my eyes are as good as gold. Through this union the international firm of Rupf has reached a pinnacle of success never before attained in my line.
(Huge columns of smoke.)

MARS: The empire is saved.

COOK: Western civilization preserved! To celebrate this day I'll roast the Flavians.

SULPHURIDES AND PHOSPHORIDOS: Your Majesty, the Ode of Joy!

BOTH TOGETHER WITH ZENO:
O Byzantium, joy be thine!
Your name and fame like flames outshine
The moon and stars and sun.

Yea, our faith and hopes have been
Wondrously fulfilled again.
Salvation is ours, O Byzantium!

TULLIUS ROTUNDUS: Stop the burning of the archives this very instant.

VOICE OF ACHILLES: The Emperor!
(The smoke clears away. The Emperor, surrounded by his Court, appears in the doorway. Achilles and Pyramus are behind him. Pyramus is carrying a flat basket. Silence.)

ROMULUS: There seems to be some excitement in my garden. What is the reason for all these goings-on?
(Silence.)

EMILIAN: Welcome, O Caesar of exalted cuisine. Greetings unto you, Emperor of fine fowl. Hail unto you whom your soldiers call Romulus the Little.

(The Emperor looks attentively at Emilian.)

ROMULUS: Hail unto you, Emilian, my daughter's bridegroom.

EMILIAN: You are the first to recognize me, Emperor Romulus. Not even your daughter knew me.

ROMULUS: Don't doubt her love, though. It's just that old age has sharper eyes. Emilian, be welcomed.

EMILIAN: Forgive me, Father of the world, for not responding perhaps to your greeting in the customary manner. I've been a prisoner of the Teutons for too long. Now I no longer know the customs of your court. But knowing Rome's history will help me. There were emperors who were hailed thus: Well won, O mighty one! And others: Well murdered, Your Majesty! and thus you shall be hailed: Well slept, Emperor Romulus!

(The Emperor sits down on an easy chair in the doorway and looks for a long time at Emilian.)

ROMULUS: Your body bears witness to great want and tribulation. You've suffered hunger and thirst.

EMILIAN: I went hungry and you ate your meals.

ROMULUS: I see your hands. You were tortured.

EMILIAN: I was tortured while your chickens flourished.

ROMULUS: You are full of despair.

EMILIAN: I escaped from my prison in Germania, Emperor of Rome. I came to you on foot, Exalted One. I measured the vast expanse of your dominions, mile after mile, step after step. I saw your empire, Father of the world . . .

ROMULUS: Ever since I've been Emperor I have not left my country residence. Tell me about my empire, Emilian.

EMILIAN: Wherever I went I saw nothing but immense decay.

ROMULUS: Tell me of my subjects.

EMILIAN: Your people have been robbed by war profiteers, cheated by black marketeers, oppressed by mercenaries, jeered at by Teutonic tribesmen.

ROMULUS: I'm not ignorant of these things.

EMILIAN: How can you know what you have never seen, Emperor of Rome?

ROMULUS: I can imagine it, Emilian. Come into my house. My daughter has been waiting for you these many years.

EMILIAN: I'm no longer worthy of your daughter, Emperor of Rome.

ROMULUS: You are not unworthy—only unhappy.

EMILIAN: I've been dishonored. The Teutons forced me to crawl beneath a blood-smeared yoke. Naked. Like a beast.

MARS: Revenge!

REA: Emilian!

(She embraces her betrothed.)

EMILIAN: I'm a Roman officer. I've lost my honor. Go to him, Daughter of the Emperor, go to the man you now belong to.

(Rea steps slowly back to Caesar Rupf.)

EMILIAN: Your daughter has become the wife of this trouser-maker, Emperor of Rome, and my disgrace has saved the empire.

(The Emperor rises.)

ROMULUS: The Emperor will not permit this marriage.

(All stand as if turned to stone.)

CAESAR RUPF: Papa!

REA: I shall marry him, Father. You cannot keep me from doing the one thing that will save my fatherland.

ROMULUS: My daughter will submit to the Emperor's will. The Emperor knows what he is doing when he throws his empire to the flames, when he drops what must break, when he crushes what is doomed.

(Rea, head bowed, goes into the house.)

ROMULUS: To our duties, Pyramus. Bring the chicken feed! Augustus! Tiberius! Trajan! Hadrian! Marcus Aurelius! Odoaker! *(He goes off to the right, scattering chicken feed. His chamberlains follow him. The rest of the Court stand motionless.)*

TULLIUS ROTUNDUS: Better start burning the archives again!

(Everything is again enveloped in heavy black smoke.)

EMILIAN: Down with the Emperor!

Act Three

The night of the Ides of March in the year 476 . . . The Emperor's bedroom with a row of windows at left and a door at the back. On the right is a bed and another door. In the center of the room stand two couches forming an angle that opens toward the audience. Between the couches stands a small, low, elegant table.

In the foreground, both on the right and left, are two wardrobes. Near midnight. Full moon. The room lies in darkness except for the light that falls through the windows on to the floor and walls. The door at the back opens. Pyramus appears with a three-armed candelabra and uses it to light a second candelabra standing by the bed. Then he places the candelabra he carries on the low table. The Emperor enters by the door on the right, dressed in a rather shabby nightshirt. Behind him Achilles.

ROMULUS: My bath tonight did me doubly good: first, because we had a fine supper, and then after such a depressing day nothing helps as much as a good bath. Days like this are not for me. I am an untragic human being, Achilles.

ACHILLES: Does Your Majesty wish to don the Emperor's toga or his dressing gown?

ROMULUS: My dressing gown. I won't be governing any more today.

ACHILLES: Your Majesty is supposed to sign the proclamation to the Roman people tonight.

ROMULUS: I'll do it tomorrow.

(Achilles wants to help him put on the dressing gown. The Emperor stops him.)

ROMULUS: Bring me my imperial dressing gown, Achilles. This one's too shabby.

ACHILLES: The Empress has already packed the imperial dressing gown. It belonged to her father.

ROMULUS: I see. Well then, help me into these rags.

(He slips on the gown and takes the wreath off his head.)

ROMULUS: What? The wreath was on my head all this time? I even forgot to take it off for my bath. Hang it up by my bed, Pyramus.

(He gives the wreath to Pyramus, who hangs it up by the bed.)

ROMULUS: How many leaves are left?

PYRAMUS: Two.

ROMULUS: My expenses today were enormous. *(The Emperor sighs and goes to the window.)* At last some fresh air. The wind has changed direction and blown the smoke away. This afternoon was a torture. But at least the archives are ashes. The only sensible order my Minister of State ever gave.

PYRAMUS: Future historians will bemoan this loss, O my Emperor.

ROMULUS: Nonsense. They'll invent better sources than our imperial archives.

(*He sits down on the couch on the right.*)

ROMULUS: Hand me Catullus, Pyramus, or has my wife already packed it, too, since it belonged to her father's library?

PYRAMUS: It was packed, my Emperor.

ROMULUS: It doesn't matter. I'll just have to try to reconstruct Catullus from memory as best I can. Good verses are never wholly forgotten. A cup of wine, Achilles.

ACHILLES: Does Your Majesty prefer wine from Falerone or from Syracuse?

ROMULUS: From Falerone. In days like these one should drink the best.

(*Achilles places a large cup in front of the Emperor. Pyramus fills it.*)

PYRAMUS: This bottle of Falerone, vintage 70, is all that's left, my Emperor.

ROMULUS: Then leave it here.

ACHILLES: The mother of our country wishes to speak to Your Majesty.

ROMULUS: The Empress may enter. I won't be needing this second candelabra.

(*The chamberlains bow and leave. Pyramus takes the candelabra standing nearest the bed. Now only the foreground is lit. The background is bathed in the growing light of the moon. Julia appears in the back.*)

JULIA: The Lord High Steward has gone over to the Teutons. I always warned you about Ebi.

ROMULUS: Well, as a Teuton was he supposed to die for us Romans?

(*Silence.*)

JULIA: I came to speak with you for the last time.

ROMULUS: You're wearing your traveling clothes, my dear wife.

JULIA: I'm leaving for Sicily tonight.

ROMULUS: Is the fishing boat ready?

JULIA: A raft.

ROMULUS: But isn't that a little dangerous?

JULIA: Staying is more dangerous.

(*Silence.*)

ROMULUS: I wish you a safe journey.

JULIA: We may not see each other for a long time.

ROMULUS: We shall never see each other again.

JULIA: I am determined to continue the resistance against the enemy from Sicily. At any price.

ROMULUS: Resistance at any price is the greatest nonsense there is.

JULIA: You are a defeatist.

ROMULUS: I only weigh the odds. If we defend ourselves, our defeat will be bloodier. That may look grandiose, but what's the sense? Why burn a world that's already lost?

(Silence.)

JULIA: Then you really don't want Rea to marry this Caesar Rupf?

ROMULUS: No.

JULIA: And you won't go to Sicily, either?

ROMULUS: The Emperor does not flee.

JULIA: It will cost you your head.

ROMULUS: Quite likely. But is that any reason why I should act as if I'd already lost it?

(Silence.)

JULIA: We've been married for twenty years, Romulus.

ROMULUS: What do you want to say with this dismal fact?

JULIA: We once loved each other.

ROMULUS: You know you're lying.

(Silence.)

JULIA: Then you only married me in order to become Emperor.

ROMULUS: Precisely.

JULIA: You dare to say this calmly to my face?

ROMULUS: Of course. Our marriage was horrible, but I never committed the crime of keeping you in doubt for a single day why I had married you. I married you in order to become Emperor and you married me to become Empress. You became my wife because I was a descendant of the highest Roman nobility, and you were the daughter of the Emperor Valentinian and a slave girl. I made you legitimate and you crowned me.

(Silence.)

JULIA: We needed each other.

ROMULUS: Precisely.

JULIA: Then it's your duty now to come with me to Sicily. We belong together.

ROMULUS: I have no more duties toward you. I gave you what you wanted from me. You became Empress.

JULIA: You cannot reproach me for anything. We both acted the same way.

ROMULUS: No, we did not both act the same way. Between your action and mine is an infinite difference.

JULIA: I don't see it.

ROMULUS: You married me out of ambition. Everything you have ever done was done out of ambition. Even now, you won't give up this lost war simply because of ambition.

JULIA: I'm going to Sicily because I love my country.

ROMULUS: You don't know your country. What you love is the abstract idea of a state that offered you the opportunity of becoming Empress by marriage.

(The two are again silent.)

JULIA: All right then, why not speak the truth? Why not be open with one another? I *am* ambitious. For me, there is nothing else but the empire. I am the great-granddaughter of Julian, the last great Emperor. And proud of it. And what are you? The son of a bankrupt patrician. But you're ambitious, too, or you wouldn't have become the Emperor of an entire world—you would have remained the nobody you were.

ROMULUS: What I did was done not out of ambition but of necessity. What was the end for you was for me a means to an end. I became Emperor purely out of political insight.

JULIA: Political insight? When did you ever have any? In the twenty years of your reign you did nothing but eat, drink, sleep, read, and raise chickens. You never left your country estate, never entered your capital, and the financial reserves of the empire were so totally used up that we now have to live like common laborers. Your only skill was to defeat with a joke any thought aimed at getting rid of you. But that your attitude is based on political insight is an enormous lie. Nero's megalomania and Caligula's madness were evidence of greater political maturity than your passion for chickens. Yours was no political insight but just plain indolence!

ROMULUS: Precisely. It was my political insight to do nothing.

JULIA: You didn't have to become Emperor for that.

ROMULUS: But that was the only way in which my doing nothing could make any sense. To do nothing as a private citizen is completely ineffectual.

JULIA: And to do nothing as Emperor jeopardizes the state.

ROMULUS: Precisely.

JULIA: What do you mean?

ROMULUS: You've discovered the meaning of my idleness.

JULIA: But you can't possibly doubt the necessity of the state.

ROMULUS: I don't doubt the necessity of the state. I merely doubt the necessity of our state. Our state has become a world empire, an institution officially engaged in murder, plunder, suppression, and oppressive taxation at the expense of other people—until I came along.

JULIA: Then I don't understand why you had to become Emperor, of all things, if that is what you thought about the Roman Empire.

ROMULUS: For hundreds of years now the Roman Empire has existed only because there was still an Emperor. Therefore, I had no other choice than to become Emperor if I wanted to liquidate the empire.

JULIA: Either you are mad or the world is.

ROMULUS: I think the latter.

JULIA: The only reason you married me then was to destroy the Roman Empire.

ROMULUS: For no other reason.

JULIA: And from the very beginning you never thought of anything but Rome's fall.

ROMULUS: Nothing else.

JULIA: You deliberately sabotaged any attempts to save the Empire?

ROMULUS: Deliberately.

JULIA: You acted the cynic and the perpetual overstuffed buffoon in order to stab us in the back?

ROMULUS: You might put it that way, if you like.

JULIA: You deceived me.

ROMULUS: You deceived yourself about me. You thought I was

just as power-hungry as you. You had it all figured out, but
your calculation was wrong.

JULIA: And yours was right, I suppose?

ROMULUS: Rome is falling.

JULIA: You are Rome's traitor.

ROMULUS: No, Rome's judge.

> (*They are silent. Then Julia cries out in despair.*)

JULIA: Romulus!

ROMULUS: You'd better leave for Sicily now. I have nothing more
to say to you.

> (*Slowly the Empress leaves. Achilles steps out of the back-
> ground.*)

ACHILLES: My Emperor.

ROMULUS: My cup is empty. Fill it again.

> (*Achilles fills the cup.*)

ROMULUS: You are trembling.

ACHILLES: Indeed, my Emperor.

ROMULUS: What's the matter with you?

ACHILLES: Your Majesty doesn't like me to discuss the military
situation.

ROMULUS: You know that I expressly forbade you to do so. The
only person I talk about the military situation with is my bar-
ber. He is the only one who understands something about it.

ACHILLES: But Capua has fallen.

ROMULUS: That is no excuse whatsoever to spill good wine.

ACHILLES: I beg your pardon.

> (*He bows.*)

ROMULUS: Now go to sleep.

ACHILLES: The Princess would like to speak to Your Majesty.

ROMULUS: My daughter may enter.

> (*Achilles leaves. Rea comes from behind.*)

REA: Father.

ROMULUS: Come, my child, sit down by me.

> (*Rea sits down by him.*)

ROMULUS: What do you want to tell me?

REA: Rome is in danger, Father.

ROMULUS: Why is it that tonight of all nights everyone wants to
discuss politics with me? That's what the noon meal is for.

REA: What shall I talk about then?

ROMULUS: About all those things one says to one's father at night. About all those things closest to your heart, my child.

REA: Rome is closest to my heart.

ROMULUS: Then you no longer love Emilian for whom you waited so long?

REA: But I do, Father.

ROMULUS: But no longer as passionately as before, no longer the way you once loved him?

REA: I love him more than my own life.

ROMULUS: Then talk to me about Emilian. If you love him, then he is more important than our rundown empire.

(Silence.)

REA: Father, let me marry Caesar Rupf.

ROMULUS: My dear daughter, I find this Rupf fellow quite congenial because he has money, but his conditions are unacceptable.

REA: He will save Rome.

ROMULUS: That is exactly what makes this man so eerie. A trouser manufacturer who wants to save the Roman Empire must be crazy.

REA: There's no other way to save our country.

ROMULUS: I admit there's no other way. The fatherland can only be saved with money, or it will surely be lost. But we must choose between a catastrophic capitalism and a capital catastrophe. So my dear child, you simply cannot marry this Caesar Rupf; you love Emilian.

(Silence.)

REA: I must leave him to serve my country.

ROMULUS: That's easily said.

REA: My country, above all.

ROMULUS: You see, you've been reading too many tragedies lately.

REA: But shouldn't one love one's country more than anything else in the world?

ROMULUS: No, one should never love it as much as one loves other human beings. In fact, the most inportant thing is to mistrust one's country. No one turns killer more easily than one's native country.

REA: Father.

ROMULUS: Yes, Daughter?

REA: I can't possibly let my country down.

ROMULUS: You have to.

REA: I can't live without a country.

ROMULUS: Can you live without your beloved? It is much more difficult to be loyal to a human being than to remain loyal to a state.

REA: It's my country, not just a state.

ROMULUS: Every state calls itself "country," or "nation," when it is about to commit murder.

REA: Our unconditional love for our country was what made Rome great.

ROMULUS: But our love did not make Rome good. We nurtured a beast with our virtues. We became drunk on the greatness of our country, but what we loved has now turned into gall and wormwood.

REA: You are ungrateful to your country.

ROMULUS: No. Only I'm not like that sire of heroes in one of your tragedies who says "bon appetit" to the state when the state wants to devour one of his children. Go, marry Emilian!

REA: Emilian has rejected me, Father.

ROMULUS: If there remains even one spark of genuine love in your body, you will not let this separate you from your lover. You remain with him even when he rejects you. You stick by him even if he's a criminal. But you can be separated from your country. Shake its dust off your feet when it has become a murderer's den and an executioner's block, because your love for your country is impotent.

(Silence. A human figure climbs through the window on the left and then hides somewhere in the dark at the back.)

REA: If I go to him now he will surely reject me again. He will always reject me.

ROMULUS: Then you have to keep on going back to him.

REA: He doesn't love me any more. He loves only Rome.

ROMULUS: Rome will come to an end and then all he'll have left is your love.

REA: I'm afraid.

ROMULUS: Learn to conquer your fears. That's the only art we have to learn to master these days. Learn to look at things fearlessly and fearlessly to do the right thing. I've been trying to practice it all my life. Now, you try it, too. Go to him.

REA: Yes, Father, I will.

ROMULUS: Well said, my child. This is how I love you. Go to Emilian. Take leave of me. You'll never see me again, for I shall die.

REA: Father!

ROMULUS: The Teutons will kill me. I have always counted on that death. That's my secret. I sacrifice Rome by sacrificing myself.

(Silence.)

REA: My Father.

ROMULUS: But you will live. Now go, my child; go to Emilian.
(Rea slowly leaves. Pyramus steps out of the background.)

PYRAMUS: My Emperor.

ROMULUS: What do you want?

PYRAMUS: The Empress has left.

ROMULUS: Fine.

PYRAMUS: Does Your Majesty wish to go to bed?

ROMULUS: Not yet. There is still another person I have to talk to. Bring me a second cup.

PYRAMUS: Yes, my Emperor.
(He brings a second cup.)

ROMULUS: Here, put it next to mine and fill it.
(Pyramus fills it.)

ROMULUS: And now mine, too.
(Pyramus fills the Emperor's cup.)

PYRAMUS: The bottle is empty, my Emperor.

ROMULUS: Then you may go to bed.
(Pyramus bows and exits. Romulus sits without moving till the chamberlain's steps are no longer heard.)

ROMULUS: Emilian, come forward. We're alone now.
(Emilian slowly comes out of the darkness, wrapped in a black cloak.)

EMILIAN: You knew I was here?

ROMULUS: A few seconds ago you climbed into my room through the window. My wine cup reflected your figure. Sit down.

EMILIAN: I'll stand.

ROMULUS: You came very late. It's midnight.

EMILIAN: Some visits can only be made at midnight.

ROMULUS: You see, I was ready to receive you. To welcome you I had this cup filled with excellent wine. Let's make a toast.

EMILIAN: So be it.

ROMULUS: To your homecoming.

EMILIAN: To that which shall be fulfilled this midnight.

ROMULUS: And what is that?

EMILIAN: Let's toast justice, Emperor Romulus.

ROMULUS: Justice is a terrible thing, Emilian.

EMILIAN: As terrible as my wounds.

ROMULUS: All right then: To justice.

EMILIAN: We're alone. Only the darkness is witness to this moment when the Emperor of Rome and a man just returned from his Teutonic prison toast justice with cups of blood-red wine.

(Romulus rises and they touch glasses. At the same instant someone cries out and from under the couch of the Emperor the head of Tullius Rotundus appears.)

ROMULUS: For heaven's sake, my dear Minister, has something happened to you?

TULLIUS ROTUNDUS: Your Majesty stepped on my fingers.

(He moans.)

ROMULUS: I'm sorry, but how was I to know you were under there? Every Minister of State cries out when justice is toasted.

TULLIUS ROTUNDUS: I merely wanted to propose to Your Majesty an all-inclusive old age insurance program for the Roman Empire.

(He crawls out from under the bed, not without some embarrassment, dressed in a black cloak similar to Emilian's.)

ROMULUS: Your hand is bleeding, Tullius Rotundus.

TULLIUS ROTUNDUS: I scratched myself with my dagger out of pure fright.

ROMULUS: My dear Tullius, one must be very careful with daggers.

(He walks toward the left.)

EMILIAN: Are you going to call your chamberlains, Emperor Romulus?

(They face one another, Emilian hostile and resolute, Romulus smiling.)

ROMULUS: What for, Emilian? You know perfectly well they're asleep by midnight. But I do want to get a bandage for my wounded Minister of State.

(*He goes to the wardrobe on the left and opens it. Inside the wardrobe stands, somewhat bent, Zeno the Isaurian.*)

ROMULUS: Forgive me, Emperor of East Rome. I didn't know you were sleeping in my wardrobe.

ZENO: You're excused. Ever since I fled Constantinople my insecure life has accustomed me to this sort of thing.

ROMULUS: I'm sincerely sorry you have such troubles.

(*Zeno climbs out of the wardrobe. He, too, is dressed in a black cloak. He looks about astonished.*)

ZENO: Why, is someone else here?

ROMULUS: Don't be disturbed. They came in quite by chance.

(*He takes a cloth from an upper shelf of the wardrobe.*)

ROMULUS: Amazing! There's somebody else in here, too.

ZENO: My chamberlain, Sulphurides.

(*Sulphurides climbs out. He is extremely tall. He is also dressed in a black cloak. He bows ceremoniously before Romulus. Romulus looks at him.*)

ROMULUS: Good evening. You really should have assigned him the other wardrobe, my Imperial Brother. And where did you put your chamberlain Phosphoridos?

ZENO: He's still under your bed, Emperor Romulus.

ROMULUS: He might as well come out, too. No need to be embarrassed.

(*Phosphoridos, who is a short man, crawls out from under the Emperor's bed. He, too, is dressed in a black cloak.*)

SULPHURIDES: We have come, Your Majesty . . .

PHOSPHORIDOS: To recite our ode of woe.

SULPHURIDES: The complete recital of which Your Majesty has not yet had the pleasure to hear.

ROMULUS: By all means, only not at this silent midnight hour.

(*Romulus sits down and gives the cloth to Tullius Rotundus.*)

ROMULUS: Bind your wounds with this cloth, my dear Minister. I don't like to see blood.

(*The door of the wardrobe on the right falls open and Spurius Titus Mamma falls full length to the floor with a crash.*)

ROMULUS: Well, even our athlete isn't asleep yet?

SPURIUS TITUS MAMMA: I'm tired, simply dead tired.

    (*He gets up unsteadily.*)

ROMULUS: You lost your dagger, Spurius Titus Mamma.

    (*Spurius Titus Mamma, with a frown, picks up his dagger, and hastily hides it under his cloak.*)

SPURIUS TITUS MAMMA: I haven't slept for one hundred and ten hours.

ROMULUS: If anyone else happens to be present, please step forward.

    (*From under the couch on the left crawls Mars, followed by a soldier. Both are wrapped in black cloaks.*)

MARS: Excuse me, my Emperor. I want to discuss total mobilization with you.

ROMULUS: And whom did you bring along for this discussion, Marshal?

MARS: My adjutant.

    (*The Cook with his tall white hat now crawls forth slowly from under the Emperor's couch. He, too, is wrapped in a black cloak. For the first time the Emperor is visibly moved.*)

ROMULUS: You, too, Cook? And with the very kitchen knife with which you slaughtered so many emperors?

    (*With downcast eyes the Cook steps into the half-circle of men around the Emperor.*)

ROMULUS: I see you've all dressed in black. You crawled out from under my bed and my couch, and out of my wardrobes, after having spent half the night there in very complicated and uncomfortable positions. Why?

    (*Deep silence.*)

TULLIUS ROTUNDUS: We want to speak with you, Emperor Romulus.

ROMULUS: The Emperor was not aware that court ceremonial prescribes gymnastics for those wishing to speak with him.

    (*He gets up and rings a bell.*)

ROMULUS: Pyramus! Achilles!

(Achilles and Pyramus, dressed in their nightshirts and caps, rush forth trembling.)

ACHILLES: My Emperor!

PYRAMUS: Your Majesty!

ROMULUS: My imperial toga, Achilles! My imperial wreath, Pyramus!

(Achilles places the toga about the Emperor's shoulders, and Pyramus the wreath upon his head.)

ROMULUS: Take the table and cups out, Achilles. This is a solemn moment.

(Achilles and Pyramus carry the table off to the right.)

ROMULUS: Now, go back to sleep.

(Pyramus and Achilles bow and leave, greatly confused and frightened.)

ROMULUS: The Emperor is ready to hear all of you. What is it you have to say to him?

TULLIUS ROTUNDUS: We demand the provinces back.

MARS: Your legions.

EMILIAN: The Empire.

(Deep silence.)

ROMULUS: The Emperor doesn't owe you an accounting.

EMILIAN: You owe Rome an accounting.

ZENO: You must answer before history.

MARS: You depended on our power.

ROMULUS: I did not depend on your power. Had I acquired the world with your help, you would be justified. But I lost a world you never won. I passed it on out of my hands like a bad coin. I am free, I have nothing to do with you. You are nothing but moths dancing about my light, shadows that will fade when I no longer shine.

(The conspirators inch away from him toward the wall.)

I owe an accounting to only *one* of you and to this one I shall now speak. Come forward, Emilian.

(Emilian slowly steps forward from the right.)

I cannot speak to you as to an officer who has lost his honor. I am a civilian and have never understood what is meant by an officer's honor. But I will speak to you as to a human being who was tortured and who suffered greatly. I love you like a son, Emilian. For me you represent the final great argument against those who, like myself, refuse to defend themselves; in you I'm willing to see the militant challenge of the people, violated again and again, the victim of power defiled a thousand times. What do you demand of your Emperor, Emilian?

EMILIAN: I demand an answer, Emperor Romulus.

ROMULUS: You shall have your answer.

EMILIAN: What did you do to keep your people from falling into the hands of the Teutons?

ROMULUS: Nothing.

EMILIAN: What have you done to keep Rome from being violated as I was?

ROMULUS: Nothing.

EMILIAN: And how will you justify yourself? You are accused of having betrayed your empire.

ROMULUS: I didn't betray my empire; Rome betrayed herself. Rome knew the truth but chose violence. Rome knew humaneness but chose tyranny. Rome doubly demeaned herself: before her own people and before the other nations in her power. You are standing before an invisible throne, Emilian; before the throne of all the Roman Emperors, of whom I am the last. Shall I touch your eyes that you may see this throne, this pyramid of skulls down whose steps cascade rivers of blood in endless waterfalls, generating Rome's power? What kind of an answer do you expect I can hand down to you, as I sit on top of the colossus that is Roman history? What can be said about your wounds by the Emperor who sits enthroned above the corpses of his own sons and the sons of strangers, above the mound of human sacrifices swept to his feet by the wars of Rome's glory and the gladiatorial games for Rome's amusement? Rome has grown weak, a tottering old hag, but her guilt has not been expiated and her crimes not erased. The new day has dawned overnight. The curses of Rome's victims are being fulfilled. The axe is put to the trunk, the rotten tree is being felled. The Teutons are coming; we have spilled the stranger's blood; now we have to pay back with our own. Don't turn away, Emilian, don't retreat before the majesty that is mine, rising before you, covered as it is with the ancient guilt of our history, making it more horrible than your own body. Now we are speaking of justice, the justice we drank to. Answer my question now: Do we still have the right to defend ourselves? Do we still have the right to be more than victims?

(*Emilian is silent.*)

You're silent.

(*Emilian slowly retreats to those surrounding the Emperor in a wide half-circle.*)

You're stepping back among those who came to me like thieves in the night. Let's be honest with each other. Let there be not one hair's breadth of a lie, not one hand's width of deceit between us. I know what all of you are hiding under your black cloaks, I know what your hands are clutching. But you made one mistake. You thought you were coming to a man who could not defend himself, while I now spring upon you with the claws of truth and grip you with the teeth of justice. You aren't attacking me, I'm attacking you. You aren't accusing me, I'm accusing you. Defend yourselves! Don't you know who's standing in front of you? In full knowledge I brought about the fall of the country you wish to defend. I broke the ice on which you stepped and burned the foundation on which you built. Why so pale, why do you cling so silently to the walls of my chamber? You have only one answer. Kill me if you believe I am in the wrong! But if in truth we no longer have a *right* to defend ourselves, then surrender to the Teutons. Answer me.

(*They remain silent.*)

Answer!

(*Emilian lifts his dagger on high.*)

EMILIAN (*shouts*): Long live Rome!

(*All draw their daggers and step toward Romulus, who remains calmly seated. The daggers close in over him. At that moment a horrifying cry of fright can be heard at the back: "The Teutons are coming!" Gripped by panic everyone rushes away through windows and doors. The Emperor does not move. Pale from fright, Pyramus and Achilles step out of the background.*)

ROMULUS: Well, where are the Teutons?

PYRAMUS: In Nola, Your Majesty.

ROMULUS: What's all the shouting about, then? They won't get here before tomorrow morning. I'm going to bed.
> *:He rises.)*

PYRAMUS: Very well, my Emperor.
> *(Pyramus takes off the Emperor's toga, his wreath, and his robe. Romulus, going to his bed, suddenly stops.)*

ROMULUS: I see one of them is still lying here in front of my bed, Achilles. Who is it?
> *(The chamberlain lights up the body with a candelabra.)*

ACHILLES: It is Spurius Titus Mamma, Your Majesty, sound asleep.

ROMULUS: Heavens be thanked. Our athlete is asleep at last. Let him be.
> *(Romulus steps over him into his bed. Pyramus blows out the candles and goes off with Achilles in the dark.)*

ROMULUS: Pyramus!

PYRAMUS: Yes, my Emperor.

ROMULUS: When the Teutons arrive, let them come in.

Act Four

The morning following the Ides of March in the year 476.

The Emperor's study is in Act One. Now only the bust of the founder of Rome, King Romulus, sits over the door at the back. Achilles and Pyramus, awaiting the Emperor, are standing by the door.

ACHILLES: A beautiful and refreshing morning.

PYRAMUS: I can't understand it: even on this day when the world's coming to an end the sun still rises.

ACHILLES: There's no depending even on nature anymore.
> *(Silence)*

PYRAMUS: We've served Rome for the past sixty years, under eleven emperors, and it seems historically incomprehensible that Rome should cease to exist during our lifetime.

ACHILLES: I'm washing my hands in innocence. I was always a perfect chamberlain.

PYRAMUS: No matter how you look at it, we were the only really solid pillars of the empire.

ACHILLES: Our exit will go down in history as the end of antiquity.

(*Silence.*)

PYRAMUS: To think the day will come when no one will speak Latin or Greek any more, but only an impossible language like this German.

ACHILLES: Imagine men at the helm of world politics, Teutonic chieftains, Chinese and Zulus, with not the smallest fraction of our education and culture. *Arma virumque cano.* I know all of Virgil by heart.

PYRAMUS: *Mehnin aeide thea,* and I, Homer!

ACHILLES: No matter how you look at it, the times about to begin will be frightful.

PYRAMUS: Yes, a literal Dark Ages. Without wishing to be a pessimist, I say mankind will never recover from the present catastrophe.

(*Romulus enters, wearing the imperial toga and wreath.*)

ACHILLES AND PYRAMUS: Hail Caesar!

ROMULUS: Hail: I am late. Yesterday's unexpectedly large number of audiences exhausted me. This morning I was so sleepy I was hardly able to climb over the athlete who's still snoring in front of my bed. I governed more last night than at any time in all the twenty years of my reign.

ACHILLES: True, my Emperor.

ROMULUS: How strangely quiet it is here this morning. How desolate! Has everyone deserted?

(*Silence.*)

ROMULUS: Where is my daughter, Rea?

(*Silence.*)

ACHILLES: The Princess . . .

PYRAMUS: And Emilian . . .

ACHILLES: And the Empress . . .

PYRAMUS: The Secretary of State, the Imperial Marshal, the cook and all the others . . .

(*Silence.*)

ROMULUS: Well?

ACHILLES: Drowned on their raft crossing to Sicily.

PYRAMUS: A fisherman brought the news.

ACHILLES: Only Zeno the Isaurian, together with his chamber-
lains, was able to escape on the ferry to Alexandria.
(*Silence. The Emperor remains calm.*)
ROMULUS: My daughter, Rea, and my son, Emilian.
(*He looks closely at the two chamberlains.*)
ROMULUS: I don't see tears in your eyes.
ACHILLES: We are old.
ROMULUS: And I must die. The Teutons will kill me. Today. No
pain can hurt me now. He who is about to die doesn't weep for
the dead. Never was I more composed, never more cheerful than
now, when it is all over. My morning repast.
PYRAMUS: Your breakfast?
ACHILLES: But the Teutons, Your Majesty. At any moment the
Teutons might—
PYRAMUS: And with all the flags in the empire at half-mast—
ROMULUS: Nonsense. There is no empire left to mourn and I shall
exit as I have lived.
PYRAMUS: Very well, my Emperor.
(*Romulus sits down on an easy chair standing in the middle of the
foreground. Pryamus brings a small table to him, laden with the
Emperor's usual breakfast. The Emperor looks contemplatively
at the breakfast dishes.*)
ROMULUS: Why do you serve my last morning meal on this cheap
tin plate and this cracked bowl?
PYRAMUS: The Empress took the imperial tableware with her. They
belonged to her father.
ACHILLES: And now they're at the bottom of the sea.
ROMULUS: Never mind. Perhaps these old dishes are more fitting
for my last meal, after all.
(*He opens a soft-boiled egg.*)
ROMULUS: Augustus, of course, didn't lay again.
(*Pyramus looks at Achilles, pleading for help.*)
PYRAMUS: Nothing, my Emperor.
ROMULUS: Tiberius?
PYRAMUS: None of the Julians.
ROMULUS: How about the Flavians?
PYRAMUS: Domitian. But Your Majesty has expressly refused to
consume her products.

ROMULUS: Then just who laid this egg? (*He spoons out the egg.*)
PYRAMUS: Marcus Aurelius, as always.
ROMULUS: Anyone else?
PYRAMUS: Odoaker.
> (*He is somewhat embarrassed.*)
ROMULUS: I declare.
PYRAMUS: Three eggs, Your Majesty.
ROMULUS: Mark my word! That one will lay a record today.
> (*The Emperor drinks his milk.*)
ROMULUS: You are both so solemn. What's on your minds?
ACHILLES: We have served Your Majesty for twenty years, now.
PYRAMUS: And for forty years before that we served Your Majesty's ten predecessors.
ACHILLES: For sixty years we accepted the direst poverty to serve our Emperors.
PYRAMUS: Every hackney driver is paid better than the imperial chamberlains. Let it be said openly this once, Your Majesty.
ROMULUS: True, true. However, you have to remember that a cab driver takes in more than an emperor.
> (*Pyramus looks at Achilles, pleading for help.*)
ACHILLES: Caesar Rupf, the industrialist, has offered us positions as valets in his house in Rome.
PYRAMUS: Four thousand sesterces a year and three afternoons off a week.
ACHILLES: Time enough to write our memoirs.
ROMULUS: A fantastic offer. You're free to go.
> (*He takes the imperial wreath off his brow and gives each a leaf.*)
Here, the last two leaves off my golden crown. This marks the last financial transaction of my reign.
> (*Battle noises are heard.*)
What's that noise?
ACHILLES: The Teutons, my Emperor. The Teutons are here!
ROMULUS: Well, then, I'll just have to receive them.
PYRAMUS: Perhaps His Majesty wants the imperial sword?
ROMULUS: I thought it was pawned!
> (*Pyramus looks pleadingly at Achilles.*)
ACHILLES: No pawnshop would take it. It's rusty, and Your Majesty had plucked out the imperial jewels a long time ago.
PYRAMUS: Shall I bring it?

ROMULUS: Imperial swords, my dear Pyramus, are best left in their corners.

PYRAMUS: Has Your Majesty finished breakfast?

ROMULUS: A little more asparagus wine, if you please.

(Pyramus pours with a shaking hand.)

ROMULUS: You both may go now. Your Emperor no longer has need of you. You were always faultless chamberlains.

(The two chamberlains go off, frightened. The Emperor drinks his glass of asparagus wine. A Teuton enters from the left. He moves about freely and unconcerned. He is quite sure of himself and there is nothing barbarian about him except his trousers. He looks at the room as if he were walking through a museum, and indeed, makes notes now and then on a small pad, which he takes out of a leather briefcase. He is wearing trousers, a loose-fitting coat, broad-brimmed travel hat, all of it very unwarlike except for the sword at his side. Behind him comes a young man, wearing a warlike uniform, which, however, must not be "operatic." The Teuton notices, as if incidentally and among other objects, the Emperor. They look at each other with astonishment.)

TEUTON: A Roman!

ROMULUS: Greetings.

(The young Teuton draws his sword.)

YOUNG WARRIOR (THEODORIC): Die, Roman!

TEUTON: Put your sword back in its sheath, dear Nephew.

YOUNG WARRIOR: As you say, dear Uncle.

TEUTON: I beg your pardon, Roman.

ROMULUS: But, of course. You're a real Teuton, aren't you?

(He looks at him dubiously.)

TEUTON: Of ancient lineage.

ROMULUS: I find it hard to imagine: Tacitus describes you people as having huge barbarian bodies, defiant cold blue eyes, and reddish hair. But when I look at you, I would easily take you for a disguised Byzantine botanist.

TEUTON: My notions of what you Romans were like were quite different, too. I'd always heard of their bravery, but you're the only one who hasn't run away.

ROMULUS: Obviously our ideas about different races and peoples are quite wrong. I suppose those things on your legs are trousers?

TEUTON: Of course.

ROMULUS: A truly remarkable garment. Where do you button it?

TEUTON: In front.

ROMULUS: Quite practical.

            (*He drinks more asparagus wine.*)

TEUTON: What are you drinking?

ROMULUS: Asparagus wine.

TEUTON: May I have a taste?

ROMULUS: I grew it myself.

   (*The Emperor fills a cup. The Teuton drinks and shudders.*)

TEUTON: Impossible stuff! This drink has no future. Beer is better.

    (*The Teuton sits down at the table next to Romulus and takes off his hat.*)

I must congratulate you on the Venus standing by the pond in your park.

ROMULUS: Why, is she something special?

TEUTON: A genuine Praxiteles.

ROMULUS: What bad luck! I always believed it was a worthless copy and now the antique dealer has already left.

TEUTON: Permit me.

    (*With professional eye, he examines the shell of the egg the Emperor has eaten.*)

TEUTON: Not bad.

ROMULUS: Are you a chicken breeder?

TEUTON: Passionate.

ROMULUS: Remarkable! I, too, am a chicken fancier!

TEUTON: You, too?

ROMULUS: Yes, me, too.

TEUTON: At last a human being with whom I can talk about my passion. Do the chickens in the park belong to you?

ROMULUS: Yes. A fine domestic breed. Imported from Gaul.

TEUTON: Do they lay well?

TEUTON: Be honest. Judging by this egg they're only average.

ROMULUS: You're right. They're laying less and less. Confidentially, between us chicken fanciers, they worry me. Only one hen is really in form.

TEUTON: The gray one with the yellow spots?

ROMULUS: How did you know?

TEUTON: Because I had this hen brought down to Italy. I wanted to know how she would fare in a southern climate.

ROMULUS: Now its my turn to congratulate you. Truly, an excellent breed.

TEUTON: I developed it myself.

ROMULUS: You seem to be a first-rate chicken breeder.

TEUTON: As the father of my country, it's part of my job, after all.

ROMULUS: The father of your country? Just who are you?

TEUTON: Odoaker, ruler of the Teutons.

ROMULUS: I'm truly pleased to meet you.

ODOAKER: And who are you?

ROMULUS: Romulus, Emperor of Rome.

ODOAKER: I, too, am pleased to make your acquaintance. Though, in fact, I knew right off who you were.

ROMULUS: You knew it?

ODOAKER: Forgive the pretense. It's somewhat embarrassing for two enemies suddenly to find themselves face to face. That's why I thought it more useful at first to talk chickens rather than politics. May I introduce my nephew? Bow, Nephew.

YOUNG WARRIOR: Yes, dear Uncle.

ODOAKER: Leave us, Nephew.

YOUNG WARRIOR: Very well, dear Uncle.

(*He exits. Silence. The two look at each other.*)

ODOAKER: So you are Romulus. You've been on my mind all these years.

ROMULUS: And you are Odoaker. I pictured you as my enemy— and now you're a chicken breeder just like me.

ODOAKER: Now the moment I waited for all these years has come.

(*The Emperor wipes his mouth with his napkin and rises.*)

ROMULUS: You find me ready.

ODOAKER: Ready for what?

ROMULUS: For death.

ODOAKER: You expected to die?

ROMULUS: The whole world knows how you Teutons deal with your prisoners.

ODOAKER: Have your thoughts about your enemies been so shallow, Emperor Romulus, that you must go by the world's judgment?

ROMULUS: What could you possibly have in mind for me other than death?

ODOAKER: You shall see. Nephew!

(*The Young Warrior enters from the right.*)

YOUNG WARRIOR: Yes, dear Uncle.

ODOAKER: Bow before the Emperor of Rome, Nephew.

YOUNG WARRIOR: Yes, dear Uncle.

(*He bows.*)

ODOAKER: Lower, Nephew.

YOUNG WARRIOR: Very well, dear Uncle.

ODOAKER: Throw yourself upon your knee before the Emperor of Rome.

YOUNG WARRIOR: As you say, dear Uncle.

(*He throws himself upon his knee.*)

ROMULUS: What's this all about?

ODOAKER: Now rise, Nephew.

YOUNG WARRIOR: Very well, dear Uncle.

ODOAKER: Now you may go again.

YOUNG WARRIOR: As you say, dear Uncle.

(*He goes off.*)

ROMULUS: I don't understand.

ODOAKER: I didn't come to kill you, Emperor of Rome. I came to subject myself and my entire people to you.

(*Odoaker, too, kneels. Romulus is frightened to death.*)

ROMULUS: This is madness!

ODOAKER: Even a Teuton may be guided by reason, Emperor of Rome.

ROMULUS: You are mocking me.

(*Odoaker rises.*)

ODOAKER: Romulus, a moment ago we talked sensibly about chickens. Isn't it possible to talk just as sensibly about nations and people?

ROMULUS: Speak.

ODOAKER: May I sit down again?

ROMULUS: Why do you ask? You're the victor.

ODOAKER: You're forgetting that I've just subjected myself to you.

(*Silence.*)

ROMULUS: Do sit down.

(*Both sit down, Romulus gloomily, Odoaker watching Romulus carefully.*)

ODOAKER: You've seen my nephew. His name is Theodoric.

ROMULUS: Of course.

ODOAKER: A polite young man. "Yes, dear Uncle; very well, dear Uncle," all day long. His conduct is faultless. He's ruining my people with his way of life. He never touches girls, drinks nothing but water, and sleeps on the bare ground. Every day he practices with his weapons. Even now, while waiting in the anteroom, he's sure to be exercising.

ROMULUS: He's a hero, that's why.

ODOAKER: He's the ideal of the Teutons. He dreams of ruling the world and the people dream with him. That's why I had to undertake this campaign. I was alone in opposing my nephew, the poets, and our public opinion, but I was forced to give in. I was hoping to conduct this war humanely. The opposition of the Romans was slight. Still, the farther south I advanced, the greater were the misdeeds of my army. Not because my army is any more cruel than any other army, but because *every* war turns men into beasts. I was shocked, I tried to call off the campaign. I was ready to accept the sum offered by the trouser-maker. Up to that point my captains could still be bribed, and I thought I might still be able to have things my way. Soon I won't be able to any more. Then we shall have become, once and for all, a people of heroes. Save me, Romulus, you're my only hope.

ROMULUS: Your hope for what?

ODOAKER: To escape with my life.

ROMULUS: Are you in danger?

ODOAKER: Right now my nephew is still tame; right now, he's still the polite young man. But one of these days, in a few years, he will kill me. I know this Teutonic loyalty.

ROMULUS: Is that why you wish to subject yourself to me?

ODOAKER: I spent my whole life looking for the true greatness of man, not that falsely acclaimed greatness of my nephew, who some day shall be called Theodoric the Great, if I know those historians. I'm a farmer and I hate war. I sought a human way of life that I could not find in the primeval Teutonic forests. I found it in you, Emperor Romulus. Your head steward, Ebius, saw through you.

ROMULUS: Ebi? At my Court? Under your orders?

ODOAKER: He was my spy, but he sent good reports: Of a true human being, of a just man, of you, Romulus.

ROMULUS: He sent you reports of a fool, Odoaker. My whole life was aimed at the day when the Roman Empire would collapse. I took it upon myself to be Rome's judge, because I was ready to die. I asked of my country an enormous sacrifice because I, myself, was willing to be sacrificed. By rendering my country defenseless, I allowed its blood to flow because my own blood was ready to be spilled. And now I am to live; my sacrifice is not being accepted. Now I am to be the only one who was able to save himself. Even worse, just before you came I received the news that my only daughter, whom I love, died together with her bridegroom, with my wife and the entire Court. I bore this news easily because I thought I was going to die. But now it hits me pitilessly and pitilessly proves me wrong. Everything I have done has become absurd. Kill me, Odoaker.

(Silence.)

ODOAKER: You are speaking in anguish. Conquer your grief and accept my submission.

ROMULUS: You are afraid. Conquer your fear and kill me.

(Silence.)

ODOAKER: You thought of your own people, Romulus, but now you must think of your enemies, too. If you do not accept my submission, if you and I do not make our way together, then the world will fall to my nephew; and a second Rome will rise, a Teutonic empire, as transitory as Rome and just as bloody. If that comes to pass your work, the fall of Rome, will truly have been absurd. You cannot escape your own greatness, Romulus. You're the only man who knows how to rule this world. Be merciful, accept my submission, become our Emperor. Protect us from Theodoric's bloody greatness.

(Silence.)

ROMULUS: I can't do it any more, Odoaker. Even if I wanted to. You've taken from me the very thing that justified my actions.

ODOAKER: Is this your last word?

(Romulus kneels.)

ROMULUS: Kill me! I beg you on my knees.

ODOAKER: I can't force you to help us. This misfortune cannot be undone. But neither can I kill you, because I love you.

ROMULUS: If you won't kill me, there is still one solution left. The only man who would still murder me is sleeping in front of my bed. I'll go and wake him.

   . (*As he rises, Odoaker rises also.*)

ODOAKER: That is no solution, Romulus. You're just desperate. Your death would be senseless. It would only make sense if the world were as you imagine it. But it isn't. Even your enemy is a human being who wants to do what is right, just as you do. You have to accept your destiny. There's no other way.

(*Silence.*)

ROMULUS: Let's sit down again.

ODOAKER What else can we do?

ROMULUS: What are you planning to do with me now?

ODOAKER: I'll send you into retirement.

ROMULUS: Into retirement?

ODOAKER: It is the only possibility left to us.

(*Silence.*)

ROMULUS: Retirement is probably the worst that could happen to me.

ODOAKER: Don't forget that I, too, am about to face the worst. You'll have to proclaim me King of Italy, and that will be the beginning of my end unless I act promptly, here and now. Whether I want to or not, I will have to begin my reign with a murder.

(*He draws his sword and starts to go off to the right.*)

ROMULUS: What are you going to do?

ODOAKER: Kill my nephew. Right now I'm still stronger than he.

ROMULUS: Now you're the desperate one, Odoaker. If you kill your nephew a thousand new Theodorics will rise. Your people think differently than you do. Your people want heroics. You can't change that.

(*Silence.*)

ODOAKER: Let's sit down again. We are caught in a vicious circle.

(*They sit down again.*)

ROMULUS: My dear Odoaker, I wanted to make my destiny and you wanted to avoid yours. Now it's our fate to be politicians who have failed. We thought we could drop the world from our hands, you, your Germania and I, my Rome. Now we have to do something with the pieces that are left. We can't let them fall. I wanted Rome's end because I feared its past; and you, you wanted the end of Germania because you shuddered at its future. We let ourselves be ruled by two specters, for we have no power over what was nor over what will be. Our only power is over the present. But we didn't think of the present and now we're foundering on it. I must now live through the present in retirement, and weighing on my conscience will be a daughter I loved, a son, a wife, and indeed many other unhappy human beings.

ODOAKER: And I shall have to reign.

ROMULUS: Reality has put our ideas right.

ODOAKER: Bitterly right.

ROMULUS: Then let's bear this bitterness. Let's try to endow the nonsense with sense! Try in the few years that remain to you to rule the world faithfully. Grant peace to the Teutons and the Romans alike. To your task then, Ruler of the Teutons. Take up your reign! There may be a few years that world history will forget because they will be unheroic years—but they will be among the happiest this confused world has ever lived through.

ODOAKER: And then I shall have to die.

ROMULUS: Take comfort. Your nephew will kill me, too. He'll never forgive me for having had to kneel before me.

ODOAKER: Then let's get on with our sad duty.

ROMULUS: Let's do it quickly. Once more and for the last time, let's play this comedy. Let's act *as if* final accounts were settled here on earth, as if the spirit won out over the material called man.

ODOAKER: Nephew.

(*The nephew enters from the right.*)

THEODORIC: Yes, dear Uncle?

ODOAKER: Call in our captains, Nephew.

THEODORIC: Yes, dear Uncle.

(*He again goes off to the right. The room fills up with Teutons, filthy and fatiqued from their long marches. They are dressed in monotonous linen clothes and simple helmets. Odoaker rises.*)

ODOAKER: Teutons! Covered with dust and tired from your long marches, burned by the sun, you have now come to the end of your campaign. You are standing before the Emperor of Rome. Show him all honors.

(*The Teutons stand at attention.*)

Teutons! You have laughed at this man and mocked him in the songs you sang all day on the highways and at night by your campfires. But I discovered his humanity. Never have I seen a greater man, and never shall you see a greater one, no matter who my successor is. Speak now, O Emperor of Rome.

ROMULUS: The Emperor is dissolving his Empire. Let all of you take one last look at this tinted globe, this dream of a great empire, floating in space, driven by the slightest breath of my lips. Look at these far-flung lands encircling the blue sea with its dancing dolphins, these rich provinces golden with wheat, these teeming cities overflowing with life. This empire was once a sun warming mankind, but at its zenith it scorched the world; now it is a harmless bubble and in the hands of the Emperor it dissolves into nothing.

(*Solemn silence. The Teutons stare in amazement at the Emperor, who rises.*)

ROMULUS: I now proclaim Odoaker, Ruler of the Teutons, King of Italy!

TEUTONS: Long live the King of Italy!

ODOAKER: I, for my part, assign to the Emperor of Rome the villa of Lucullus in the Campania. Furthermore, he is to receive a yearly pension of six thousand gold coins.

ROMULUS: The Emperor's years of hunger are over. Take this wreath and the imperial toga. You'll find the imperial sword among the garden tools and the Senate in the catacombs of Rome. Will someone fetch me my namesake off the wall, the bust of King Romulus, the founder of Rome?

(*A Teuton brings him the bust.*)

ROMULUS: Thanks.

(*He puts the bust under his arm.*)

I'll leave you now, Ruler of the Teutons. I'm going into retirement.

TEUTONS: Long live Romulus the Great.

(*Spurious Titus Mamma, carrying a drawn sword, bursts in from behind.*)

SPURIOUS TITUS MAMMA: Where is the Emperor? I'll kill him.

(*The King of Italy steps up to him with dignity.*)

ODOAKER: Put your sword away, Captain. There is no emperor any more.

SPURIOUS TITUS MAMMA: The empire?

ODOAKER: Is dissolved.

SPURIUS TITUS MAMMA: Then the last imperial officer slept right through the fall of his homeland?

(*Spurius Titus Mamma sinks down upon the Emperor's seat, downcast and broken-hearted.*)

ROMULUS: And with that, gentlemen, the Roman Empire has ceased to exist.

(*The Emperor goes off slowly with bent head, carrying the bust under his arm. The Teutons stand by respectfully.*)

NOTES

This is a difficult comedy, because seemingly a light one! What is the devotee of German literature to make of it? Style is what sounds solemn. Our devotee will think of *Romulus* as a kind of farce, and will place it somewhere between Theo Lingen and Shaw. And yet, such a fate is not entirely unfitting for Romulus. He played the fool for twenty years and the world around him did not realize there was a method to his madness. That itself is something to think about. My characters must emerge from the way they appear. This applies to the actors and the director. Practically speaking: how should Emilian be portrayed? He has been on the road for days, perhaps weeks, along secret paths, through destroyed cities, and finally he reaches the Emperor's villa which, after all, he knows very well. But he asks: is this the Emperor's villa in Campania? If we do not feel his unbelievable astonishment at seeing the Emperor's villa so dilapidated and looking like a chicken coop, which it in fact is, then the question will seem merely rhetorical; this also holds when he asks his beloved, with fear and hesitancy: who are you? He really does not know her any more. He has truly forgotten her, but still he suspects that he once knew and loved this girl. Emilian is the counterpart to Romulus. His fate must be seen with human eyes, with the eyes, as it were, of the Emperor. For the Emperor can see behind Emilian's façade of the dishonored officer, "the victim of power, defiled a thousand times." Romulus takes Emilian seriously, knowing him to be a human being who was captured and tortured, and who is unhappy. What Romulus will not accept is Emilian's demand that his beloved "get a knife," or that he is willing to barter off his own beloved to save his country. If an actor does not discover the humanity within each of my characters, he cannot represent any of them. This is true for all my plays. But there is an additional difficulty facing the actor playing Romulus, and it is simply that he must not allow the audience to feel sympathetic toward Romulus too quickly. That is easily said and perhaps almost impossible to achieve, but it should be kept in mind as a tactical approach. What the Emperor really stands for should only be revealed in the third act. In the first act it should be quite understandable why the Captain of the Cavalry calls him "a disgrace to Rome" just as understandable should be Emilian's verdict at the end of Act Two, "Down with the Emperor." If Romulus sits in judgment over the world in Act Three, the world sits in judgment over him in Act Four. Look closely at what kind of person I have sketched here: surely, a witty man, a man at ease and humane, but in the last analysis, a human being who proceeds with the utmost firmness and lack of consideration for others, a man who does not shrink from demanding the same absoluteness of purpose from others. He is a dangerous fellow, a man determined to die. That is the terror lying within this imperial chicken breeder, this judge of the world disguised as a fool. His tragedy lies in the comedy of his end; in his retirement. But then—and this alone is what makes him great—he has the wisdom and the insight to accept his fate.

F.D.

Translated by Gerhard Nellhaus

THE VISIT

A Tragic Comedy
in Three Acts

CHARACTERS

Visitors:
  CLAIRE ZACHANASSIAN,
  née Wascher, Armenian
  oil billionairess
  HER HUSBANDS, *VII–IX*
  BUTLER
  TOBY⎱ *gum-chewers*
  ROBY⎰
  KOBY⎱ *blind*
  LOBY⎰

Visited:
  ILL
  HIS WIFE
  HIS SON
  HIS DAUGHTER
  MAYOR
  PASTOR
  SCHOOLMASTER
  DOCTOR
  POLICEMAN
  MAN ONE
  MAN TWO
  MAN THREE
  MAN FOUR
  PAINTER
  FIRST WOMAN
  SECOND WOMAN
  MISS LOUISA

Extras:
  STATIONMASTER
  TICKET INSPECTOR

  GUARD
  MARSHAL

Distractors:
  FIRST REPORTER
  SECOND REPORTER
  RADIO COMMENTATOR
  CAMERAMAN

PLACE: *Guellen, a small town*

TIME: *The Present*

(*Interval after Act Two*)

Act One

Clangor of railway station bell before curtain rises to discover legend: "Guellen." Obviously name of small, skimpily depicted township in background: a tumbledown wreck. Equally ramshackle station buildings may or may not be cordoned off, according to country, and include a rusty signal cabin, its door marked "No Entry." Also depicted in bare outline, center, the piteous Station Road. Left, a barren little building with tiled roof and mutilated posters on its windowless walls. A sign, at left corner: "Ladies." Another, at right corner: "Gents." This entire prospect steeped in hot autumn sun. In front of little building, a bench. On it, four men. An unspeakably ragged fifth (so are the other four) is inscribing letters in red paint on a banner clearly intended for some procession: "Welcome Clarie." Thunderous pounding din of express train rushing through. Men on bench show interest in express train by following its headlong rush with head movements from left to right.

MAN ONE: The Gudrun. Hamburg-Naples.

MAN TWO: The Racing Roland gets here at eleven twenty-seven. Venice-Stockholm.

MAN THREE: Our last remaining pleasure: watching trains go by.

MAN FOUR: Five years ago the Gudrun and the Racing Roland stopped in Guellen. And the Diplomat. And the Lorelei. All famous express trains.

MAN ONE: World famous.

MAN TWO: Now not even the commuter trains stop. Just two from Kaffigen and the one-thirteen from Kalberstadt.

MAN THREE: Ruined.

MAN FOUR: The Wagner Factory gone out of business.

MAN ONE: Bockmann bankrupt.

MAN TWO: The Foundry on Sunshine Square shut down.

MAN THREE: Living on the dole.

MAN FOUR: On Poor Relief soup.

MAN ONE: Living?

MAN TWO: Vegetating.

MAN THREE: And rotting to death.

MAN FOUR: The entire township.

(Bell rings.)

MAN TWO: It's more than time that billionairess got here. They say she founded a hospital in Kalberstadt.

MAN THREE: And a kindergarten in Kaffigen. And a memorial church in the Capital.

PAINTER: She had Zimt do her portrait. That Naturalistic dabbler.

MAN ONE: She and her money. She owns Armenian Oil, Western Railways, North Broadcasting Company and the Hong Kong— uh—Amusement District.

(Train clatter. Station master salutes. Men move heads from right to left after train.)

MAN FOUR: The Diplomat.

MAN THREE: We were a city of the Arts, then.

MAN TWO: One of the foremost in the land.

MAN ONE: In Europe.

MAN FOUR: Goethe spent a night here. In the Golden Apostle.

MAN THREE: Brahms composed a quartet here.

(Bell rings.)

MAN TWO: Bertold Schwarz invented gunpowder here.

PAINTER: And I was a brilliant student at the Ecole des Beaux Arts. And what am I doing here now? Sign-painting!

(Train clatter. Guard appears, left, as after jumping off train.)

GUARD *(long-drawn wail)*: Guellen!

MAN ONE: The Kaffigen commuter.

(One passenger has got off, left. He walks past men on bench, disappears through doorway marked "Gents.")

MAN TWO: The Marshal.

MAN THREE: Going to place a lien on the Town Hall.

MAN FOUR: We're even ruined politically.

STATION MASTER *(waves green flag, blows whistle)*: Stand clear!

(*Enter from town, Mayor, Schoolmaster, Priest and Ill—
a man of near sixty-five; all shabbily dressed.*)

MAYOR: The guest of honor will be arriving on the one-thirteen commuter from Kalberstadt.

SCHOOLMASTER: We'll have the mixed choir singing; the Youth Club.

PASTOR: And the fire bell ringing. It hasn't been pawned.

MAYOR: We'll have the town band playing on Market Square. The Athletics Club will honor the billionairess with a pyramid. Then a meal in the Golden Apostle. Finances unfortunately can't be stretched to illuminating the Cathedral for the evening. Or the Town Hall.

(*Marshal comes out of little building.*)

MARSHAL: Good morning, Mister Mayor, a very good morning to you.

MAYOR: Why, Mister Glutz, what are you doing here?

MARSHAL: You know my mission, Mister Mayor. It's a colossal undertaking I'm faced with. Just you try placing a lien on an entire town.

MAYOR: You won't find a thing in the Town Hall. Apart from one old typewriter.

MARSHAL: I think you're forgetting something, Mister Mayor. The Guellen History Museum.

MAYOR: Gone three years ago. Sold to America. Our coffers are empty. Not a single soul pays taxes.

MARSHAL: It'll have to be investigated. The country's booming and Guellen has the Sunshine Foundry. But Guellen goes bankrupt.

MAYOR: We're up against a real economic enigma.

MAN ONE: The whole thing's a Freemasons' plot.

MAN TWO: Conspired by the Jews.

MAN THREE: Backed by High Finance.

MAN FOUR: International Communism's showing its colors.

(*Bell rings.*)

MARSHAL: I always find something. I've got eyes like a hawk. I think I'll take a look at the Treasury.

(*Exit.*)

MAYOR: Better let him plunder us first. Not after the billionairess's visit.

(*Painter has finished painting his banner.*)

ILL: You know, Mister Mayor, that won't do. This banner's too familiar. It ought to read, "Welcome Claire Zachanassian."

MAN ONE: But she's Clarie!

MAN TWO: Clarie Wascher!

MAN THREE: She was educated here!

MAN FOUR: Her dad was the builder.

PAINTER: O.K., so I'll write "Welcome Claire Zachanassian" on the back. Then if the billionairess seems touched we can turn it round and show her the front.

MAN TWO: It's the Speculator. Zürich-Hamburg.

(Another express train passes. Right to left.)

MAN THREE: Always on time, you can set your watch by it.

MAN FOUR: Tell me who still owns a watch in this place.

MAYOR: Gentlemen, the billionairess is our only hope.

PASTOR: Apart from God.

MAYOR: Apart from God.

SCHOOLMASTER: But God won't pay.

MAYOR: You used to be a friend of hers, Ill, so now it all depends on you.

PASTOR: But their ways parted. I heard some story about it—have you no confession to make to your Pastor?

ILL: We were the best of friends. Young and hotheaded. I used to be quite a guy, gentlemen, forty-five years ago. And she, Clara, I can see her still: coming towards me through the shadows in Petersens' Barn, all aglow. Or walking barefoot in the Konradsweil Forest, over the moss and the leaves, with her red hair streaming out, slim and supple as a willow, and tender, ah, what a devilish beautiful little witch. Life tore us apart. Life. That's the way it is.

MAYOR: I ought to have a few details about Madam Zachanassian for my little after-dinner speech in the Golden Apostle.

(Takes a small notebook from pocket.)

SCHOOLMASTER: I've been going through the old school reports. Clara Wascher's marks, I'm sorry to say, were appalling. So was her conduct. She only passed in botany and zoology.

MAYOR *(takes note)*: Good. Botany and zoology. A pass. That's good.

ILL: I can help you here, Mister Mayor. Clara loved justice. Most decidedly. Once when they took a beggar away she flung stones at the police.

MAYOR: Love of justice. Not bad. It always works. But I think we'd better leave out that bit about the police.

ILL: She was generous too. Everything she had she shared. She stole potatoes once for an old widow.

MAYOR: Sense of generosity. Gentlemen, I absolutely must bring that in. It's the crucial point. Does anyone here remember a building her father built? That'd sound good in my speech.

ALL: No. No one.

(*Mayor shuts his little notebook.*)

MAYOR: I'm fully prepared, for my part. The rest is up to Ill.

ILL: I know. Zachanassian has to cough up her millions.

MAYOR: Millions—that's the idea. Precisely.

SCHOOLMASTER: It won't help us if she only founds a nursery school.

MAYOR: My dear Ill, you've been the most popular personality in Guellen for a long while now. In the spring, I shall be retiring. I've sounded out the Opposition: we've agreed to nominate you as my successor.

ILL: But Mister Mayor.

SCHOOLMASTER: I can confirm that.

ILL: Gentlemen, back to business. First of all, I'll tell Clara all about our wretched plight.

PASTOR: But do be careful—do be tactful.

ILL: We've got to be clever. Psychologically acute. If we make a fiasco of the welcome at the station, we could easily wreck everything else. You won't bring it off by relying on the municipal band and the mixed choir.

MAYOR: Ill's right, there. It'll be one of the decisive moments. Madam Zachanassian sets foot on her native soil, she's home again, and how moved she is, there are tears in her eyes, ah, the old familiar places. The old faces. Not that I'll be standing here like this in my shirtsleeves. I'll be wearing my formal black coat and a top hat. My wife beside me, my two grandchildren in front of me, all in white. Holding roses. My God, if only it all works out according to plan!

(*Bell rings.*)

MAN ONE: It's the Racing Roland.

MAN TWO: Venice-Stockholm eleven twenty-seven.

PASTOR: Eleven twenty-seven! We still have nearly two hours to get suitably dressed.

MAYOR: Kuhn and Hauser hoist the "Welcome Claire Zachanassian" banner. (*Points at four men.*) You others better wave your hats. But please: no shouting like last year at the Government Mission, it hardly impressed them at all and so far we've had no subsidy. This is no time for wild enthusiasm; the mood you want is an inward, an almost tearful sympathy for one of our children, who was lost, and has been found again. Be relaxed. Sincere. But above all, time it well. The instant the choir stops singing, sound the fire alarm. And look out . . .

(*His speech is drowned by thunder of oncoming train. Squealing brakes. Dumbfounded astonishment on all faces. The five men spring up from bench.*)

PAINTER: The Express!

MAN ONE: It's stopping!

MAN TWO: In Guellen!

MAN THREE: The lousiest—

MAN FOUR: Most poverty-stricken—

MAN ONE: Desolate dump on the Venice-Stockholm line!

STATIONMASTER: It's against the Laws of Nature. The Racing Roland ought to materialize from around the Leuthenau bend, roar through Guellen, dwindle into a dark dot over at Pückenried Valley, and vanish.

(*Enter, right, Claire Zachanassian. Sixty-three, red hair, pearl necklace, enormous gold bangles, unbelievably got up to kill and yet by the same token a Society Lady with a rare grace, in spite of all the grotesquerie. Followed by her entourage, comprising Butler Boby, aged about eighty, wearing dark glasses, and Husband VII, tall and thin with a black moustache, sporting a complete angler's outfit. Accompanying this group, an excited Ticket Inspector, peaked cap, little red satchel.*)

CLAIRE ZACHANASSIAN: Is it Guellen?

TICKET INSPECTOR: Madam. You pulled the Emergency Brake.

CLAIRE ZACHANASSIAN: I always pull the Emergency Brake.

TICKET INSPECTOR: I protest. Vigorously. No one ever pulls the Emergency Brake in this country. Not even in case of emergency. Our first duty is to our timetable. Will you kindly give me an explanation.

CLAIRE ZACHANASSIAN: It is Guellen, Moby. I recognize the wretched dump. That's Konradsweil Forest yonder, with a stream you can fish—pike and trout; that roof on the right is Petersens' Barn.

ILL (*as if awakening*): Clara.

SCHOOLMASTER: Madam Zachanassian.

ALL: Madam Zachanassian.

SCHOOLMASTER: And the choir and the Youth Club aren't ready!

MAYOR: The Athletics Club! The Fire Brigade!

PASTOR: The Sexton!

MAYOR: My frock coat, for God's sake, my top hat, my grand-children!

MAN ONE: Clarie Wascher's here! Clarie Wascher's here!
        (*Jumps up, rushes off towards town.*)

MAYOR (*calling after him*): Don't forget my wife!

TICKET INSPECTOR: I'm waiting for an explanation. In my official capacity. I represent the Railway Management.

CLAIRE ZACHANASSIAN: You're a simpleton. I want to pay this little town a visit. What d'you expect me to do, hop off your express train?

TICKET INSPECTOR: You stopped the Racing Roland just because you wanted to visit Guellen?

CLAIRE ZACHANASSIAN: Of course.

TICKET INSPECTOR: Madam. Should you desire to visit Guellen, the twelve-forty commuter from Kalberstadt is at your service. Please use it. Like other people. Arrival in Guellen one thirteen p.m.

CLAIRE ZACHANASSIAN: The ordinary passenger train? The one that stops in Loken, Brunnhübel, Beisenbach and Leuthenau? Are you really and truly asking me to go puffing round this countryside for half an hour?

TICKET INSPECTOR: You'll pay for this, Madam. Dearly.

CLAIRE ZACHANASSIAN: Boby, give him a thousand.

ALL (*murmuring*): A thousand.
        (*Butler gives Ticket Inspector a thousand.*)

TICKET INSPECTOR (*perplexed*): Madam.

CLAIRE ZACHANASSIAN: And three thousand for the Railway Widows' Fund.

ALL (*murmuring*): Three thousand.
        (*Ticket Inspector receives three thousand from Butler.*)

TICKET INSPECTOR (*staggered*): Madam. No such fund exists.

CLAIRE ZACHANASSIAN: Then found one.

(*The supreme Civic Authority whispers a word or two in Ticket Inspector's ear.*)

TICKET INSPECTOR (*all confusion*): Madam is Madam Claire Zachanassian? Oh, do excuse me. Of course it's different in that case. We'd have been only too happy to stop in Guellen if we'd had the faintest notion. Oh, here's your money back, Madam, four thousand, my God.

ALL (*murmuring*): Four thousand.

CLAIRE ZACHANASSIAN: Keep it, it's nothing.

ALL (*murmuring*): Keep it.

TICKET INSPECTOR: Does Madam require the Racing Roland to wait while she visits Guellen? I know the Railway Management would be only too glad. They say the Cathedral portals are well worth a look. Gothic. With the Last Judgment.

CLAIRE ZACHANASSIAN: Will you and your express train get the hell out of here?

HUSBAND VII (*whines*): But the Press, my angel, the Press haven't got off yet. The Reporters have no idea. They're dining up front in the saloon.

CLAIRE ZACHANASSIAN: Let them dine, Moby, let them dine. I can't use the Press in Guellen yet, and they'll come back later on, don't worry.

(*Meanwhile Man Two has brought Mayor his frock coat. Mayor crosses ceremoniously to Claire Zachanassian. Painter and Man Four stand on bench, hoist banner: "Welcome Claire Zachanassi"* . . . *Painter did not quite finish it.*)

STATIONMASTER (*whistles, waves green flag*): Stand clear!

TICKET INSPECTOR: I do trust you won't complain to the Railway Management, Madam. It was a pure misunderstanding.

(*Train begins moving out. Ticket Inspector jumps on.*)

MAYOR: Madam Zachanassian, my dear lady. As Mayor of Guellen, it is my honor to welcome you, a child of our native town . . .

(*Remainder of Mayor's speech drowned in clatter of express train as it begins to move and then to race away. He speaks doggedly on.*)

CLAIRE ZACHANASSIAN: I must thank you, Mister Mayor, for your fine speech.

(*She crosses to Ill who, somewhat embarrassed, has moved toward her.*)

ILL: Clara.

CLAIRE ZACHANASSIAN: Alfred.

ILL: It's nice you've come.

CLAIRE ZACHANASSIAN: I'd always planned to. All my life. Ever since I left Guellen.

ILL (*unsure of himself*): It's sweet of you.

CLAIRE ZACHANASSIAN: Did you think about me too?

ILL: Of course. All the time. You know I did, Clara.

CLAIRE ZACHANASSIAN: They were wonderful, all those days we used to spend together.

ILL (*proudly*): They sure were. (*to Schoolmaster*) See, Professor, I've got her in the bag.

CLAIRE ZACHANASSIAN: Call me what you always used to call me.

ILL: My little wildcat.

CLAIRE ZACHANASSIAN (*purrs like an old cat*): And what else?

ILL: My little sorceress.

CLAIRE ZACHANASSIAN: I used to call you my black panther.

ILL: I still am.

CLAIRE ZACHANASSIAN: Nonsense. You've grown fat. And gray. And a lush.

ILL: But *you're* still the same, my little sorceress.

CLAIRE ZACHANASSIAN: Don't be silly. I've grown old and fat as well. And lost my left leg. An automobile accident. Now I only travel in express trains. But they made a splendid job of the artificial one, don't you think? (*She pulls up her skirt, displays left leg.*) It bends very well.

ILL (*wipes away sweat*): But my little wildcat, I'd never have noticed it.

CLAIRE ZACHANASSIAN: Would you like to meet my seventh husband, Alfred? Tobacco Plantations. We're very happily married.

ILL: But by all means.

CLAIRE ZACHANASSIAN: Come on, Moby, come and make your bow. As a matter of fact his name's Pedro, but Moby's much nicer. In any case it goes better with Boby; that's the butler's name. And you get your butlers for life, so husbands have to be named accordingly.

(*Husband VII bows.*)

Isn't he nice, with his little black moustache? Think it over, Moby.

> (*Husband VII thinks it over.*)

Harder.

> (*Husband VII thinks it over harder.*)

Harder still.

HUSBAND VII: But I can't think any harder, darling, really I can't.

CLAIRE ZACHANASSIAN: Of course you can. Just try.

> (*Husband VII thinks harder still. Bell rings.*)

You see. It works. Don't you agree, Alfred, he looks almost demonic like that. Like a Brazilian. But no! He's Greek-Orthodox. His father was Russian. We were married by a Pope. Most interesting. Now I'm going to have a look round Guellen.

> (*She inspects little house, left, through jewel-encrusted lorgnette.*)

My father built these public toilets, Moby. Good work, painstakingly executed. When I was a child I spent hours on that roof, spitting. But only on the Gents.

> (*Mixed choir and Youth Club have now assembled in background. Schoolmaster steps forward wearing top hat.*)

SCHOOLMASTER: Madam. As Headmaster of Guellen College, and lover of the noblest Muse, may I take the liberty of offering you a homely folksong, rendered by the mixed choir and the Youth Club.

CLAIRE ZACHANASSIAN: Fire away, Schoolmaster, let's hear your homely folksong.

> (*Schoolmaster takes up tuning fork, strikes key. Mixed choir and Youth Club begin ceremoniously singing, at which juncture another train arrives, left. Stationmaster salutes. Choir struggles against cacophonous clatter of trains; Schoolmaster despairs; train, at long last, passes.*)

MAYOR (*despondent*): The fire alarm, sound the fire alarm!

CLAIRE ZACHANASSIAN: Well sung, Guelleners! That blond bass out there on the left, with the big Adam's apple, he was really most singular.

> (*A Policeman elbows a passage through mixed choir, draws up to attention in front of Claire Zachanassian.*)

POLICEMAN: Police Inspector Hahncke, Madam. At your service.

CLAIRE ZACHANASSIAN (*inspects him*): Thank you. I don't want to arrest anybody. But Guellen may need you soon. Can you close an eye to things from time to time?

POLICEMAN: Sure I can, Madam. Where would I be in Guellen if I couldn't!

CLAIRE ZACHANASSIAN: Start learning to close them both.

(*Policeman goggles at her, perplexed.*)

ILL (*laughing*): Just like Clara! Just like my little wildcat!

(*Slaps thigh with enjoyment. Mayor perches Schoolmaster's top hat on his own head, ushers pair of grandchildren forward. Twin seven-year-old girls, blond plaits.*)

MAYOR: My grandchildren, Madam. Hermione and Adolfina. My wife is the only one not present.

(*Mops perspiration. The two little girls curtsy for Madam Zachanassian and offer her red roses.*)

CLAIRE ZACHANASSIAN: Congratulations on your kids, Mister Mayor. Here!

(*She bundles roses into Stationmaster's arms. Mayor stealthily hands top hat to Priest, who puts it on.*)

MAYOR: Our Pastor, Madam.

(*Pastor raises top hat, bows.*)

CLAIRE ZACHANASSIAN: Ah, the Pastor. Do you comfort the dying?

PASTOR (*startled*): I do what I can.

CLAIRE ZACHANASSIAN: People who've been condemned to death as well?

PASTOR (*perplexed*): The death sentence has been abolished in this country, Madam.

CLAIRE ZACHANASSIAN: It may be reintroduced.

(*Pastor, with some consternation, returns top hat to Mayor, who dons it again.*)

ILL (*laughing*): Really, little wildcat! You crack the wildest jokes.

CLAIRE ZACHANASSIAN: Now I want to go into town.

(*Mayor attempts to offer her his arm.*)

What's all this, Mister Mayor? I don't go hiking miles on my artificial leg.

MAYOR (*shocked*): Immediately, immediately, Madam. The doctor owns a car. It's a Mercedes. The nineteen thirty-two model.

POLICEMAN (*clicking heels*): I'll see to it, Mister Mayor. I'll have the car commandeered and driven round.

CLAIRE ZACHANASSIAN: That won't be necessary. Since my accident I only go about in sedan chairs. Roby, Toby, bring it here. (*Enter, left, two herculean gum-chewing brutes with sedan chair. One of them has a guitar slung at his back.*) Two gangsters. From Manhattan. They were on their way to Sing Sing. To the electric chair. I petitioned for them to be freed as sedan bearers. Cost me a million dollars per petition. The sedan chair came from the Louvre. A gift from the French President. Such a nice man; he looks exactly like his pictures in the newspapers. Roby, Toby, take me into town.

ROBY/TOBY (*in unison*): Yes Mam.

CLAIRE ZACHANASSIAN: But first of all to the Petersens' Barn, and then to Konradsweil Forest. I want to take Alfred to visit our old haunts. In the meanwhile have the luggage and the coffin put in the Golden Apostle.

MAYOR: (*startled*): The coffin?

CLAIRE ZACHANASSIAN: Yes, I brought a coffin with me. I may need it. Roby, Toby, off we go!

(*The pair of gum-chewing brutes carry Claire Zachanassian away to town. Mayor gives signal, whereon all burst into cheers which spontaneously fade as two more servants enter, bearing an elaborate black coffin, cross stage and exeunt, towards Guellen. Now, undaunted and unpawned, the fire-alarm bell starts ringing.*)

MAYOR: At last! The fire bell.

(*Populace gathers round coffin. It is followed in by Claire Zachanassian's maidservants and an endless stream of cases and trunks, carried by Guelleners. This traffic is controlled by Policeman, who is about to follow it out when enter at that point a pair of little old fat soft-spoken men, both impeccably dressed.*)

THE PAIR: We're in Guellen. We can smell it, we can smell it, we can smell it in the air, in the Guellen air.

POLICEMAN: And who might you be?

THE PAIR: We belong to the old lady, we belong to the old lady. She calls us Koby and Loby.

POLICEMAN: Madam Zachanassian is staying at the Golden Apostle.

THE PAIR (*gay*): We're blind, we're blind.

POLICEMAN: Blind? O.K., I'll take you two there.

THE PAIR: Oh, thank you Mister Policeman, thank you very much.

POLICEMAN (*with surprise*): If you're blind, how did you know I was a policeman?

THE PAIR: By your tone of voice, your tone of voice, all policemen have the same tone of voice.

POLICEMAN (*with suspicion*): You fat little men seem to have had a bit of contact with the police.

THE PAIR (*incredulous*): Men, he thinks we're men!

POLICEMAN: Then what the hell are you?

THE PAIR: You'll soon see, you'll soon see!

POLICEMAN (*baffled*): Well, at least you are cheerful.

THE PAIR: We get steak and ham, every day, every day.

POLICEMAN: Yeah. I'd get up and dance for that too. Come on, give me your hands. Funny kind of humor foreigners have. (*Goes off to town with pair.*)

THE PAIR: Off to Boby and Moby, off to Roby and Toby!

(*Open scene change: façade of station and adjacent little building soar into flies. Interior of the Golden Apostle: a hotel sign might well be let down from above, an imposing gilded Apostle, as emblem, and left to hang in midair. Faded, outmoded luxury. Everything threadbare, tattered, dusty and musty and gone to seed. Interminable processions of porters taking interminable pieces of luggage upstairs: first a cage, then the case and trunks. Mayor and Schoolmaster seated in foreground drinking Schnapps.*)

MAYOR: Cases, cases, and still more cases. Mountains of them. And a little while ago they came in with a cage. There was a panther in it. A black, wild animal.

SCHOOLMASTER: She had the coffin put in a special spare room. Curious.

MAYOR: Famous women have their whims and fancies.

SCHOOLMASTER: She seems to want to stay here quite a while.

MAYOR: So much the better. Ill has her in the bag. He was calling her his little wildcat, his little sorceress. He'll get thousands out of her. Her health, Professor. And may Claire Zachanassian restore the Bockmann business.

SCHOOLMASTER: And the Wagner Factory.

MAYOR: And the Foundry on Sunshine Square. If they boom we'll all boom—my Community and your College and the Standard of Living.

(*He has called a toast; they clink glasses.*)

SCHOOLMASTER: I've been correcting the Guellen schoolchildren's Latin and Greek exercises for more than two decades, Mister Mayor, but let me tell you, Sir, I only learned what horror is one hour ago. That old lady in black robes getting off the train was a gruesome vision. Like one of the Fates; she made me think of an avenging Greek goddess. Her name shouldn't be Claire; it should be Clotho. I could suspect her of spinning destiny's webs herself.

(*Enter Policeman. Hangs cap on peg.*)

MAYOR: Pull up a chair, Officer.

(*Policeman pulls up a chair.*)

POLICEMAN: Not much fun patroling in this dump. But maybe now it'll rise from the ashes. I've just been to Petersens' Barn with the billionairess and that shopkeeper Ill. I witnessed a moving scene. Both parties maintained a meditative pause, as in church. I was embarrassed. I therefore did not follow them when they went to Konradsweil Forest. Say, that was a real procession. The sedan chair first, then Ill walking beside it, then the Butler, then her seventh husband last with his fishing rod.

SCHOOLMASTER: That conspicuous consumption of husbands; she's a second Laïs.

POLICEMAN: And those two little fat men. The devil knows what it all means.

SCHOOLMASTER: Sinister. An ascent from the infernal regions.

MAYOR: I wonder what they're after in Konradsweil Forest.

POLICEMAN: The same as in Petersens' Barn, Mister Mayor. They're visiting the places where their passion used to burn, as they say.

SCHOOLMASTER: Flame, flame. Remember Shakespeare: Romeo and Juliet. Gentlemen: I'm stirred. I sense the grandeur of antiquity in Guellen. I've never sensed it here before.

MAYOR: Gentlemen: we must drink a special toast to Ill—a man who's doing all a man can to better our lot. To our most popular citizen: to my successor!

(*The Hotel Apostle floats away, back into the flies. Enter the four citizens, left, with a simple, backless wooden bench, which they set down, left. Man One, with a huge, pasteboard heart hanging from his neck, on it the letters AC, climbs onto the bench. The others stand round him in a half circle, holding twigs at arm's length to designate trees.)*

MAN ONE.
We are trees, we're pine and spruce
MAN TWO:
We are beech, and dark-green fir
MAN THREE:
Lichen, moss and climbing ivy
MAN FOUR:
Undergrowth and lair of fox
MAN ONE:
Drifting cloud and call of bird
MAN TWO:
We are the woodland wilderness
MAN THREE:
Toadstool, and the timid deer
MAN FOUR:
And rustling leaves; and bygone dreams

(The two gum-chewing brutes emerge from background bearing sedan chair with Claire Zachanassian, Ill at her side. Behind her, Husband VII. Butler brings up rear, leading blind pair by the hand.)

CLAIRE ZACHANASSIAN: It's the Konradsweil Forest. Roby, Toby, stop a moment.

BLIND PAIR: Stop, Roby and Toby, stop Boby and Moby.
(Claire Zachanassian descends from sedan chair, surveys wood.)

CLAIRE ZACHANASSIAN: There's the heart with our two names on it, Alfred. Almost faded away, and grown apart. And the tree's grown. The trunk and branches have thickened. The way we have ourselves.
(Claire Zachanassian crosses to other trees.)
A German forest. It's a long time since I last walked through these woods, in my young days, frolicking in the foliage and the purple ivy. You brutes just go and chew your gum behind the

bushes, and take your sedan chair with you; I don't want to look at your mugs all the time. And Moby, stroll away over to that stream on the right, there, and look at the fish.

(*Exit brutes, left, with sedan-chair. Exit Husband VII, right. Claire Zachanassian sits on bench.*)

Look, a doe.

(*Man Three springs off.*)

ILL: It's the close season.

(*He sits next to her.*)

CLAIRE ZACHANASSIAN: We kissed each other on this spot. More than forty-five years ago. We loved each other under these boughs, under these bushes, among these toadstools on the moss. I was seventeen, and you weren't quite twenty. Then you married Matilda Blumhard with her little general store, and I married old Zachanassian with his billions from Armenia. He found me in a brothel. In Hamburg. It was my red hair took his fancy; the old, gold lecher!

ILL: Clara!

CLAIRE ZACHANASSIAN: Boby, a Henry Clay.

BLIND PAIR: A Henry Clay, a Henry Clay.

(*Butler comes out of background, passes her a cigar, lights it.*)

CLAIRE ZACHANASSIAN: I'm fond of cigars. I suppose I ought to smoke my husband's produce; but I don't trust them.

ILL: It was for your sake I married Matilda Blumhard.

CLAIRE ZACHANASSIAN: She had money.

ILL: You were young and beautiful. The future belonged to you. I wanted you to be happy. So I had to renounce being happy myself.

CLAIRE ZACHANASSIAN: And now the future's here.

ILL: If you'd stayed here, you'd have been ruined like me.

CLAIRE ZACHANASSIAN: Are you ruined?

ILL: A broken-down shopkeeper in a broken-down town.

CLAIRE ZACHANASSIAN: Now it's me who has money.

ILL: I've been living in hell since you went away from me.

CLAIRE ZACHANASSIAN: And I've grown into hell itself.

ILL: Always squabbling with my family. They blame me for being poor.

CLAIRE ZACHANASSIAN: Didn't little Matilda make you happy?

ILL: Your happiness is what matters.

CLAIRE ZACHANASSIAN: Your children?

ILL: No sense of ideals.

CLAIRE ZACHANASSIAN: They'll develop one soon.

(*He says nothing. Both gaze at the wood of childhood memory.*)

ILL: I lead a laughable life. Never once really managed to leave this township. One trip to Berlin and one to Tessin. That's all.

CLAIRE ZACHANASSIAN: Why bother, anyway. I know what the world's like.

ILL: Because you've always been able to travel.

CLAIRE ZACHANASSIAN: Because I own it.

(*He says nothing; she smokes.*)

ILL: Everything's going to be different now.

CLAIRE ZACHANASSIAN: Sure.

ILL (*watches her*): Are you going to help us?

CLAIRE ZACHANASSIAN: I won't leave my home town in the lurch.

ILL: We need millions.

CLAIRE ZACHANASSIAN: That's nothing.

ILL (*enthusiastically*): My little wildcat!

(*Moved, he slaps her on left thigh, then painfully withdraws hand.*)

CLAIRE ZACHANASSIAN: That hurt. You hit one of the straps for my artificial leg.

(*Man One pulls pipe and rusty door key from trousers pocket, taps on pipe with key.*)

A woodpecker.

ILL: Now it's the way it used to be when we were young and bold, when we went out walking in Konradsweil Forest, in the days of our young love. And the sun was a dazzling orb, above the pine trees. And far away a few wisps of cloud, and somewhere in the woodland you could hear a cuckoo calling.

MAN FOUR: Cuckoo, cuckoo!

(*Ill lays hand on Man One.*)

ILL: Cool wood, and the wind in the boughs, churning like the surf.

(*The three men who are trees begin blowing and waving their arms up and down.*)

Ah, my little sorceress, if only time could be rolled back. If only life hadn't put us asunder.

CLAIRE ZACHANASSIAN: Would you wish that?

ILL: That above all, above all. I do love you!

> (*Kisses her right hand.*)

The same, cool white hand.

CLAIRE ZACHANASSIAN: No, you're wrong. It's artificial too. Ivory.

> (*Ill, horrified, releases her hand.*)

ILL: Clara, are you all artificial?

CLARE ZACHANASSIAN: Practically. My plane crashed in Afghanistan. I was the only one who crawled out of the wreckage. Even the crew died. I'm unkillable.

BLIND PAIR: She's unkillable, she's unkillable.

> (*Ceremonial oompah music. The Hotel Apostle descends again. Guelleners bring in tables, wretched, tattered table-cloths, cutlery, crockery, food. One table, center, one left, and one right, parallel to audience. Clergyman comes out of background. More Guelleners flock in, among them a Gymnast. Mayor, Schoolmaster and Policeman reappear. The Guelleners applaud. Mayor crosses to bench where Claire Zachanassian and Ill are sitting; the trees have metamorphosed back into citizens and moved away upstage.*)

MAYOR: The storm of applause is for you, my dear lady.

CLAIRE ZACHANASSIAN: It's for the town band, Mister Mayor. It was a capital performance; and the Athletics Club did a wonderful pyramid. I love men in shorts and leotards! They look so natural.

MAYOR: May I escort you to your place?

> (*He escorts Claire Zachanassian to her place at table, center, introduces her to his wife.*)

My wife.

> (*Claire Zachanassian examines wife through lorgnette.*)

CLAIRE ZACHANASSIAN: Annie Dummermut, top of our class.

> (*Mayor introduces her to a second woman, as worn out and embittered as his wife.*)

MAYOR: Mrs. Ill.

CLAIRE ZACHANASSIAN: Matilda Blumhard. I can remember you lying in wait for Alfred behind the shop door. You've grown very thin and pale, my dear.

> (*Doctor hurries in, right; a squat, thick-set fifty-year-old;*

moustachioed, bristly black hair, scarred face, threadbare frock coat.)

DOCTOR: Just managed to do it, in my old Mercedes.

MAYOR: Doctor Nuesslin, our physician.

(*Claire Zachanassian examines Doctor through lorgnette as he kisses her hand.*)

CLAIRE ZACHANASSIAN: Interesting. Do you make out Death Certificates?

DOCTOR (*taken off guard*): Death Certificates?

CLAIRE ZACHANASSIAN: If someone should die?

DOCTOR: Of course, Madam. It's my duty. As decreed by the authorities.

CLAIRE ZACHANASSIAN: Next time, diagnose heart attack.

ILL (*laughs*): Delicious, simply delicious.

(*Claire Zachanassian turns from Doctor to inspect Gymnast, clad in shorts and leotards.*)

CLAIRE ZACHANASSIAN: Do another exercise.

(*Gymnast bends knees, flexes arms.*)

Marvelous muscles. Ever used your strength for strangling?

GYMNAST (*stiffens in consternation at knee-bend position*): For strangling?

CLAIRE ZACHANASSIAN: Now just bend your arms back again, Mister Gymnast, then forward into a press-up.

ILL (*laughs*): Clare has such a golden sense of humor! I could die laughing at one of her jokes!

DOCTOR (*still disconcerted*): I wonder. They chill me to the marrow.

ILL (*stage whisper*): She's promised us millions.

MAYOR (*gasps*): Millions?

ILL: Millions.

DOCTOR: God Almighty.

(*The billionairess turns away from Gymnast.*)

CLAIRE ZACHANASSIAN: And now, Mister Mayor, I'm hungry.

MAYOR: We were just waiting for your husband, my dear lady.

CLAIRE ZACHANASSIAN: You needn't. He's fishing. And I'm getting a divorce.

MAYOR: A divorce?

CLAIRE ZACHANASSIAN: Moby'll be surprised too. I'm marrying a German film star.

MAYOR: But you told us it was a very happy marriage.

CLAIRE ZACHANASSIAN: All my marriages are happy. But when I was a child I used to dream of a wedding in Guellen Cathedral. You should always fulfill your childhood dreams. It'll be a grand ceremony.

(*All sit. Claire Zachanassian takes her place between Mayor and Ill. Ill's wife beside Ill, Mayor's wife beside Mayor. Schoolmaster, Pastor, and Policeman at separate table, right. The four citizens, left. In background, more guests of honor, with wives. Above, the banner: "Welcome Claire." Mayor stands, beaming with joy, napkin already in position, and taps on his glass.*)

MAYOR: My dear lady, fellow citizens. Forty-five years have flowed by since you left our little town, our town founded by Crown Prince Hasso the Noble, our town so pleasantly nestling between Konradsweil and Pückenried Valley. Forty-five years, more than four decades, it's a long time. Many things have happened since then, many bitter things. It has gone sadly with the world, gone sadly with us. And yet we have never, my dear lady—our Claire (*applause*)—never forgotten you. Neither you, nor your family. Your mother, that magnificent and robustly healthy creature (*Ill whispers something to him*) tragically and prematurely torn from our midst by tuberculosis, and your father, that popular figure, who built the building by the station which experts and laymen still visit so often (*Ill whispers something to him*)—still admire so much, they both live on in our thoughts, for they were of our best, our worthiest. And you too, my dear lady: who, as you romped through our streets—our streets, alas, so sadly decrepit nowadays—you, a curly-headed, blonde (*Ill whispers something to him*)—redheaded tomboy, who did not know you? Even then, everyone could sense the magic in your personality, foresee your approaching rise to humanity's dizzy heights. (*Takes out his notebook.*) You were never forgotten. Literally never. Even now, the staff at school holds up your achievements as an example to others, and in nature studies—the most essential ones—they were astonishing, a revelation of your sympathy for every living creature, indeed for all things in need of protection. And even then, people far and wide were moved to wonder at your love of justice, at your sense of generosity. (*Huge applause.*) For did not our Claire obtain food for an old widow, buying potatoes with that pocket-money so hardly earned from neighbors, and thereby save the old lady from dying of hunger, to mention but one of her deeds of charity. (*Huge applause.*) My dear lady, my dear Guelleners, that happy temperament has now developed from those tender seeds to an impressive flowering, and our redheaded madcap has become a lady whose generosity stirs the world; we need only think of her social work, of her maternity homes and her soup kitchens, of her art foundations and her children's nurseries, and now, therefore, I ask you to give three cheers for the prodigal returned: Hip, Hip, Hip, Hurrah! (*Applause.*)

(*Claire Zachanassian gets to her feet.*)

CLAIRE ZACHANASSIAN: Mister Mayor, Guelleners. I am moved by your unselfish joy in my visit. As a matter of fact I was somewhat different from the child I seem to be in the Mayor's speech. When I went to school, I was beaten. And I stole the potatoes for Widow Boll, aided by Ill; not to save the old bitch from dying of hunger, but just for once to sleep with Ill in a more comfortable bed than Konradsweil Forest or Petersens' Barn. Nonetheless, as my contribution to this joy of yours, I want to tell you I'm ready to give Guellen one billion. Five hundred million for the town and five hundred million to be shared among each family.

(*Deathly silence.*)

MAYOR (*stammers*): One billion.

(*Everyone still dumbstruck.*)

CLAIRE ZACHANASSIAN: On one condition.

(*Everyone bursts into indescribable jubilation, dancing round, standing on chairs, Gymnast performing acrobatics, etc. Ill pounds his chest enthusistically.*))

ILL: There's Clara for you! What a jewel! She takes your breath away! Just like her, O my little sorceress!

(*Kisses her.*)

MAYOR: Madam: you said, on one condition. May I ask, on what condition?

CLAIRE ZACHANASSIAN: I'll tell you on what condition. I'm giving you one billion, and I'm buying myself justice.

(*Deathly silence.*)

MAYOR: My dear lady, what do you mean by that?

CLAIRE ZACHANASSIAN: What I said.

MAYOR: Justice can't be bought.

CLAIRE ZACHANASSIAN: Everything can be bought.

MAYOR: I still don't understand.

CLAIRE ZACHANASSIAN: Boby. Step forward.

> (*Butler steps forward, from right to center, between the three tables. Takes off his dark glasses.*)

BUTLER: I don't know if any of you here still recognize me.

SCHOOLMASTER: Chief Justice Courtly.

BUTLER: Right. Chief Justice Courtly. Forty-five years ago, I was Chief Justice in Guellen. I was later called to the Kaffigen Court of Appeal until, twenty-five years ago it is now, Madam Zachanassian offered me the post of Butler in her service. A somewhat unusual career, indeed, I grant you, for an academic man, however, the salary involved was really quite fantastic . . .

CLAIRE ZACHANASSIAN: Get to the point, Boby.

BUTLER: As you may have gathered, Madam Claire Zachanassian is offering you the sum of one billion, in return for which she insists that justice be done. In other words, Madam Zachanassian will give you all one billion if you right the wrong she was done in Guellen. Mr. Ill, if you please.

> (*Ill stands. He is pale, startled, wondering.*)

ILL: What do you want of me?

BUTLER: Step forward, Mr. Ill.

ILL: Sure.

> (*Steps forward, to front of table, right. Laughs uneasily. Shrugs.*)

BUTLER: The year was nineteen ten. I was Chief Justice in Guellen. I had a paternity claim to arbitrate. Claire Zachanassian, at the time Clara Wascher, claimed that you, Mr. Ill, were her child's father.

> (*Ill keeps quiet.*)

At that time, Mr. Ill, you denied paternity. You called two witnesses.

ILL: Oh, it's an old story. I was young, thoughtless.

CLAIRE ZACHANASSIAN: Toby and Roby, bring in Koby and Loby.

> (*The two gum-chewing giants lead the pair of blind eunuchs on to center of stage, blind pair gaily holding hands.*)

BLIND PAIR: We're on the spot, we're on the spot!

BUTLER: Do you recognize these two, Mr. Ill?
        (Ill keeps quiet.)
BLIND PAIR: We're Koby and Loby, we're Koby and Loby.
ILL: I don't know them.
BLIND PAIR: We've changed a lot, we've changed a lot!
BUTLER: Say your names.
FIRST BLIND MAN: Jacob Chicken, Jacob Chicken.
SECOND BLIND MAN: Louis Perch, Louis Perch.
BUTLER: Now, Mr. Ill.
ILL: I know nothing about them.
BUTLER: Jacob Chicken and Louis Perch, do you know Mr. Ill?
BLIND PAIR: We're blind, we're blind.
BUTLER: Do you know him by his voice?
BLIND PAIR: By his voice, by his voice.
BUTLER: In nineteen ten, I was Judge and you the witnesses. Louis
    Perch and Jacob Chicken, what did you swear on oath to the
    Court of Guellen?
BLIND PAIR: We'd slept with Clara, we'd slept with Clara.
BUTLER: You swore it on oath, before me. Before the Court. Be-
    fore God. Was it the truth?
BLIND PAIR: We swore a false oath, we swore a false oath.
BUTLER: Why, Jacob Chicken and Louis Perch?
BLIND PAIR: Ill bribed us, Ill bribed us.
BUTLER: With what did he bribe you?
BLIND PAIR: With a bottle of brandy, with a bottle of brandy.
CLAIRE ZACHANASSIAN: And now tell them what I did with you,
    Koby and Loby.
BUTLER: Tell them.
BLIND PAIR: The lady tracked us down, the lady tracked us down.
BUTLER: Correct. Claira Zachanassian tracked you down. To the
    ends of the earth. Jacob Chicken had emigrated to Canada and
    Louis Perch to Australia. But she tracked you down. And then
    what did she do with you?
BLIND PAIR: She gave us to Toby and Roby, she gave us to Toby
    and Roby.
BUTLER: And what did Toby and Roby do to you?
BLIND PAIR: Castrated and blinded us, castrated and blinded us.
BUTLER: And there you have the full story. One Judge, one ac-
    cused, two false witnesses: a miscarriage of justice in the year
    nineteen ten. Isn't that so, plaintiff?

CLAIRE ZACHANASSIAN (*stands*): That is so.

ILL (*stamping on floor*): It's over and done with, dead and buried! It's an old, crazy story.

BUTLER: What happened to the child, plaintiff?

CLAIRE ZACHANASSIAN (*gently*): It lived one year.

BUTLER: What happened to you?

CLAIRE ZACHANASSIAN: I became a prostitute.

BUTLER: What made you one?

CLAIRE ZACHANASSIAN: The judgment of that court made me one.

BUTLER: And now you desire justice, Claire Zachanassian?

CLAIRE ZACHANASSIAN: I can afford it. A billion for Guellen if someone kills Alfred Ill.

(*Deathly silence. Mrs. Ill rushes to Ill, flings her arms round him.*)

MRS. ILL: Freddy!

ILL: My little sorceress! You can't ask that! It was long ago. Life went on.

CLAIRE ZACHANASSIAN: Life went on, but I've forgotten nothing, Ill. Neither Konradsweil Forest, nor Petersens' Barn; neither Widow Boll's bedroom, nor your treachery. And now we're old, the pair of us. You decrepit, and me cut to bits by the surgeons' knives. And now I want accounts between us settled. You chose your life, and forced me into mine. A moment ago you wanted time turned back, in that wood so full of the past, where we spent our young years. Well, I'm turning it back now, and I want justice. Justice for a billion.

(*Mayor stands, pale, dignified.*)

MAYOR: Madam Zachanassian: you forget, this is Europe. You forget, we are not savages. In the name of all citizens of Guellen, I reject your offer; and I reject it in the name of humanity. We would rather have poverty than blood on our hands.

(*Huge applause.*)

CLAIRE ZACHANASSIAN: I'll wait.

Act Two

The little town only in outline. In background, the Golden Apostle Hotel, exterior view. Faded "art nouveau" architecture. Bal-

cony. Right, a sign, "Alfred Ill: General Store," above a grimy shop counter backed by shelves displaying old stock. Whenever anyone enters the imaginary door, a bell rings, tinnily. Left, a sign, "Police," above a wooden table, on it a telephone. Two chairs. It is morning. Roby and Toby, chewing gum, enter, left, bearing wreaths and flowers as at a funeral, cross stage and enter, back, the hotel. Ill at a window, watching them. His daughter on her knees scrubbing floor. His son puts a cigarette in his mouth.

ILL: Wreaths.

SON: They bring them in from the station every morning.

ILL: For the empty coffin in the Golden Apostle.

SON: It doesn't scare anyone.

ILL: The town's on my side.

> *(Son lights cigarette.)*

Mother coming down for breakfast?

DAUGHTER: She's staying upstairs. Says she's tired.

ILL: You've a good mother, children. That's a fact. I just want you to know. A good mother. Let her stay upstairs, rest, save her energy. In that case, *we'll* have breakfast together. It's a long time since we've done that. I suggest eggs and a tin of American ham. We'll go all out. Like in the good old days, when the Sunshine Foundry was still booming.

SON: You'll have to excuse me.

> *(Stubs out cigarette.)*

ILL: Aren't you going to eat with us, Karl?

SON: I'm going to the station. One of the railroad workers is out sick. Maybe they want a replacement.

ILL: Railroad work in the blazing sun is no job for my boy.

SON: It's better than no job.

> *(Exit Son. Daughter stands.)*

DAUGHTER: I'm going too, father.

ILL: You too? I see. Where, mademoiselle, if one may ask?

DAUGHTER: To the Employment Office. They may have a vacancy.

> *(Exit Daughter. Ill, upset, takes out handkerchief, blows nose.)*

ILL: Good kids, fine kids.

> *(A few bars of guitar music are heard from balcony.)*

VOICE OF CLAIRE ZACHANASSIAN: Boby, pass me my left leg.

VOICE OF BUTLER: I can't find it, Madam.

VOICE OF CLAIRE ZACHANASSIAN: On the chest of drawers behind the wedding flowers.

(Enter Man One, as first customer; he goes through imaginary door into Ill's shop.)

ILL: 'Morning, Hofbauer.

MAN ONE: Cigarettes.

ILL: Same as usual?

MAN ONE: Not those, I want the green ones.

ILL: They cost more.

MAN ONE: Charge it.

ILL: Since it's you, Hofbauer, and we should all stick together.

MAN ONE: That's a guitar playing.

ILL: One of those Sing Sing gangsters.

(Blind pair walk out of hotel carrying rods and other fishing gear.)

BLIND PAIR: Lovely morning, Alfred, lovely morning.

ILL: Go to hell.

BLIND PAIR: We're going fishing, we're going fishing.

(Exit blind pair, left.)

MAN ONE: They're going to Guellen Creek.

ILL: With the fishing tackle of her seventh husband.

MAN ONE: They say he's lost his tobacco plantations.

ILL: They belong to the billionairess, too.

MAN ONE: The eighth wedding will be gigantic. She announced their engagement yesterday.

(Claire Zachanassian appears on balcony in background, dressed for the morning. Moves her right hand, her left leg. Sporadic notes plucked on the guitar accompany the balcony scene that follows, after the fashion of opera recitative, pointing the text now with a waltz, now with snatches of national or traditional songs, anthems, etc.)

CLAIRE ZACHANASSIAN: I'm assembled again. Roby, the Armenian folk-song!

(Guitar music.)

Zachanassian's favorite tune. He used to love listening to it. Every morning. An exemplary man, that old tycoon. With a veritable navy of oil tankers. And racing stables. And millions more in cash. So a marriage was worthwhile. A great teacher, and a great dancer; a real devil. I've copied him completely.

(*Two women come in, hand Ill milk-cans.*)
FIRST WOMAN: Milk, Mr. Ill.
SECOND WOMAN: My can, Mr. Ill.
ILL: A very good morning to you. A quart of milk for the ladies.
(*Opens a milk drum, prepares to ladle milk.*)
FIRST WOMAN: Whole milk, Mr. Ill.
SECOND WOMAN: Two quarts of whole milk, Mr. Ill.
ILL: Whole milk.
(*Opens another drum, ladles milk.*)

(*Claire Zachanassian assesses morning critically through lorgnette.*)
CLAIRE ZACHANASSIAN: A fine autumn morning. Light mist in the streets, a silvery haze, and the sky above precisely the shade of violet-blue Count Holk used to paint. My third husband. The Foreign Minister. He used to spend his holidays painting. They were hideous paintings.
(*She sits, with elaborate ceremony.*)
Everything about the Count was hideous.

FIRST WOMAN: And butter. Half a pound.
SECOND WOMAN: And super-bread. Four large loaves.
ILL: I see we've had a legacy, ladies.
THE TWO WOMEN: Charge it.
ILL: Share the rough and share the smooth.
FIRST WOMAN: And a bar of chocolate.
SECOND WOMAN: Two bars.
ILL: Charge it?
FIRST WOMAN: Charge it.
SECOND WOMAN: We'll eat those here, Mr. Ill.
FIRST WOMAN: It's much nicer here, Mr. Ill.
(*They sit at back of shop eating chocolate.*)

CLAIRE ZACHANASSIAN: A Winston. I'll try that brand my seventh husband made, just once, now I've divorced him; poor Moby, with his fishing passion. He must be so sad sitting in the Portugal Express.

(*Butler hands her a cigar, gives her a light.*)

MAN ONE: Look, sitting on the balcony, puffing at her cigar.

ILL: Always some outrageously expensive brand.

MAN ONE: Sheer extravagance. She ought to be ashamed, in front of the poor.

CLAIRE ZACHANASSIAN (*smoking*): Curious. Quite smokeable.

ILL: Her plan's misfired. I'm an old sinner, Hofbauer—who isn't. It was a mean trick I played on her when I was a kid, but the way they all rejected the offer, all the Guelleners in the Golden Apostle unanimously, that was the finest moment of my life.

CLAIRE ZACHANASSIAN: Boby! Whisky. Neat.

(*Enter Man Two, as second customer, poor and tattered and torn, like everyone else.*)

MAN TWO: 'Morning. It'll be a hot day.

MAN ONE: Very fine and warm for the time of the year.

ILL: Quite a few customers this morning. Not a soul for weeks and suddenly these past few days they're flocking in.

MAN ONE: We'll stick by you. We'll stick by *our* Ill. Come what may.

THE TWO WOMEN (*munching chocolate*): Come what may, Mr. Ill, come what may.

MAN TWO: Remember, you're the town's most popular personality.

MAN ONE: Our most important personality.

MAN TWO: You'll be elected Mayor in spring.

MAN ONE: That's for sure.

THE TWO WOMEN (*munching chocolate*): Dead certain, Mr. Ill, dead certain.

MAN TWO: Brandy.

(*Ill reaches to shelf.*)

(*Butler serves whisky.*)

CLAIRE ZACHANASSIAN: Wake the new guy. Can't bear my husbands sleeping all the time.

ILL: Three sixty.

MAN TWO: Not that.

ILL: It's what you always drink.

MAN TWO: Cognac.

ILL: That's eighteen ninety-five. No one can afford that.

MAN TWO: Got to give yourself a treat sometimes.

(*A half-naked girl rushes headlong over stage, pursued by Toby.*)

FIRST WOMAN (*munching chocolate*): It's a scandal, the way Louisa behaves.

SECOND WOMAN (*munching chocolate*): And to make matters worse she's engaged to that blond musician in Gunpowder Street.

(*Ill takes down Cognac.*)

ILL: Cognac.

MAN TWO: And tobacco. For my pipe.

ILL: Tobacco.

MAN TWO: The Export.

(*Ill totals account.*)

(*Husband VIII appears on balcony—the film star, tall, slender, red moustache, bathrobe. May be played by same actor as Husband VII.*)

HUSBAND VIII: Isn't it divine, Hopsi. Our first engagement breakfast. Really a dream. A little balcony, the lime tree rustling, the Town Hall fountain softly plashing, a few hens scampering right across the sidewalk, housewives' voices chattering away over their little daily cares and there, beyond the rooftops, the Cathedral spires!

CLAIRE ZACHANASSIAN: Sit down, Hoby. Stop babbling. I can see the landscape. And thoughts aren't your strong point.

MAN TWO: She's sitting up there with her husband now.

FIRST WOMAN (*munching chocolate*): Handsome gentleman. Acts in films. My daughter saw him as the poacher in a country-life feature.

FIRST WOMAN: I saw him when he was the priest in a Graham Greene.

(*Claire Zachanassian is kissed by Husband VIII. Guitar chords.*)

MAN TWO: You can get anything you want with money.

(*Spits.*)

MAN ONE: Not from us. (*Bangs fist on table.*)

ILL: Twenty-three dollars ten.

MAN TWO: Charge it.

ILL: I'll make an exception this week; just make sure you pay on the first, when the dole's due.

(*Man Two crosses to door.*)

ILL: Helmesberger!

(*Man Two halts. Ill goes after him.*)

You're wearing new shoes. New yellow shoes.

MAN TWO: So what?

(*Ill stares at Man One's feet.*)

ILL: You too, Hofbauer. You're wearing new shoes too.

(*His gaze alights on the women; he walks slowly towards them, terror-stricken.*)

You too. New shoes. New yellow shoes.

MAN ONE: What's so extraordinary about new shoes?

MAN TWO: You can't go around in the same old shoes for ever.

ILL: New shoes. How did you all get new shoes?

THE TWO WOMEN: We got them on credit, Mr. Ill, we got them on credit.

ILL: You got them on credit. You got things on credit from me too. Better tobacco, better milk, Cognac. Why are all the shops suddenly giving you credit?

MAN TWO: You're giving us credit too.

ILL: How are you going to pay?

(*Silence. He begins throwing his wares at the customers. They all run away.*)

How are you going to pay? How are you going to pay? How? How?

(*He rushes off, back.*)

HUSBAND VII: Township's getting rowdy.

CLAIRE ZACHANASSIAN: Village life.

HUSBAND VIII: Seems to be trouble in the shop down there.

CLARE ZACHANASSIAN: Probably haggling over the price of meat.

(*Chords on guitar, fortissimo. Husband VIII leaps up, horrified.*)

HUSBAND VIII: Hopsi, for heaven's sake! Did you hear that?

CLAIRE ZACHANASSIAN: The Black Panther. Hissing a little.

HUSBAND VIII (*awestruck*): A Black Panther?

CLAIRE ZACHANASSIAN: From the Pasha of Marakeesh. A present. He's loping around in the sitting room next door. A great wicked cat with flashing eyes. I'm very fond of him.
(*Policeman sits down at table, left. Drinks beer. Slow, portentous manner of speech. Ill arrives from back of stage.*)
CLAIRE ZACHANASSIAN: You may serve, Boby.
POLICEMAN: Ill. What can I do for you? Take a seat.
(*Ill remains standing.*)
You're trembling.
ILL: I demand the arrest of Claire Zachanassian.
(*Policeman thumbs tobacco into his pipe, lights it, comfortably.*)
POLICEMAN: Peculiar. Highly peculiar.
(*Butler serves breakfast, brings mail.*)
ILL: I demand it as future Mayor.
POLICEMAN (*puffing clouds of smoke*): We have not yet held the elections.
ILL: Arrest that woman on the spot.
POLICEMAN: What you mean is, you wish to charge this lady. It is then for the police to decide whether or not to arrest her. Has she broken any laws?
ILL: She's inciting the people of our town to kill me.
POLICEMAN: So now you want me to walk up to the lady and arrest her.
(*Pours himself beer.*)
CLAIRE ZACHANASSIAN: The mail. One from Ike. Nehru. They send congratulations.
ILL: It's your duty.
POLICEMAN: Peculiar. Highly peculiar.
(*Drinks beer.*)
ILL: It's only natural. Perfectly natural.
POLICEMAN: My dear Ill, it's not as natural as all that. Now let's examine the matter soberly. The lady makes an offer of one billion to the town of Guellen in exchange for your—you know what I'm talking about, of course. True, true, I was there. All this notwithstanding, no sufficient grounds are thereby constituted for the police taking action against Mrs. Claire Zachanassian. After all, we must abide by the law.
ILL: Incitement to murder.

POLICEMAN: Now listen here, Ill. We would only have a case of incitement to murder if the proposal to murder you were meant seriously. So much is obvious.

ILL: That's what I'm saying.

POLICEMAN: Exactly. Now, this proposal cannot be meant seriously, because one billion is an exorbitant price, you have to admit that yourself. People offer a hundred, or maybe two hundred, for a job like that, not a penny more, you can bet your life on it. Which again proves the proposal wasn't meant seriously, and even if it had been the police couldn't take the lady seriously, because in that case she'd be mad. Get it?

ILL: Inspector. This proposal threatens *me,* whether the woman happens to be mad or not. That's only logical.

POLICEMAN: Illogical. You can't be threatened by a proposal, only by the execution of a proposal. Show me one genuine attempt to execute that proposal, for example one man who's been pointing a gun at you, and I'll be on the spot in a flash. But no one, in point of fact, has any wish to execute the proposal; quite the contrary. That demonstration in the Golden Apostle was extremely impressive. It was a while ago now, but allow me to congratulate you.

(*Drinks beer.*)

ILL: I'm not quite so sure, Officer.

POLICEMAN: Not quite so sure?

ILL: My customers are buying better milk, better bread, better cigarettes.

POLICEMAN: But you ought to be overjoyed! That means your business is picking up.

(*Drinks beer.*)

CLAIRE ZACHANASSIAN: Boby, buy up Dupont Shares.

ILL: Helmesberger's been in buying Cognac. A man who hasn't earned a cent for years and lives on Poor Relief soup.

POLICEMAN: I'll have some of that Cognac this evening. Helmesberger's invited me over.

(*Drinks beer.*)

ILL: Everyone's wearing new shoes. New yellow shoes.

POLICEMAN: Whatever can you have against new shoes? I've got a new pair on myself.

(Displays feet.)

ILL: You too.

POLICEMAN: Look.

ILL: Yellow as well. And you're drinking Pilsener Beer.

POLICEMAN: Tastes good.

ILL: You always used to drink local beer.

POLICEMAN: Filthy stuff.

(Radio music.)

ILL: Listen.

POLICEMAN: What?

ILL: Music.

POLICEMAN: *The Merry Widow.*

ILL: A radio.

POLICEMAN: It's Hagholzer next door. He ought to keep his window shut.

(Makes note in little notebook.)

ILL: How did Hagholzer get a radio?

POLICEMAN: That's his business.

ILL: And you, Officer, how are you going to pay for your Pilsener Beer and your new shoes?

POLICEMAN: That's my business.

(Telephone on table rings. Policeman picks up receiver.)

POLICEMAN: Guellen Police Station.

CLAIRE ZACHANASSIAN: Boby, telephone the Russians and tell them I accept their offer.

POLICEMAN: O.K., we'll see to it.

ILL: And how are my customers going to pay?

POLICEMAN: That doesn't concern the police.

(Stands, takes rifle from back of chair.)

ILL: But it does concern me. Because it's me they're going to pay with.

POLICEMAN: Nobody's threatening you.

(Begins loading rifle.)

ILL: The town's getting into debt. The greater the debt, the higher the standard of living. The higher the standard of living, the greater the need to kill me. And all that woman has to do is sit on her balcony, drink coffee, smoke cigars, and wait. That's all. Just wait.

POLICEMAN: You're imagining things.

ILL: You're all just waiting.

(Bangs on table.)

POLICEMAN: You've been drinking too much brandy.

(Checks rifle.)

There. Now it's loaded. Set your mind at rest. The police are here to enforce respect for the law, to maintain order and protect the individual. They know their duty. If the faintest suspicion of a threat to you arises, wheresoever it arises, from whatsoever source, the police will step in, Mr. Ill, you can rely upon it.

ILL *(softly)*: Then how do you explain that gold tooth in your mouth, Officer?

POLICEMAN: What?

ILL: A gleaming new gold tooth.

POLICEMAN: Are you crazy?

(At this point Ill perceives the gun barrel is now directed at himself, and his hands go slowly up.)

I've no time to argue over your ravings, man. I've got to go. That screwy billionairess has lost her little lap-dog. The black panther. Now I have to hunt it down.

(Goes towards back of stage and off.)

ILL: It's me you're hunting down, me.

(Claire Zachanassian is reading a letter.)

CLAIRE ZACHANASSIAN: He's coming, my dress designer's coming. My fifth husband, my best-looking man. He still creates all my wedding gowns. Roby, a minuet.

(Guitar plays a minuet.)

HUSBAND VIII: But your fifth was a surgeon.

CLAIRE ZACHANASSIAN: My sixth.

(Opens another letter.)

From the Boss of Western Railways.

HUSBAND VIII *(astonished)*: I've not heard of that one at all.

CLAIRE ZACHANASSIAN: My fourth. Impoverished. His shares belong to me. I seduced him in Buckingham Palace.

HUSBAND VIII: But that was Lord Ishmael.

CLAIRE ZACHANASSIAN: So it was. You're right, Hoby. I forgot all about him and his castle in Yorkshire. Then this letter must be

from my second. Met him in Cairo. We kissed beneath the
Sphinx. A most impressive evening.

> (*Scene change, right. The legend "Town Hall" descends.
> Man Three enters, carries off cash register and shifts
> counter into position as desk. Mayor enters. Puts revolver
> on table, sits. Ill enters, left. A construction plan is affixed
> to wall.*)

ILL: I want to talk to you, Mister Mayor.
MAYOR: Take a seat.
ILL: As man to man. As your successor.
MAYOR: By all means.
> (*Ill stays standing, watches revolver.*)
Mrs. Zachanassian's panther has escaped. It's climbing around
in the Cathedral. So it's best to be armed.
ILL: Sure.
MAYOR: I've called up all men owning weapons. We're not letting
the children go to school.
ILL (*suspiciously*): Somewhat drastic measures.
MAYOR: It's big game hunting.
> (*Enter Butler.*)
BUTLER: The World Bank President, Madam. Just flown in from
New York.
CLAIRE ZACHANASSIAN: I'm not at home. Tell him to fly away
again.
MAYOR: What's on your mind? Go on, feel free, unburden your-
self.
ILL (*suspiciously*): That's a fine brand you're smoking there.
MAYOR: A Pegasus. Virginia.
ILL: Pretty expensive.
MAYOR: Well worth the money.
ILL: You used to smoke another brand.
MAYOR: Sailor's Mates.
ILL: Cheaper.
MAYOR: Far too strong.
ILL: New tie?
MAYOR: Silk.
ILL: And I suppose you bought a pair of shoes?

MAYOR: I had some made in Kalberstadt. That's funny, how did you know?

ILL: That's why I've come to see you.

MAYOR: Whatever's the matter with you? You look pale. Are you sick?

ILL: I'm scared.

MAYOR: Scared?

ILL: Living standards are going up.

MAYOR: That's real news to me. I'd be glad if they were.

ILL: I demand official protection.

MAYOR: Eh! Whatever for?

ILL: You know very well what for.

MAYOR: Don't you trust us?

ILL: There's a billion on my head.

MAYOR: Why don't you go to the police?

ILL: I've been to the police.

MAYOR: And that reassured you.

ILL: When the Police Inspector opened his mouth, I saw a gleaming new gold tooth.

MAYOR: You're forgetting you're in Guellen. A city of Humanist traditions. Goethe spent a night here. Brahms composed a quartet here. We owe allegiance to our lofty heritage.

(*Man Three enters, left, carrying typewriter.*)

MAN: The new typewriter, Mister Mayor. An IBM.

MAYOR: It's to go in the office.

(*Man exits, right.*)

We've not deserved your ingratitude. If you're unable to place any trust in our community, I regret it for your sake. I didn't expect such a nihilistic attitude from you. After all, we live under the rule of law.

ILL: Then arrest that woman.

MAYOR: Peculiar. Highly peculiar.

ILL: The Police Officer said that too.

MAYOR: God knows, the lady isn't acting so unreasonably. You did bribe two men to commit perjury and fling a young girl into wretched misery.

ILL: That wretched misery turned out to be several billions, after all, Mister Mayor.

(*Silence.*)

MAYOR: Let me say a few frank words to you.

ILL: I wish you would.

MAYOR: As man to man, the way you wanted. You haven't any moral right to demand the arrest of that lady, and furthermore there's no question of your becoming Mayor. I'm extremely sorry to have to tell you.

ILL: Officially?

MAYOR: At the behest of all parties.

ILL: I understand.

(*Crosses slowly to window, left, turns back on Mayor, and stares out.*)

MAYOR: The fact that we condemn the lady's proposal does not mean we condone the crime which led to that proposal. The post of Mayor requires certain guarantees of good moral character which you can no longer furnish. You must realize that. We shall continue of course to show you the same friendship and regard as ever. That goes without saying.

(*Roby and Toby enter, left, with more wreaths and flowers. They cross the stage and disappear into the Golden Apostle.*)

The best thing is to pass over the whole affair in silence. I've also requested the local paper not to let any of it get into print.

(*Ill turns.*)

ILL: They've already begun adorning my coffin, Mister Mayor. For me, silence is too dangerous.

MAYOR: But my dear Ill, what makes you think that? You ought to be thankful we're spreading a cloak of forgetfulness over the whole nasty business.

ILL: If I talk, I still have a chance of getting off.

MAYOR: That's the limit. Who in the world would be threatening you?

ILL: One of you.

(*The Mayor gets up.*)

MAYOR: Whom do you suspect? Tell me the name and I'll investigate. Rigorously.

ILL: Each of you.

MAYOR: In the name of the city, I solemnly protest against this allegation.

ILL: No one wants to kill me. Everyone hopes that someone will do it. And consequently someone will do it someday.

MAYOR: You're seeing things.

ILL: I see a blueprint on the wall—the new town hall?
(He taps on the blueprint.)

MAYOR: My God, there's not yet a law against planning?

ILL: You are already speculating on my death.

MAYOR: My good man, you can depend on it, if I, as a politician, no longer had the right of believing in a better future without simultaneously having to think of a crime, I'd resign.

ILL: You've already condemned me to death.

MAYOR: Mr. Ill!

ILL: That plan proves it! Proves it.

CLAIRE ZACHANASSIAN: Onassis will be coming. The Prince and the Princess. Aga.

HUSBAND VIII: Ali?

CLAIRE ZACHANASSIAN: All the Riviera crowd.

HUSBAND VIII: Reporters?

CLAIRE ZACHANASSIAN: From all over the world. The Press always attend when I get married. They need me, and I need them.
(Opens another letter.)

From Count Holk.

HUSBAND VIII: Hopsi, this is our first breakfast together. Must you really spend it reading letters from your former husbands?

CLAIRE ZACHANASSIAN: I have to keep them under observation.

HUSBAND VIII: I have problems too.
(Rises to his feet, stares down into town.)

CLAIRE ZACHANASSIAN: Something wrong with your Porsche?

HUSBAND VIII: Small towns like this get me down. I know the lime tree's rustling, the birds are singing, the fountain's splashing, but they were all doing all that half an hour ago. And nothing else is happening at all, either to the landscape or to the people, it's all a picture of deep, carefree peace and contentment and cosy comfort. No grandeur, no tragedy. Not a trace of the spiritual dedication of a great age.

(Enter Pastor, left, with a rifle slung round his shoulder. Over the table formerly occupied by Policeman he spreads

a white cloth marked with a black cross. Leans rifle against wall of hotel. Sexton helps him on with soutane. Darkness.)

PASTOR: Come in, Ill, come into the sacristy.

(*Ill comes in, left.*)

It's dark in here, dark but cool.

ILL: I don't want to bother you, Reverend.

PASTOR: The doors of the Church are open to all.

(*Perceives that Ill's gaze has settled on the rifle.*)

Don't be surprised at this weapon. Mrs. Zachanassian's black panther is on the prowl. It's just been up in the choirloft. Now it's in Petersens' Barn.

ILL: I need help.

PASTOR: What kind of help?

ILL: I'm scared.

PASTOR: Scared? Of whom?

ILL: People.

PASTOR: That the people will kill you, Ill?

ILL: They're hunting me as if I were a wild animal.

PASTOR: You should fear not people, but God; not death in the body, but in the soul. Sexton, button the back of my soutane.

(*The citizens of Guellen materialize round the entire periphery of the stage; Policeman first, then Mayor, and four men, Painter, Schoolmaster, on patrol, rifles at the ready, stalking round.*)

ILL: My life's at stake.

PASTOR: Your eternal life.

ILL: There's a rise in the standard of living.

PASTOR: It's the specter of your conscience rising.

ILL: The people are happy. The young girls are decking themselves out. The boys have put on bright shirts. The town's getting ready to celebrate my murder, and I'm dying of terror.

PASTOR: All they're doing is affirming life, that's all they're doing, affirming life.

ILL: It's Hell.

PASTOR: You are your own Hell. You are older than I am, and you think you know people, but in the end one only knows oneself. Because you once betrayed a young girl for money, many years ago, you believe people will betray you for money too. You impute your own nature to others. All too naturally. The cause of our fear and our sin lies in our own hearts. Once you have acknowledged that, you will have conquered your torment and acquired a weapon whereby to master it.

ILL: The Siemethofers have acquired a washing machine.

PASTOR: Don't let that trouble you.

ILL: On credit.

PASTOR: You should rather be troubled by your soul's immortality.

ILL: And the Stockers, a television set.

PASTOR: Pray to God. Sexton, my bands.

(*Sexton positions bands round Pastor.*)

Examine your conscience. Go the way of repentance, or the world will relight the fires of your terror again and again. It is the only way. No other way is open to us.

(*Silence. Men and rifles disappear. Shadows round rim of stage. Fire bell begins clanging.*)

Now I must discharge my office, Ill, I have a baptism. The Bible, Sexton, the Liturgy, the Book of Psalms. When little children begin to cry they must be led to safety, into the only ray of light which illumines the world.

(*A second bell begins to sound.*)

ILL: A second bell?

PASTOR: Hear it? Splendid tone. Rich and powerful. Just affirming life.

ILL (*cries out*): You too, Reverend! You too!

(*Pastor flings himself on Ill, clings to him.*)

PASTOR: Flee! We are all weak, believers and unbelievers. Flee! The Guellen bells are tolling, tolling for treachery. Flee! Lead us not into temptation with your presence.

(*Two shots are fired. Ill sinks to ground, Pastor kneels beside him.*)

Flee! Flee!

CLAIRE ZACHANASSIAN: Boby. They're shooting.

BUTLER: Yes, Madam, they are.

CLAIRE ZACHANASSIAN: What at?

BUTLER: The black panther escaped, Madam.

CLAIRE ZACHANASSIAN: Did they hit him?

BUTLER: He's dead, Madam, stretched out in front of Ill's shop.

CLAIRE ZACHANASSIAN: Poor little animal. Roby, play a funeral march.

> (*Funeral march on guitar. Balcony disappears. Bell rings. Stage set as for opening of Act One. The station. On wall, however, is a new, untorn timetable and, stuck almost anywhere, a great poster depicting brilliant yellow sun, with the legend "Travel South." Further along same wall, another, with the legend "Visit the Passion Plays in Oberammergau." Amidst buildings in background, a few cranes and a few new rooftops. Thunderous pounding din of express train rushing through. Stationmaster standing on station salutes. Ill emerges from background, one hand clutching little, old suitcase, and looks around. As if by chance, citizens of Guellen come gradually closing in on him from all sides. Ill moves hesitantly, stops.*)

MAYOR: Hallo, Ill.

ALL: Hallo! Hallo!

ILL (*hesitant*): Hallo.

SCHOOLMASTER: Where are you off to with that suitcase?

ALL: Where are you off to?

ILL: To the station.

MAYOR: We'll take you there.

ALL: We'll take you there! We'll take you there!

> (*More Guelleners keep arriving.*)

ILL: You don't need to, you really don't. It's not worth the trouble.

MAYOR: Going away, Ill?

ILL: I'm going away.

POLICEMAN: Where are you going?

ILL: I don't know. First to Kalberstadt, then a bit further to—

SCHOOLMASTER: Ah! Then a bit further?

ILL: To Australia, preferably. I'll get the money somehow.

> (*Walks on towards station.*)

ALL: To Australia! To Australia!

MAYOR: But why?

ILL (*uneasily*): You can't live in the same place for ever—year in, year out.

(*Begins running, reaches station. The others amble over in his wake, surround him.*)

MAYOR: Emigrating to Australia. But that's ridiculous.

DOCTOR: The most dangerous thing you could do.

SCHOOLMASTER: One of those two little eunuchs emigrated to Australia.

POLICEMAN: This is the safest place for you.

ALL: The safest place, the safest place.

(*Ill peers fearfully round like a cornered animal.*)

ILL: I wrote to the Governor in Kaffigen.

POLICEMAN: And?

ILL: No answer.

SCHOOLMASTER: Why are you so suspicious? It's incomprehensible.

MAYOR: No one wants to kill you.

ALL: No one, no one.

ILL: The Post Office didn't send the letter.

PAINTER: Impossible.

MAYOR: The Postmaster is a member of the Town Council.

SCHOOLMASTER: An honorable man.

ALL: An honorable man! An honorable man!

ILL: Look at this poster: "Travel South."

DOCTOR: What about it?

ILL: "Visit the Passion Plays in Oberammergau."

SCHOOLMASTER: What about it?

ILL: They're building!

MAYOR: What about it?

ILL: And you're all wearing new trousers.

MAN ONE: What about it?

ILL: You're all getting richer, you all own more!

ALL: What about it?

(*Bell rings.*)

SCHOOLMASTER: But you must see how fond we are of you.

MAYOR: The whole town's brought you to the station.

ALL: The whole town! The whole town!

ILL: I didn't ask you to come.

MAN TWO: We're surely allowed to come and say goodbye to you.

MAYOR: As old friends.

ALL: As old friends! As old friends!

(*Noise of train. Stationmaster takes up flag. Guard appears, left, as after jumping down from train.*)

GUARD (*with long-drawn wail*): Guellen!

MAYOR: Here's your train.

ALL: Your train! Your train!

MAYOR: Well, have an enjoyable trip, Ill.

ALL: An enjoyable trip, an enjoyable trip!

DOCTOR: And long life and prosperity to you!

ALL: Long life and prosperity!

(*The citizens of Guellen flock round Ill.*)

MAYOR: It's time. Get on the Kalberstadt train, and God be with you.

POLICEMAN: And good luck in Australia!

ALL: Good luck, good luck!

(*Ill stands motionless staring at his compatriots.*)

ILL (*softly*): Why are you all here?

POLICEMAN: Now what do you want?

STATIONMASTER: Take your seats please!

ILL: Why are you all crowding me?

MAYOR: We're not crowding you at all.

ILL: Let me pass.

SCHOOLMASTER: But we're letting you pass.

ALL: We're letting you pass, we're letting you pass.

ILL: Someone'll stop me.

POLICEMAN: Nonsense. All you need do is get on the train, and you'll see it's nonsense.

ILL: Get out of the way.

(*No one moves. Several stand where they are, hands in pockets, and stare at him.*)

MAYOR: I don't know what you're trying to do. It's up to you to go. Just get on the train.

ILL: Get out of the way!

SCHOOLMASTER: It's simply ridiculous of you to be afraid.

(*Ill falls on knees.*)

ILL: Why have you all come so close to me!

POLICEMAN: The man's gone mad.

ILL: You want to stop me from going.

MAYOR: Go on! Get on the train!

ALL: Get on the train! Get on the train!

(*Silence.*)

ILL (*softly*): If I get on the train one of you will hold me back.

ALL (*emphatically*): No, we won't! No, we won't!

ILL: I know you will.

POLICEMAN: It's nearly time.

SCHOOLMASTER: My dear man, will you please get on the train.

ILL: I know, I know. Someone will hold me back, someone will hold me back.

STATIONMASTER: Stand clear!

(*Waves green flag, blows whistle. Guard assumes position to jump on train as Ill, surrounded by the citizens of Guellen, his head in his hands, collapses.*)

POLICEMAN: Look! Now you've missed it.

(*Leaving Ill crumpled in collapse, all walk slowly towards back of stage and disappear.*)

ILL: I am lost!

Act Three

Petersens' Barn. Claire Zachanassian seated, left, immobile in sedan chair, clad in white wedding gown, veil, etc. Further left, a ladder. Further back, a haycart, an old carriage, straw. Center, small cask. Rags and mouldering sacks hang from beams. Enormous outspun spiders' webs. Enter Butler from back.

BUTLER: The Doctor and the Schoolmaster.

CLAIRE ZACHANASSIAN: Show them in.

(*Enter Doctor and Schoolmaster, groping through the gloom. When at last they locate the billionairess, they bow. Both are clad in good, solid, almost fashionable clothes.*)

DOCTOR/SCHOOLMASTER: Madam.

(*Claire Zachanassian raises lorgnette, inspects them.*)

CLAIRE ZACHANASSIAN: You appear to be covered in dust, gentlemen.

(*Both rub away dust with hands.*)

SCHOOLMASTER: Excuse us. We had to climb in over an old carriage.

CLAIRE ZACHANASSIAN: I've retired to Petersens' Barn. I need peace and quiet. I found the wedding in Guellen Cathedral a strain. I'm not exactly a teenager any more. You can sit on that cask.

SCHOOLMASTER: Thank you.

(He sits on it. Doctor remains standing.)

CLAIRE ZACHANASSIAN: Pretty hot here. Stifling. Still, I love this barn, and the smell of hay and straw and axle grease. Memories. The dung fork. The carriage. That busted haycart, and all the other implements. They were all here when I was a child.

SCHOOLMASTER: A remarkable place.

(Mops away sweat.)

CLAIRE ZACHANASSIAN: An uplifting sermon by the clergyman.

SCHOOLMASTER: First Corinthians, thirteen.

CLAIRE ZACHANASSIAN: And a very solid performance on your part, Professor, with the mixed choir. It sounded grand.

SCHOOLMASTER: Bach. From the Saint Matthew Passion. My head is still spinning with it all. The place was packed with High Society, Financiers, Film Stars . . .

CLAIRE ZACHANASSIAN: Society went whizzing back to the Capital in its Cadillacs. For the wedding breakfast.

SCHOOLMASTER: My dear lady: we don't wish to take up more of your precious time than necessary. Your husband will be growing impatient.

CLAIRE ZACHANASSIAN: Hoby? I've sent him back to Geiselgasteig in his Porsche.

DOCTOR *(staggered)*: To Geiselgasteig?

CLAIRE ZACHANASSIAN: My lawyers have already filed the divorce.

SCHOOLMASTER: But Madam, the wedding guests!

CLAIRE ZACHANASSIAN: They're used to each other. It's my second-shortest marriage. Only the one with Lord Ishmael was shorter. What brings you here?

SCHOOLMASTER: We've come to discuss the Ill affair.

CLAIRE ZACHANASSIAN: Oh, has he died?

SCHOOLMASTER: Madam! We're still loyal to our Western principles.

CLAIRE ZACHANASSIAN: Then what do you want?

SCHOOLMASTER: The Guelleners have most, most regrettably acquired a number of new possessions.

DOCTOR: A considerable number.

(*Both mop off sweat.*)

CLAIRE ZACHANASSIAN: In debt?

SCHOOLMASTER: Hopelessly.

CLAIRE ZACHANASSIAN: In spite of your principles?

SCHOOLMASTER: We're only human.

DOCTOR: And now we must pay our debts.

CLAIRE ZACHANASSIAN: You know what you have to do.

SCHOOLMASTER (*bravely*): Madam Zachanassian. Let's be frank with each other. Pur yourself in our melancholy position. For two decades, I have been sowing the Humanities' tender seeds in this poverty-stricken population, and our doctor too for two decades has been trundling around curing its rickets and consumption in his antediluvian Mercedes. Why such agony of sacrifice? For the money? Hardly. Our fee is minimal. Furthermore I received and flatly rejected an offer from Kalberstadt College, just as the doctor here turned down a chair in Erlangen University. Out of pure love for our fellow beings? No, no, that would also be saying too much. No. We, and this entire little township with us, have hung on all these endless years because of a single hope: the hope that Guellen would rise again, in all its ancient grandeur, and the untold wealth in our native soil be once again exploited. Oil is waiting under Pückenried Valley, and under the forest at Konradsweil there are minerals for the mining. Madam, we are not poor; we are merely forgotten. We need credit, confidence, contracts, then our economy and culture will boom. Guellen has much to offer: the Foundry on Sunshine Square.

DOCTOR: Bockmann's.

SCHOOLMASTER: The Wagner Factory. Buy them. Revive them. And Guellen will boom. Invest a few hundred thousand, carefully, systematically. They'll produce a good return. Don't simply squander a billion!

CLAIRE ZACHANASSIAN: I've two more.

SCHOOLMASTER: Don't condemn us to a lifelong struggle in vain. We haven't come begging for alms. We've come to make a business proposition.

CLAIRE ZACHANASSIAN: Really. As business goes, it wouldn't be bad.

SCHOOLMASTER: My dear lady! I knew you wouldn't leave us in the lurch.

CLAIRE ZACHANASSIAN: Only it can't be done. I can't buy Sunshine Square, because I own it already.

SCHOOLMASTER: *You* own it?

DOCTOR: And Bockmann's?

SCHOOLMASTER: The Wagner Factory?

CLAIRE ZACHANASSIAN: I own those too. And all the factories, Pückenried Valley, Petersons' Barn, the entire township; street by street and house by house. I had my agents buy the whole ramshackle lot and shut every business down. Your hopes were lunacy, your perseverance pointless, and your self-sacrifice foolish; your lives have been a useless waste.

(Silence.)

DOCTOR: What a monstrous thing.

CLAIRE ZACHANASSIAN: It was winter, long ago, when I left this little town, in a schoolgirl sailor suit and long red braids, pregnant seven months, and the townsfolk sniggering at me. I sat in the Hamburg Express and shivered; but as I watched the silhouette of Petersens' Barn sinking away on the other side of the frosty windows, I swore to myself, I would come back again, one day. I've come back now. Now it's me imposing the conditions. Me driving the bargain. *(calls)* Roby and Toby, to the Golden Apostle. Husband number nine's on the way with his books and manuscripts.

(The two giants emerge from background, lift sedan chair.)

SCHOOLMASTER: Madam Zachanassian! You're a woman whose love has been wounded. You demand absolute justice. You make me think of a heroine from antiquity: of Medea. We feel for you, deeply; we understand; but because we do, we are inspired to demand even more of you: cast away those evil thoughts of revenge, don't try us till we break. Help these poor, weak yet worthy people lead a slightly more dignified life. Let your feeling for humanity prevail!

CLAIRE ZACHANASSIAN: Feeling for humanity, gentlemen, is cut for the purse of an ordinary millionaire; with financial resources like mine you can afford a new world order. The world turned me into a whore, now I shall turn the world into a brothel. If you can't fork out when you want to dance, you have to put off dancing. You want to dance. They alone are eligible who pay. And I'm paying. Guellen for a murder, a boom for a body. Come on, the pair of you, off we go!

(*She is borne away into background.*)

DOCTOR: My God. What shall we do?

SCHOOLMASTER: Follow the dictates of our conscience, Doctor Nuesslin.

(*Ill's shop appears in foreground, right. New sign. Glittering new shop counter, new register, costlier stock. Whenever anyone enters the imaginary door, a bell rings, magnificently. Behind shop counter, Mrs. Ill. Enter, left, Man One—a thriving butcher. Scattered bloodstains on his new apron.*)

MAN ONE: That was a ceremony. The whole of Guellen was on Cathedral Square watching it.

MRS. ILL: Clarie deserves a little happiness, after all she's been through.

MAN ONE: Every bridesmaid was a film starlet. With breasts like this.

MRS. ILL: They're in fashion today.

MAN ONE: And newspapermen. They'll be coming here too.

MRS. ILL: We're simple people, Mr. Hofbauer. They won't want anything from us.

MAN ONE: They pump everybody. Cigarettes.

MRS. ILL: Green?

MAN ONE: Camels. And a bottle of aspirin. Went to a party at Stocker's last night.

MRS. ILL: Charge it?

MAN ONE: Charge it.

MRS. ILL: How's business?

MAN ONE: Coming along.

MRS. ILL: I can't complain either.

MAN ONE: I've got more staff.

MRS. ILL: I'm getting someone on the first.

(*Miss Louisa walks across stage in stylish clothes.*)

MAN ONE: She's got her head full of dreams dressing up like that. She must imagine we'd murder Ill.

MRS. ILL: Shameless.

MAN ONE: Where is he, by the way? Haven't seen him for quite a while.

MRS. ILL: Upstairs.

(*Man One lights cigarette, cocks ear toward ceiling.*)

MAN ONE: Footsteps.

MRS. ILL: Always walking around in his room. Has been for days.

MAN ONE: It's his bad conscience. Nasty trick he played on poor Madam Zachanassian.

MRS. ILL: It's upset me terribly too.

MAN ONE: Getting a young girl in trouble. Rotten bastard. (*Speaks with decision.*) Mrs. Ill, I hope your husband will keep his mouth shut in front of the reporters.

MRS. ILL: I certainly hope so.

MAN ONE: What with his character.

MRS ILL: It's difficult for me, too, Mr. Hofbauer.

MAN ONE: If he tries showing up Clara, and telling lies, claiming she offered something for his death, or some such story, when it was only a figure of speech for unspeakable suffering, then we'll *have* to step in. Not because of the billion. (*He spits.*) But because of public indignation. God knows he's already put that sweet Madam Zachanassian through enough. (*He looks round.*) Is that a way up to the apartment?

MRS. ILL: It's the only way up. Most inconvenient. But we're having another one built in the spring.

MAN ONE: I'd better just plant myself here. You can't be too sure.

(*Man One plants himself there, very upright stance, arms folded, quietly, like a warden. Enter Schoolmaster.*)

SCHOOLMASTER: Ill?

MAN ONE: Upstairs.

SCHOOLMASTER: It really isn't like me, but I need some kind of strong, alcoholic drink.

MRS. ILL: How nice of you to come and see us, Professor. We've a new Steinhäger in. Would you like to try it?

SCHOOLMASTER: A small glass.

MRS. ILL: You too, Mr. Hofbauer?

MAN ONE: No thanks. Still have to drive my Volkswagen into Kaffigen. There's pork to buy.

(*Mrs. Ill pours a glassful. Schoolmaster drinks.*)

MRS. ILL: But you're trembling, Professor.

SCHOOLMASTER: I've been drinking too much lately.

MRS. ILL: One more won't harm.

SCHOOLMASTER: Is that him walking about?
              (*Cocks ear toward ceiling.*)

MRS. ILL: Up and down, all the time.

MAN ONE: God will punish him.
    (*Enter, left, Painter with picture under arm. New corduroys, colorful scarf, black beret.*)

PAINTER: Watch out. Two reporters asked me about this shop.

MAN ONE: Suspicious.

PAINTER: I acted ignorant.

MAN ONE: Clever.

PAINTER: For you, Mrs. Ill. Fresh off the easel. The paint's still wet.
    (*Exhibits picture. Schoolmaster pours himself another drink.*)

MRS. ILL: It's my husband.

PAINTER: Art's beginning to boom in Guellen. How's that for painting, eh?

MRS ILL: A real likeness.

PAINTER: Oils. Last for ever.

MRS. ILL: We could hang it in the bedroom. Over the bed. Alfred'll be old one day. And you never know what might happen, it's a comfort to have a souvenir.
    (*The two women from Act Two, passing by outside, stop and examine wares in imaginary shop window. Both elegantly dressed.*)

MAN ONE: Look at those women. Going to the movies in broad daylight. The way they behave, you'd think we were sheer murderers!

MRS ILL: Expensive?

PAINTER: Two hundred.

MRS. ILL: I can't pay now.

PAINTER: Doesn't matter. I'll wait, Mrs. Ill, I'll be happy to wait.

SCHOOLMASTER: Those footsteps, those footsteps all the time.
              (*Enter Man Two, left.*)

MAN TWO: The Press.

MAN ONE: All stick together. It's life or death.

PAINTER: Watch out he doesn't come down.

MAN ONE: That's taken care of.
> (*The Guelleners gather to right. Schoolmaster having now drunk half the bottle remains standing at counter. Enter two Reporters carrying cameras.*)

FIRST REPORTER: 'Evening, folks.

GUELLENERS: How do you do.

FIRST REPORTER: Question one: How do you all feel, on the whole?

MAN ONE (*uneasily*): We're very happy of course about Madam Zachanassian's visit.

PAINTER: Moved.

MAN TWO: Proud.

FRIST REPORTER: Proud.

SECOND REPORTER: Question two for the lady behind the counter: the story goes, you were the lucky woman instead of Madam Zachanassian.
> (*Silence. Guelleners manifestly shocked.*)

MRS. ILL: Where did you get that story?
> (*Silence. Both Reporters write impassively in notebooks.*)

FIRST REPORTER: Madam Zachanassian's two fat blind little mannikins.
> (*Silence.*)

MRS. ILL (*hesitant*): What did the mannikins tell you?

SECOND REPORTER: Everything.

PAINTER: Goddam.
> (*Silence.*)

SECOND REPORTER: Forty years ago Claire Zachanassian and the owner of this shop nearly married. Right?

MRS. ILL: That's right.

SECOND REPORTER: Is Mr. Ill here?

MRS. ILL: He's in Kalberstadt.

ALL: He's in Kalberstadt.

FIRST REPORTER: We can imagine the Ro-mance. Mr. Ill and Claire Zachanassian grow up together, maybe they're next-door kids, they go to school together, go for walks in the wood, share the first kisses, they're like brother and sister, and so it goes on till Mr. Ill meets you, lady, and you're the new woman, his mystery, his passion.

MRS. ILL: Passion. Yes, that's how it happened, just the way you said.

FIRST REPORTER: Elmentary, Mrs. Ill. Claire Zachanassian grasps the situation, in her quiet, noble fashion she renounces her claims, and you marry . . .

MRS. ILL: For love.

GUELLENERS (*on whom light dawns*): For love.

FIRST REPORTER: For love.

(*Enter, right, Roby leading the pair of eunuchs by their ears.*)

THE PAIR (*wailing*): We won't tell any more stories, we won't tell any more stories.

(*They are dragged towards back of stage, where Toby awaits them with whip.*)

SECOND REPORTER: About your husband, Mrs. Ill, doesn't he now and then, I mean, it'd be only human for him, now and then, to feel a few regrets.

MRS. ILL: Money alone makes no one happy.

SECOND REPORTER (*writing*): No one happy.

FIRST REPORTER: That's a truth we in this modern world can't repeat often enough.

(*Enter Son, left, wearing suede jacket.*)

MRS. ILL: Our son Karl.

FIRST REPORTER: Splendid youngster.

SECOND REPORTER: Does he know about the relationship? . . .

MRS. ILL: There are no secrets in our family. What we always say is, anything God knows our children ought to know.

SECOND REPORTER (*writing*): Children ought to know.

(*Daughter walks into shop, wearing tennis outfit, carrying tennis racket.*)

MRS. ILL: Our daughter Ottilie.

SECOND REPORTER: Charming.

(*Schoolmaster now calls up courage.*)

SCHOOLMASTER: Guelleners. I am your old schoolmaster. I've been quietly drinking my Steinhäger and keeping my thoughts to myself. But now I want to make a speech. I want to talk about the old lady's visit to Guellen.

(*Scrambles onto the little cask left over from the scene in Petersens' Barn.*)

MAN ONE: Have you gone mad?

MAN TWO: Stop him!

SCHOOLMASTER: Guelleners! I want to reveal the truth, even if our poverty endures for ever!

MRS. ILL: You're drunk, Professor, you ought to be ashamed of yourself!

SCHOOLMASTER: Ashamed? You're the one to be ashamed, woman! You're paving your way to betray your own husband!

SON: Shut up!

MAN ONE: Drag him down!

MAN TWO: Kick him out!

SCHOOLMASTER: You've nearly contrived your doom!

DAUGHTER (*Supplicating*): Please, Professor!

SCHOOLMASTER: Child, you disappoint me. It was up to you to speak out, and now your old schoolmaster must unleash the voice of thunder!

(*Painter breaks painting over his head.*)

PAINTER: There! You'll sabotage all my commissions!

SCHOOLMASTER: I protest! I wish to make a public appeal to world opinion! Guellen is planning a monstrous deed!

(*The Guelleners launch themselves at him as, simultaneously, in an old tattered suit, Ill enters, right.*)

ILL: Just what's going on here, in my shop!

(*The Guelleners fall back from Schoolmaster to stare at Ill, shocked. Deathly silence.*)

Professor! What are you up to on that cask!

(*Schoolmaster beams at Ill in happy relief.*)

SCHOOLMASTER: The truth, Ill. I'm telling the gentlemen of the Press the truth. Like an archangel I'm telling them, in forceful ringing tones. (*wavers*) Because I'm a humanist, a lover of the ancient Greeks, an admirer of Plato.

ILL: Hold your peace.

SCHOOLMASTER: Eh?

ILL: Get down.

SCHOOLMASTER: But humanitarianism—

ILL: Sit down.

(*Silence.*)

SCHOOLMASTER (*sobered*): Humanitarianism has to sit down. By all means—if you're going to betray truth as well.

(*Steps down from cask, sits on it, picture still round his neck.*)

ILL: Excuse this. The man's drunk.

FIRST REPORTER: Mr. Ill?

ILL: What is it?

FIRST REPORTER: We're very glad we finally got to meet you. We need a few pictures. May we? (*Glances round.*) Groceries, household wares, hardware—I've got it: we'll take you selling an axe.

ILL (*hesitant*): An axe?

FIRST REPORTER: To the butcher. You gotta have Realism for a punch. Give me that homicidal weapon here. Your client takes the axe, weighs it in his hand, he puts an appraising expression on his face, while you lean across the counter, you're discussing it with him. O.K., let's go.

(*He arranges the shot.*)

More natural, folks, more relaxed.

(*Reporters click their cameras.*)

That's fine, just fine.

SECOND REPORTER: Now if you don't mind please, one arm round your good wife's shoulders. Son on the left, daughter on the right. That's fine. O.K., now, you're radiant with happiness, please, just brimming over with it, radiant, radiant and contented deep down inside, quietly, happily radiant.

FIRST REPORTER: Great, great, that sure was radiant.

(*Several Photographers come running in, downstage left, cross the boards and go running out, upstage left. One photographer shouts into shop—*)

PHOTOGRAPHER: Zachanassian's got a new one. They're taking a walk in Konradsweil Forest, right now.

SECOND REPORTER: A new one!

FIRST REPORTER: That's good for a cover on *Life* magazine.

(*The two Reporters race out of shop. Silence. Man One is left still gripping axe.*)

MAN ONE (*relieved*): That was a bit of luck.

PAINTER: Forgive us, Professor. If we still hope to settle this affair amicably, we've got to exclude the Press. Agreed?

(*Exit, followed by Man Two. But passing Ill, Man Two pauses.*)

MAN TWO: Smart. Very smart you didn't shoot your mouth. No one would believe a word a bastard like you said anyway.

(*Exit Man Two.*)

MAN ONE: We'll be in the magazines, Ill.

ILL: Yes.

MAN ONE: We'll be famous.

ILL: In a manner of speaking.

MAN ONE: A Corona.

ILL: Certainly.

MAN ONE: Charge it.

ILL: Of course.

MAN ONE: Let's face it: what you did to little Clara was the work of a bastard.

(Begins to go.)

ILL: Hofbauer. The axe.

(Man One hesitates, then returns axe to Ill. Silence in shop. Schoolmaster is still sitting on his cask.)

SCHOOLMASTER: I apologize. I've been trying the Steinhäger. Must have had two or three.

ILL: It's all right.

(The family cross to right, and exit.)

SCHOOLMASTER: I wanted to help you. But they shouted me down, and you didn't want my help either. *(Disengages himself from picture.)* Ah, Ill. What kind of people are we. That infamous billion is burning up our hearts. Pull yourself together, fight for your life. Enlist the sympathy of the Press. You haven't any more time to lose.

ILL: I'm not fighting any more.

SCHOOLMASTER *(amazed)*: Tell me, has fear driven you completely out of your senses?

ILL: I've realized I haven't any right.

SCHOOLMASTER: No right? No right campared to that damned old woman, that brazen arch-whore changing husbands while we watch, and making a collection of our souls?

ILL: That's all my fault, really.

SCHOOLMASTER: Your fault?

ILL: I made Clara what she is, and I made myself what I am, a failing shopkeeper with a bad name. What shall I do, School-master? Play innocent? It's all my own work, the Eunuchs, the Butler, the coffin, the billion. I can't help myself and I can't help any of you, any more.

(Takes up torn painting and examines it.)

My portrait.

SCHOOLMASTER: Your wife wanted to hang it in your bedroom. Over the bed.

ILL: Kuhn will paint another.

(*Lays picture down on counter. Schoolmaster stands with an effort, sways.*)

SCHOOLMASTER: I'm sober. All at once.

(*He reels across to Ill.*)

You are right. Absolutely. It's all your fault. And now I want to tell you something, Alfred Ill, something fundamental.

(*Stands facing Ill, stiff as a ramrod and hardly swaying at all.*)

They will kill you. I've known it from the beginning, and you've known it too for a long time, even if no one else in Guellen wants to admit it. The temptation is too great and our poverty is too wretched. But I know something else. I shall take part in it. I can feel myself slowly becoming a murderer. My faith in humanity is powerless to stop it. And because I know all this, I have also become a drunk. I too am scared, Ill, just as you have been scared. And finally I know that one day an old lady will come for us too, and then what happened to you will also happen to us, but soon, perhaps in a few hours, I shall have lost that knowledge. (*Silence.*) Another bottle of Steinhäger.

(*Ill gets him a bottle, Schoolmaster hesitates, then firmly takes and clutches bottle.*)

Put it on my account.

(*Walks slowly out.*)

The family return. Ill looks round at his shop as if dreaming.)

ILL: It's all new. Our place looks so modern now. Clean. Inviting. I've always dreamed of having a shop like this.

(*Takes Daughter's tennis racket from her hand.*)

D'you play tennis?

DAUGHTER: I've had a couple of lessons.

ILL: Early mornings, eh? Instead of going to the Employment Office?

DAUGHTER: All my friends play tennis.

(*Silence.*)

ILL: I was looking out of my bedroom window, Karl, and I saw you in an automobile.

SON: It's only an Opel, they aren't so expensive.

ILL: When did you learn to drive?

(*Silence.*)

Instead of looking for work on the railroad in the blazing sun, eh?

SON: Sometimes.

(*Son, embarrassed, crosses to cask on which the drunk has been sitting, shoves it to right and out.*)

ILL: I was looking for my Sunday suit. I found a fur coat hanging beside it.

MRS. ILL: It's on approval.

(*Silence.*)

Everyone's making debts, Freddy. You're the only one throwing fits of hysterics. It's simply ridiculous of you to be scared. It's so obvious the thing's going to be settled peacefully, without anyone harming a hair of your head. Claire won't go the whole way, I know her, she's too goodhearted.

DAUGHTER: Of course, father.

SON: Surely you realize that.

(*Silence.*)

ILL (*slowly*): It's Saturday. Karl, I'd like to go for a drive in your automobile, just once. In *our* automobile.

SON (*uncertainly*): You'd like that?

ILL: Put on your best clothes. We'll all go for a drive together.

MRS. ILL (*uncertainly*): Am I to go with you? But surely that wouldn't do.

ILL: And why wouldn't it do? Go and put on your fur coat, this'll be an opportunity to christen it. I'll be seeing to the cash register in the meantime.

(*Exit Mother and Daughter, right. Exit Son, left. Ill busies himself at register. Enter, left, Mayor carrying rifle.*)

MAYOR: Good evening, Ill. Don't let me trouble you. I'll just have a quick look round.

ILL: By all means.

(*Silence.*)

MAYOR: Brought you a gun.

ILL: Thanks.

MAYOR: It's loaded.

ILL: I don't need it.

(*Mayor leans gun against counter.*)

MAYOR: There's a public meeting this evening. In the Golden Apostle. In the auditorium.

ILL: I'll be there.

MAYOR: Everyone'll be there. We're dealing with your case. We're under a certain amount of pressure.

ILL: That's what I feel.

MAYOR: The motion will be rejected.

ILL: Possibly.

MAYOR: People make mistakes, of course.

ILL: Of course.

(*Silence.*)

MAYOR (*cautiously*): In such a case, Ill, would you then submit to the judgment? Since the Press will be present.

ILL: The Press?

MAYOR: And the Radio. And the Television and Newsreel cameras. Very ticklish situation. Not only for you. For us too, believe you me. We're famous as the old lady's native town, and also because of her marriage in the Cathedral here. So now they're going to run a commentary on our ancient democratic institutions.

(*Ill busies himself at register.*)

ILL: Are you making public knowledge of the lady's offer?

MAYOR: Not directly. Only the initiated will grasp the full meaning of the procedure.

ILL: The fact that my life is at stake.

(*Silence.*)

MAYOR: I've let a few hints leak out to the Press that Madam Zachanassian may—there's just a possibility she may make an endowment and that you, Ill, as her childhood friend, will have negotiated that endowment. Of course, it's well known by now that you in fact were her childhood friend. This means that so far as appearances go, you'll have an absolutely clean record.

ILL: That's kind of you.

MAYOR: To be quite frank, I didn't do it for your sake. I was really thinking of your fine, upright, honest family.

ILL: I see.

MAYOR: You've got to admit we're playing fair with you. Up to now, you've kept quiet. Good. But will you go on keeping quiet?

If you intend to talk, we'll have to settle the whole business without a public meeting.

ILL: I understand.

MAYOR: Well?

ILL: I'm glad to hear an open threat.

MAYOR: I'm not threatening you, Ill, you're threatening us. If you talk, we'll have to act accordingly. First.

ILL: I'll keep quiet.

MAYOR: However the decision turns out at the meeting?

ILL: I'll accept it.

MAYOR: Good.

(Silence.)

I'm glad you'll abide by the ruling of our community court, Ill. You still have a certain glimmer of honor in you. But wouldn't it be better if we didn't even have to call on that community court to assemble?

ILL: What are you trying to say?

MAYOR: When I came in, you said you didn't need the gun. But now, perhaps, you do need it.

(Silence.)

We might then tell the lady we had brought you to justice and that way, just the same, receive the money. You can imagine the sleepless nights I've spent on that suggestion. But isn't it your duty, as a man of honor, to draw your own conclusions and make an end of your life? If only out of public spirit, and your love for your native town. You're well aware of our wretched privations, the misery here, and the hungry children . . .

ILL: You're all doing very well.

MAYOR: Ill!

ILL: Mister Mayor! I have been through Hell. I've watched you all getting into debt, and I've felt death creeping towards me, nearer and nearer with every sign of prosperity. If you had spared me that anguish, that gruesome terror, it might all have been different, this discussion might have been different, and I might have taken the gun. For all your sakes. Instead, I shut myself in. I conquered my fear. Alone. It was hard, and now it's done. There is no turning back. You *must* judge me, now. I shall accept your judgment, whatever it may be. For me, it will be justice; what it will be for you, I do not know. God grant you find your judgment justified. You may kill me, I will not complain and I will not protest, nor will I defend myself. But I cannot spare you the task of the trial.

> (*Mayor takes back gun.*)

MAYOR: Pity. You're missing a chance to redeem youself and be a more or less decent human being. I might have known it was too much to ask you.

ILL: Have a light, Mister Mayor.

> (*Lights cigarette for Mayor. Exit Mayor.*
> *Enter Mrs. Ill in fur coat, Daughter in red dress.*)

You look very distinguished, Matilda.

MRS. ILL: Persian lamb.

ILL: Like a real lady.

MRS. ILL: Quite expensive.

ILL: Pretty dress, Ottilie. But isn't it a little bold?

DAUGHTER: O silly Daddy. You should just take a peek at my evening dress.

> (*Shop disappears. Son drives up in motorcar.*)

ILL: Fine automobile. You know, I toiled a lifetime to get a little property, a mite of comfort, say for example an automobile like this, and now, my times's up, but still, I'd like to know how it feels to be inside one of these. Matilda, get in the back with me, you in the front, Ottilie, next to Karl.

> (*They get into motorcar.*)

SON: It'll do eighty.

ILL: Not so fast. I want to see a bit of the scenery, a bit of the town where I've lived for nearly seventy years. They've cleaned up the old streets. Lot of reconstruction, already. Gray smoke, coming out of those chimneys. Geraniums there in the window boxes. Sunflowers. The Goethe Arch, they've planted roses in the gardens. Don't the children look happy; and sweethearts, all over the place. Brahms Square, that's a new apartment block.

MRS. ILL: They're redoing the Café Hodel.

DAUGHTER: There goes the Doctor, in his Mercedes 300.

ILL: Look at the plain, and the light on the hills beyond, all golden, today. Impressive, when you go into the shadows and then out again into the light. Those cranes on the horizon by the Wagner Factory look like giants; and the Bockmann chimneys too.

SON: They're starting up again.

ILL: What's that?

SON (*louder*): They're starting up again.

(*Hoots horn.*)

MRS. ILL: Funny little car.

SON: Bubble-car: Messerschmidt. Every other guy has to have one.

DAUGHTER: C'est terrible.

MRS. ILL: Ottilie's taking advanced courses in French and English.

ILL: Useful. Sunshine Square. The Foundry. Long time since I've been out here.

SON: They're going to build a bigger one.

ILL: You'll have to talk louder at this speed.

SON (*louder*): They're going to build a bigger one. Stocker again, who else. Passing everybody in his Buick.

DAUGHTER: Un nouveau riche.

ILL: Now drive through Pückenried Valley. Go past the Moor and down Poplar Boulevard, round Prince Hasso's Hunting Lodge. Colossal clouds in the sky, banks of them, real summertime castles. It's a beautiful country in a soft twilight. I feel I'm seeing it today the first time.

DAUGHTER: Atmosphere like Tennyson.

ILL: Like what?

MRS. ILL: Ottilie's studying literature too.

ILL: It'll give her advantages.

SON: Hofbauer in his Volkswagen. Coming back from Kaffigen.

DAUGHTER: With the pork.

MRS. ILL: Karl drives well. Very smart, the way he cut that corner. You don't feel frightened with him.

SON: First gear. The road's getting steep.

ILL: I always used to get out of breath walking up here.

MRS. ILL: I'm so glad I brought my fur coat. It's getting quite chilly.

ILL: You've come the wrong way. This road goes to Beisenbach. You'll have to go back and then left, into Konradsweil Forest.

(*Motorcar reverses into background. Enter, carrying wooden bench, and wearing dress suits now, the four citizens who designate trees.*)

MAN ONE:
We're standing in for trees again,
A spruce, a fir, a beech, a pine,
MAN TWO:
We're bird and beast, we're timid deer,
We're woodpeckers;
MAN THREE:
The cuckoos here
Sing songs of bygone nights and dawns,
MAN FOUR:
Outraged today by motor horns.

SON (*hoots horn*): Another deer. That animal just won't get off the road.

(*Man Three jumps off the road.*)

DAUGHTER: They're so trusting. The poaching's stopped.

ILL: Stop under these trees.

SON: Sure.

MRS. ILL: What do you want to do?

ILL: Walk through the woods. (*He gets out.*) The Guellen bells are ringing. They sound so good from here. Time to stop work.

SON: Four of them. First time they sound like real bells.

ILL: Everything's yellow. The autumn's really here. The leaves on the ground are like layers of gold.

(*He tramples among leaves on the ground.*)

SON: We'll wait for you down by Guellen Bridge.

ILL: You needn't wait. I shall walk through the wood into town. To the public meeting.

MRS. ILL: In that case we'll drive into Kalberstadt, Freddy, and see a movie.

SON: 'Bye, father.

DAUGHTER: Au revoir, papa.

MRS. ILL: See you soon! See you soon!

(*Motorcar with family in it disappears, returns in reverse, the family waving; Ill watches them out of sight. Sits on wooden bench, left.*

Rush of wind. Enter Roby and Toby, right, bearing sedan chair in which Claire Zachanassian is seated, wearing her customary clothes. Roby carries guitar slung at his back.

*Husband IX comes striding in beside her—the Nobel Prize-
winner, tall, slender, hair peppered grey, moustache. [May
also be played by same actor as earlier husbands.] Butler
brings up rear.)*

CLAIRE ZACHANASSIAN: It's the Konradsweil Forest. Roby and
Toby, stop a moment.

*(Claire Zachanassian descends from sedan chair, inspects
wood through lorgnette, and strokes back of Man One.)*

Bark-beetle. This tree's withering away. *(Notices Ill.)* Alfred!
How nice to see you! I'm visiting my Forest.

ILL: Does Konradsweil Forest belong to you as well?

CLAIRE ZACHANASSIAN: Yes, it does. May I sit down beside you?

ILL: By all means. I've just said goodbye to my family. They've
gone to the cinema. Karl's got himself an automobile.

CLAIRE ZACHANASSIAN: Progress.

(Sits down beside Ill, right.)

ILL: Ottilie's taking a course in literature. French and English as
well.

CLAIRE ZACHANASSIAN: You see, they have developed a sense of
ideals after all. Zoby, come and make your bow. My ninth husband. Nobel Prize-winner.

ILL: Very glad to meet you.

CLAIRE ZACHANASSIAN: He's particularly interesting when he stops
thinking. Stop thinking a moment, Zoby.

HUSBAND IX: But Precious . . .

CLAIRE ZACHANASSIAN: No showing off.

HUSBAND IX: Oh, all right.

(Stops thinking.)

CLAIRE ZACHANASSIAN: See? Now he looks like a diplomat. Re-
minds me of Count Holk, except that he couldn't write books.
He wants to go into retirement, publish his memoirs, and manage my property.

ILL: Congratulations.

CLAIRE ZACHANASSIAN: I feel uneasy about it. You only have husbands for display purposes, they shouldn't be useful. Zoby, go
away and do some research. You'll find the historical ruins on
the left.

*(Husband IX goes away to do some research. Ill
glances round.)*

ILL: What's happened to the two Eunuchs?

CLAIRE ZACHANASSIAN: They were getting garrulous. I had them shipped off to Hong Kong. Put in one of my opium dens. They can smoke and they can dream. The Butler will follow them soon. I shan't be needing him either, any more. Boby, a Romeo and Juliet.

(*Butler emerges from background, passes her a cigarette case.*)

Would you like one, Alfred?

ILL: Thank you.

CLAIRE ZACHANASSIAN: Here, then. Give us a light, Boby.

(*They smoke.*)

ILL: Smells good.

CLAIRE ZACHANASSIAN: We often smoked together in this wood; do you remember? You used to buy the cigarettes from little Matilda. Or steal them.

(*Man One taps key on pipe.*)

That woodpecker again.

MAN FOUR: Cuckoo! Cuckoo!

CLAIRE ZACHANASSIAN: Would you like Roby to play for you on his guitar?

ILL: Please.

CLAIRE ZACHANASSIAN: My pardoned killer plays well. I need him for meditative moments. I hate record players. And radios.

ILL: There's an army marching in an African valley.

CLAIRE ZACHANASSIAN: Your favorite song. I taught it to him.

(*Silence. They smoke. Cuckoo call, forest sounds, etc. Roby plays ballad.*)

ILL: You had—I mean, we had a child.

CLAIRE ZACHANASSIAN: True.

ILL: Was it a boy or a girl?

CLAIRE ZACHANASSIAN: A girl.

ILL: And what name did you give it?

CLAIRE ZACHANASSIAN: Genevieve.

ILL: Pretty name.

CLAIRE ZACHANASSIAN: I only saw the thing once. At birth. Then they took it away. The Salvation Army.

ILL: Eyes?

CLAIRE ZACHANASSIAN: Not yet open.

ILL: Hair?

CLAIRE ZACHANASSIAN: I think it had black hair. But then new-born babies often have black hair.

ILL: Yes, they often do.

(*Silence. They smoke. Guitar plays.*)

Where did it die?

CLAIRE ZACHANASSIAN: With some people. I've forgotten their name.

ILL: What of?

CLAIRE ZACHANASSIAN: Meningitis. Perhaps it was something else. I did receive a card from the authorities.

ILL: In cases of death you can rely on them.

(*Silence.*)

CLAIRE ZACHANASSIAN: I've talked about our little girl. Now you talk about me.

ILL: About you?

CLAIRE ZACHANASSIAN: The way I was, when I was seventeen, when you loved me.

ILL: I had to look for you a long while once in Petersens' Barn; I found you in the old carriage with nothing on but a blouse and a long straw between your lips.

CLAIRE ZACHANASSIAN: You were strong and brave. You fought that railwayman when he tried to paw me. I wiped the blood off your face with my red petticoat.

(*Guitar stops playing.*)

The ballad has ended.

ILL: One more: "Home Sweet Home."

CLAIRE ZACHANASSIAN: Yes, Roby can play that.

(*Guitar resumes play.*)

ILL: Thank you for the wreaths, and for the chrysanthemums and roses. They'll look fine on the coffin in the Golden Apostle. Distinguished. They fill two rooms already. Now the time has come. It is the last time we shall sit in our old wood and hear the cuckoo calling and the sound of the wind. They are meeting this evening. They will sentence me to death, and one of them will kill me. I don't know who it will be, and I don't know where it will happen, I only know that my meaningless life will end.

CLAIRE ZACHANASSIAN: I shall take you in your coffin to Capri. I have had a mausoleum built, in my Palace Park. It is surrounded by cypress trees. Overlooking the Mediterranean.

ILL: I only know it from pictures.

CLAIRE ZACHANASSIAN: Deep blue. A grandiose panorama. You will remain there. A dead man beside a stone idol. Your love died many years ago. But my love could not die. Neither could it live. It grew into an evil thing, like me, like the pallid mushrooms in this wood, and the blind, twisted features of the roots, all overgrown by my golden billions. Their tentacles sought you out, to take your life, because your life belonged to me, forever. You are in their toils now, and you are lost. You will soon be no more than a dead love in my memory, a gentle ghost haunting the wreckage of a house.

ILL: "Home Sweet Home" has ended now as well.

(*Husband* IX *returns.*)

CLAIRE ZACHANASSIAN: Here's the Nobel Prize-winner. Back from his ruins. Well, Zoby?

HUSBAND IX: Early Christian. Sacked by the Huns.

CLAIRE ZACHANASSIAN: What a pity. Give me your arm. Roby, Toby, the sedan.

(*Gets into sedan chair.*)

Goodbye, Alfred.

ILL: Goodbye, Clara.

(*The sedan chair is borne away to background. Ill remains seated on bench. The trees put away their twigs. Portal descends, with usual curtains and draperies, also inscription:* LIFE IS SERIOUS, ART SERENE. *Policeman emerges from background in swashbuckling new uniform, sits beside Ill. A Radio Commentator enters, begins talking into microphone while the Guelleners assemble. Everyone in new evening gowns and dress suits. Hordes of Press Photographers, Reporters, Cameramen.*)

RADIO COMMENTATOR: Ladies and gentlemen: Radio Newsreel has been bringing you a Scene from the Birthplace and a Conversation with the Pastor, and now it's time to go over to the Public Meeting. We're nearing the climax of this visit which Madam Claire Zachanassian has kindly accorded to her charming, friendly little hometown. Of course it's unfortunate the famous lady won't be putting in a personal appearance; on the other hand we will be hearing the Mayor, because he's slated to make an important announcement in her name. Right now we're coming to you from the auditorium of the Golden Apostle, an hotel that can boast of a bed where Goethe once spent the night. And now the townsmen are assembling on the stage, in less exciting days the scene of local club gatherings and guest shows by the Kalberstadt Repertory Players. The Mayor's just informed me this is an old custom. The women are all down in the auditorium—it seems this is an old custom too. I can't tell you what a solemn atmosphere it is, the tension's really extraordinary. All the newsreel cameras are here, I can see my colleagues from TV, there are reporters from all over the world, and now here comes the Mayor and he's going to begin his speech, we're crossing over to him now!

(*Radio Commentator crosses over to Mayor, who is standing in center of stage, around him in a semicircle the men of Guellen.*)

MAYOR: Ladies and gentlemen, Citizens of Guellen. I'm very happy to welcome you all here this evening. I declare this meeting open. We have one single item on our agenda. It is my privilege to announce that Madam Claire Zachanassian, daughter of our worthy fellow-citizen Godfrey Wascher—the architect—intends to make us a donation of one billion dollars.

(*Whispers among the Press.*)

Five hundred million for the town and five hundred million to be shared among all citizens.

(*Silence.*)

RADIO COMMENTATOR (*subdued*): What a sensation, listeners, what a colossal sensation. One endowment, and every inhabitant of this little town has suddenly become a well-to-do citizen. It must constitute one of the greatest social experiments of our age. The public here are gasping for breath, there's a deathly silence, Oh, they're awestruck, you can see it on every face.

MAYOR: I leave the floor to the President of our Community College.

(*Radio Commentator crosses with microphone to Schoolmaster.*)

SCHOOLMASTER: Guelleners: I want to raise one point we must all clearly understand—namely, in making her donation, Madam Claire Zachanassian has a definite aim. What is her aim? Is it her aim to make us happy with money? Is it merely her aim to heap gold on our heads? To revive the Wagner Factory and Bockmann's and the Foundry on Sunshine Square? You know very well it is not. Madam Claire Zachanassian has a more important aim. Her aim is to have the spirit of this community transformed—transformed to the spirit of justice. We, staggered by this demand, ask: have we not always been a just community?

VOICE ONE: Never!

VOICE TWO: We fostered a crime!

VOICE THREE: A false judgment!

VOICE FOUR: A perjury!

WOMAN'S VOICE: A villain!

OTHER VOICES: Hear! Hear!

SCHOOLMASTER: O people of Guellen! Such is the bitter truth! We have condoned injustice! I am of course fully aware of the material possibilities inherent for all of us in a billion. Nor am I blind to the fact that poverty is the root of much evil, nay, of great hardship. And yet, and yet: we are not moved by the money (*huge applause*): we are not moved by ambitious thoughts of prosperity and good living, and luxury: we are moved by this matter of justice, and the problem of how to apply it. Nor yet by justice alone, but also by all those ideals, for which our forebears lived and fought, and for which they died; and which constitute the values of our Western World. (*Huge applause.*) When individual persons slight the ideal of brotherly love, disobey the commandment to succor the weak, spurn the marriage vow, deceive the courts and plunge young mothers into misery, then Freedom is at stake. (*Catcalls.*) Now, in God's name, we must take our ideals seriously, even unto death. (*Huge applause.*) For what would be the sense of wealth, which created not a wealth of grace? Yet grace can only be accorded those who hunger after grace. People of Guellen, do you have that hunger? Or is all your hunger common hunger, physical and profane? That is the question. As President of your Community College, I put it to you all. Only if you refuse to abide any evil, refuse to live any longer under any circumstances in a world that connives at injustice, can you accept a billion from Madam

Zachanassian, and thereby fulfill the conditions attaching to her endowment.

(*Thunderous applause.*)

RADIO COMMENTATOR: Just listen to it, ladies and gentlemen, just listen to that applause. We're all overwhelmed. That speech by the President evinced a moral grandeur we don't find everywhere these days. And a very brave denunciation it was too, aimed at all the little misdemeanors and injustices we find in every community, alas, all over the world.

MAYOR: Alfred Ill . . .

RADIO COMMENTATOR: It's the Mayor, I think he's going to take the floor again.

MAYOR: Alfred Ill, I would like to ask you one question.

(*Policeman gives Ill a shove. Ill stands. Radio Commentator crosses with microphone to Ill.*)

RADIO COMMENTATOR: Ah. Now we're going to hear the voice of the man responsible for the Zachanassian endowment: it's the voice of Alfred Ill, our prodigal lady's childhood friend. Alfred Ill—a vigorous man around seventy, an upright Guellener of the old school, and of course he's deeply moved, full of gratitude, full of quiet satisfaction.

MAYOR: Alfred Ill: it is owing to you we have been offered this endowment. Are you aware of that?

(*Ill says something in an undertone.*)

RADIO COMMENTATOR: My dear sir, would you kindly speak a shade louder, our listeners are so eager to hear you.

ILL: All right.

MAYOR: Will you respect our decision as to acceptance or refusal of the Claire Zachanassian Endowment?

ILL: I shall respect it.

MAYOR: Are there any questions to Alfred Ill?

(*Silence.*)

The Church?

(*Pastor says nothing.*)

The Medical Profession?

(*Doctor says nothing.*)

The Police?

(*Policeman says nothing.*)

The Opposition Party?
> (*No one says anything.*)

I shall now put the issue to vote.
> (*Silence. Hum of movie cameras, flash of flashbulbs.*)

All those pure in heart who want justice done, raise their hands.
> (*All except Ill raise their hands.*)

RADIO COMMENTATOR: There's a devout silence in the auditorium. Nothing but a single sea of hands, all raised, as if making one, mighty pledge for a better, juster world. Only the old man has remained seated, absolutely motionless, he's overcome with joy. His ambition has been fulfilled, and thanks to the generosity of his childhood friend the endowment's finally assured.

MAYOR: The Claire Zachanassian Endowment is accepted. Unanimously. Not for the sake of the money,

CITIZENS: Not for the sake of the money,

MAYOR: But for justice

CITIZENS: But for justice

MAYOR: And for conscience' sake.

CITIZENS: And for conscience' sake.

MAYOR: For we cannot connive at a crime:

CITIZENS: For we cannot connive at a crime:

MAYOR: Let us then root out the wrongdoer,

CITIZENS: Let us then root out the wrongdoer,

MAYOR: And deliver our souls from evil

CITIZENS: And deliver our souls from evil

MAYOR: And all our most sacred possessions.

CITIZENS: And all our most sacred possessions.

ILL (*screams*): My God!

(*Everyone remains standing solemnly with raised hands, but at this point, however, the newsreel camera jams.*)

CAMERAMAN: What a shame, Mister Mayor. There's a short in the light cable. Would you just do that last vote again, please?

MAYOR: Do it again?

CAMERAMAN: For the newsreel.

MAYOR: Oh, yes, certainly.

CAMERAMAN: O.K., spots?

A VOICE: O.K.

CAMERAMAN: O.K., shoot!

(*Mayor assumes pose.*)

MAYOR: The Claire Zachanassian Endowment is accepted. Unanimously. Not for the sake of the money,

CITIZENS: Not for the sake of the money,

MAYOR: But for justice

CITIZENS: But for justice

MAYOR: And for conscience' sake.

CITIZENS: And for conscience' sake.

MAYOR: For we cannot connive at a crime:

CITIZENS: For we cannot connive at a crime:

MAYOR: Let us then root out the wrongdoer,

CITIZENS: Let us then root out the wrongdoer,

MAYOR: And deliver our souls from evil

CITIZENS: And deliver our souls from evil

MAYOR: And all our most sacred possessions.

CITIZENS: And all our most sacred possessions.

(*Silence.*)

CAMERAMAN (*stage whisper*): Hey! Ill! Come on!

(*Silence.*)

(*Disappointed*) O.K., so he won't. Pity we didn't get his cry of joy the first time. That "My God" was most impressive.

MAYOR: And now we invite the gentlemen of the Press, Cinema, and Radio to a little Refreshment. In the Restaurant. The easiest way out of the auditorium is through the stage door. Tea is being served for the ladies on the Golden Apostle lawn.

(*Those of the Press, Cinema, and Radio cross to background, right, and go off. Men of Guellen remain on stage, immobile. Ill stands, moves to go.*)

POLICEMAN: You stay here!

(*He pushes Ill down onto bench.*)

ILL: Were you going to do it today?

POLICEMAN: Of course.

ILL: I'd have thought it would be better at my place.

POLICEMAN: It'll be done here.

MAYOR: No one left in the stalls?

(*Man Three and Man Four peer down into stalls.*)

MAN THREE: No one.

MAYOR: What about the gallery?

MAN FOUR: Empty.

MAYOR: Lock the doors. Don't let anyone else into the auditorium.

(*Man Three and Man Four step down into stalls.*)

MAN THREE: Locked.

MAN FOUR: Locked.

MAYOR: Put out the lights. The moon is shining through the gallery window. It's enough.

(*The stage dims. In the pale moonlight, people are only dimly visible.*)

Form a lane.

(*Men of Guellen form a lane: it ends at Gymnast, clad now in elegant white slacks and vest, round which a red scarf.*)

Reverend. If you please.

(*Pastor crosses slowly to Ill, sits beside him.*)

PASTOR: Now, Ill, your hardest hour is at hand.

ILL: Give me a cigarette.

PASTOR: Mister Mayor, a cigarette.

MAYOR (*warmly*): But of course. A good one.

(*Passes packet to Priest, who offers it to Ill, who takes a cigarette; Policeman proffers light, Pastor returns packet to Mayor.*)

PASTOR: As the prophet Amos said—

ILL: Please don't.

(*Ill smokes.*)

PASTOR: Are you not afraid?

ILL: Not much, any more.

(*Ill smokes.*)

PASTOR: (*helpless*): I'll pray for you.

ILL: Pray for Guellen.

(*Ill smokes. Pastor gets slowly to his feet.*)

PASTOR: God have mercy upon us.

(*Pastor slowly rejoins the Guelleners' ranks.*)

MAYOR: Alfred Ill. Stand up.

(*Ill hesitates.*)

POLICEMAN: Get up, you bastard.

(*Drags Ill to his feet.*)

MAYOR: Officer, control yourself.

POLICEMAN: Sorry. It just slipped out.

MAYOR: Alfred Ill. Come here.

(*Ill drops cigarette, treads it out. Then walks slowly to center of stage, turns his back to audience.*)

Walk down that line.

(*Ill hesitates.*)

POLICEMAN: Get moving.

(*Ill walks slowly into lane of silent men. When he gets to the end, he comes up against Gymnast planted facing him. Ill stops, turns round, and seeing lane close mercilessly in on him, sinks to his knees. The lane becomes a silent knot of men, swelling up, then slowly crouching down. Silence. Enter Reporters, downstage, left. Lights up.*)

FIRST REPORTER: What's going on here?

(*The knot of men opens, loosed. The men assemble quietly in background. Only Doctor remains, kneeling beside a corpse over which is spread a checkered table-cloth as used in restaurants. Doctor stands, puts away stethoscope.*)

DOCTOR: Heart attack.

(*Silence.*)

MAYOR: Died of joy.

FIRST REPORTER: Died of joy.

SECOND REPORTER: Life writes the most beautiful stories.

FIRST REPORTER: Better get to work.

(*Reporters hurry off to background, right. Enter, left, Claire Zachanassian, followed by Butler. She sees corpse, stops, then walks slowly to center of stage, turns to face audience.*)

CLAIRE ZACHANASSIAN: Bring him here.

(*Enter Roby and Toby with stretcher, on which they lay Ill, then bring him to Claire Zachanassian's feet.*)

(*Unmoving*) Uncover him, Boby.

(*Butler uncovers Ill's face. She examines it at length, does not move.*)

Now he looks the way he was, a long while ago: the black panther. Cover him.

(*Butler covers face.*)

Carry him to the coffin.

(Roby and Toby carry out body, left.)

Take me to my room, Boby. Get the bags packed. We are going to Capri.

(Butler offers her his arm, she walks slowly out to left, then stops.)

Mayor.

(Mayor emerges from ranks of silent men in background, comes slowly forward.)

The check.

(She passes him a piece of paper; and exit, with Butler.)

(As the clothing, that outward visible form of a mounting standard of living, improves by degrees discreet and unobtrusive yet less and less to be ignored, and as the stage grows more inviting, while rung by rung it scales the social ladder and metamorphoses into wealth, like a gradual change of house from a slum to a well-to-do neighborhood, so the epitome of that ascent occurs in the concluding tableau. The erstwhile gray and dreary world has been transformed; it has grown rich and dazzling new, a flashy incarnation of up-to-the-minute technics, as if the world and all were ending happily. Flags and streamers, posters, neon lights now surround the renovated railway station, and the men and women of Guellen clad in evening gowns and dress suits form two choruses, resembling those of Greek tragedy, nor is this an accident but rather to orientate the close, as if some stricken ship, borne far, far away, were sending out its last signals.)

CHORUS ONE:

Many, many the monstrous things on earth,
The volcano spewing and spitting its fire,
The shattering earthquake and the tidal wave,
And wars:

Across the corn the clatter of tanks
While the radiant mushroom grows
From the spoor of the atom bomb.

CHORUS TWO:

These monstrous things
do not exceed

The monstrous plight
      of poverty
Which excites
      no tragic deed
Is not heroic
      but condemns
Our human race
      to barren days
After hopeless
      yesterdays.
          THE WOMEN:
The mothers are helpless, they watch
      Their loved ones pining away;
          THE MEN:
But the men rumor rebellion.
      The men think treachery.
          MAN ONE:
In worn-out shoes they pace the town.
          MAN THREE:
Cigarette butts in their mouths.
          CHORUS ONE:
For the jobs, the jobs that earned them bread,
      The jobs are gone.
          CHORUS TWO:
And the station scorned by the screaming trains.
          ALL:
Now God be praised
          MRS. ILL:
For kindly fate
          ALL:
Has changed all that.
          THE WOMEN:
Our tender forms are clad in fitting frocks,
          SON:
Young guys with any future drive a Sports,
          THE MEN:
The businessmen relax in limousines,
          DAUGHTER:
All tennis-girls play tennis on hard courts.

DOCTOR:

Our operating theaters are the best:
The instruments are new, the tiles green;
Medical morale will stand the test.

ALL:

Our suppers now are simmering at home
And Everyman, contented and well shod,
Buys cigarettes of quality at last.

SCHOOLMASTER:

Assiduous students study their studies,

MAN TWO:

Dynamic tycoons amass fortunes,

ALL:

Rembrandts after Rubens,

PAINTER:

And the painters of today
Get an excellent living in Art.

PASTOR:

At Christmas and at Easter and at Whitsun
The Cathedral is packed to the portals
With Flocks of the Christian religion.

ALL:

And the trains, the trains come haughtily roaring
  In on the iron
    Railway to Guellen
Hurrying people from town to town,
  Commuting,
    Stopping.
     (Enter Guard, left.)

GUARD:

Guellen!

STATIONMASTER:

Guellen-Rome Express! All seats please!
  Diner up front!
  *(Enter from background Claire Zachanassian seated im-
  mobile in sedan chair, like an old stone idol, and moves
  downstage with retinue, between the two Choruses.)*

MAYOR:

Our lady and her noble retinue,

ALL:

Her wealth endowed on Guellen town,

DAUGHTER:

The benefactrice of us all

MAYOR:

Is leaving now!

(*Exit Claire Zachanassian, right, followed last and very slowly by servants bearing coffin.*)

MAYOR:

Long may she live.

ALL:

She bears a precious charge.

STATIONMASTER:

(*Whistles, waves green flag.*)

Stand clear!

PASTOR:

Now let us pray to God

ALL:

To protect us all

MAYOR:

In these hustling, booming, prosperous times:

ALL:

Protect all our sacred possessions,
Protect our peace and our freedom,
Ward off the night, nevermore
Let it darken our glorious town
Grown out of the ashes anew.
Let us go and enjoy our good fortune.

POSTSCRIPT

The Visit is a story that takes place in a small town somewhere in Central Europe. It is told by someone who by no means feels removed from the people involved, and who is not so sure he would have acted differently. Any further meaning imputed to the story needs no mention here, and should not be imposed on the stage production. This applies even to the final scene, where the people, admittedly, speak in a more formal fashion than might be found in reality, more in the so-called poetical manner, and use what could be described as fine words, but this is merely because the Guelleners have just acquired riches and speak as befits the newly rich, in a more select language. I have described people, not marionettes; an action, not an allegory. I have presented a world, not pointed a moral (as I have been accused of doing), and what is more I have not even tried to force my play on the public, for all that happens quite naturally in any case, so long as the audience too belongs in the theater. In my view, a play is acted in the theater according to the limits and possibilities of the stage; it is not confined within the garb of some special style. When the Guelleners act trees, therefore, this is no Surrealism. Rather is it a somewhat distressing love story, enacted in that wood: an old man's attempt to approach an old woman; and this is placed in a "poetical" setting in order to make it more bearable. I write with an inherent confidence in the theater and its actors—this is my fundamental inspiration; the material draws me into its charmed circle. To play his character, the actor needs little: only the very outer skin, the text, which of course has to ring true. That is to say, just as any creature is sealed off inside its skin, so the play is sealed off inside speech. For speech is all the dramatist provides. It is his end product. And it is consequently impossible to work on the element of speech alone, but only on that which gives rise to speech, such as thought and action; only dilettantes work on speech alone. I think the actor should aim to present that end product afresh, whereby all that is art should seem to be nature. If the foreground I have provided is correctly played, the background will emerge of its own accord. I don't account myself a member of the contemporary avant-grade. I admit I have my Theory of Art as well—one indulges in a lot of things as a hobby—but I keep it to myself as my private opinion (otherwise I'd be obliged to practice it) and prefer being regarded as a somewhat lunatic child of nature lacking a proper sense of form and structure. Producers and directors will probably come nearest the mark if they stage my plays after the style of folk plays, and treat me as a kind of conscious Nestroy. They should follow the flights of my fancy and let the deeper meanings take care of themselves; they should change the sets without pause or curtain, play even the car scene simply and preferably with a stage vehicle, equipped only with what the action requires: seats, steering wheel, bumpers, the car seen from the front, rear seats raised and, of course, everything brand new, like the shoes, etc. (This scene hasn't anything to do with Wilder—why not? Dialectical exercise for critics.) Claire Zachanassian doesn't represent Justice or the Marshall Plan or even the Apocalypse, she's purely and simply what she is, namely, the richest woman in the world and, thanks to her finances, in a position to act as the Greek tragic heroines acted, absolutely, terribly, something like Medea. She can afford to. This lady has a sense of humor and it mustn't be overlooked, for she is quite detached from people as saleable objects and detached from herself as well, and she has a rare grace, more, she has a wicked charm. Nonetheless, moving as she does outside the human pale, she has grown into someone unalterable and rigid, contains within herself no further possibility of development and, in consequence is cast in a mold of stone, to be represented as a stone idol. She's a poetical apparition, so is her retinue, and her eunuchs too. The latter are not to be given a realistically unappetizing interpretation, complete with high-pitched gelded voices, but made on the contrary to seem quite improbable, legendary, fantastic, soft and ghostly in their vegetable contentment, a sacrifice to total revenge, logical as the lawbooks of antiquity. (To facilitate the playing of these roles the blind pair may speak alternately, instead of together, in which case they needn't repeat every phrase.) While Claire Zachanassian, fixed and unmoving, is a heroine from the very beginning, her onetime sweetheart still has to develop into a hero. At first, a disreputable shopkeeper, he is her unsuspecting victim and, guilty, believes life has been its own expiation of that guilt; he is a thoughtless figure of a man, a simple man in whose mind something slowly dawns, by the agency of fear and terror, something highly personal; a man who in recognizing his guilt lives out justice and who, in death, achieves greatness. (His death should not be without a certain monumental quality.) That death is both meaningful and meaningless. It would only have been entirely meaningful in the mythological kingdom of some ancient *polis*. But the action of this story unfolds in Guellen. In the present. The Guelleners who swarm around the hero are people like the rest of us. They must not, emphatically not, be portrayed as wicked. At first, they are firmly resolved to reject the offer, and although they incur debts that is not because they intend to kill Ill, but out of thoughtless irresponsibility and the feeling that somehow things will come to a happy settlement. Act Two should be directed accordingly. And then in the station scene, Ill is the only one to see his own plight and be afraid; not a harsh word has yet been uttered; events only take their decisive trun during the scene in Petersens' Barn. Disaster can no longer be averted. From that moment onward, the Guelleners steadily pave their way to the murder, waxing indignant over Ill's guilt, etc. The family alone keep on to the end trying to convince themselves things will somehow turn out all right; for they aren't wicked either, only weak, like everyone. It's a community slowly yielding to temptation, as in the Schoolmaster's case; but the yielding must be comprehensible. The temptation is too strong, the poverty too wretched. *The Visit* is a wicked play, and for precisely that reason mustn't be played wicked; it has to be rendered as human as possible, not with anger but with sorrow and humor, for nothing could harm this comedy with a tragic end more than heavy seriousness.

F.D.

Translated by Patrick Bowles

THE PHYSICISTS

Editor's note: Rigidly observing the three dramatic unities, Dürrenmatt's ninth play (a comedy in two acts, written in 1962, first performed in New York, 1964, under the direction of Peter Brook) confines its action to a single day spent in a sanatorium among three apparently mad physicists and its hunchbacked owner, the psychiatrist Miss von Zahnd. At the core of the play, as in Brecht's *Galileo,* is the question of responsibility and possible guilt of the modern scientist. Möbius, a nuclear physicist, has taken refuge behind the mask of insanity because he fears that his discoveries are too dangerous. With him in the insane asylum are two other scientists, also pretending to be mad, who in fact are secret agents of rival political powers trying to ferret out Möbius's secrets. For different reasons, each scientist feels compelled to murder his nurse to prevent being discovered. Eventually Möbius convinces the other two that they have to "take back their knowledge" and remain in the asylum, for "either we stay in this madhouse or the world becomes one." But, like Emperor Romulus, Möbius finds in the end that no individual can change the course of history by his solitary act of conviction. Even the insane asylum turns out to be no refuge. All three have fallen into a trap: they are at the mercy of Dr. von Zahnd, the truly mad psychiatrist and literary descendant of Claire Zachanassian, who uses them and their secrets for her own irresponsible purposes. Having fled the world because they feared the destructive potential of their discoveries in hands of "normal" power brokers, they and their terrible secret find themselves in the hands of a madwoman. The proud history of Western science ends in the vision of tragedy, precipitated by an insane coincidence: "Somewhere, round a small, yellow, nameless star there circles, pointlessly, everlastingly, the radioactive earth."

21 Points to *The Physicists*

1. I don't start out with a thesis but with a story.

2. If you start out with a story you must think it to its conclusion.

3. A story has been thought to its conclusion when it has taken its worst possible turn.

4. The worst possible turn is not foreseeable. It occurs by coincidence.

5. The art of the playwright consists in employing coincidence as effectively as possible within the action.

6. The bearers of a dramatic action are human beings.

7. Coincidence in a dramatic action consists in when and where who happens to meet whom coincidentally.

8. The more human beings proceed according to plan, the more effectively they may be hit by coincidence.

9. Human beings proceeding according to plan wish to reach a specific goal. They are most severely hit by coincidence when through it they reach the opposite of their goal: the very thing they feared, what they sought to avoid (i.e., Oedipus).

10. Such a story, though grotesque, is not absurd (contrary to meaning).

11. It is paradoxical.

12. Playwrights are as little able as logicians to avoid the paradoxical.

13. Physicists are as little able as logicians to avoid the paradoxical.

14. A drama about physicists must be paradoxical.

15. It cannot have as its goal the content of physics but only its effect.

16. The content of physics is the concern of physicists, its effect the concern of all men.

17. What concerns everyone can only be resolved by everyone.

18. Every attempt by an individual to resolve for himself what is the concern of everyone is doomed to fail.

19. Within the paradoxical, reality appears.

20. He who confronts the paradoxical exposes himself to reality.

21. Drama can dupe the spectator into exposing himself to reality but cannot compel him to withstand it or even to master it.

Translated by James Kirkup

THE JUDGE
AND HIS
HANGMAN

A Novel

On the morning of November 3, 1948, Alphonse Clenin, a local policeman of the village of Twann, came upon a blue Mercedes by the side of the road just where the highway from Lamboing emerges from the woods that surround the gorge of the Twann River. It was one of those foggy mornings of which there were many in the late autumn of that year. Clenin had actually walked past the car when something made him stop and turn back. In passing he glanced through the fog-dimmed window and got a blurred impression of the driver collapsed over the wheel. Being a decent sort who did not discount the obvious, Clenin thought the man was drunk and thus strode slowly back to the car to arouse the stranger and offer a few fatherly rather than official words of advice. He was even considering driving the man into Twann and leaving him to sober up over a breakfast of black coffee and porridge in the Bear Hotel. After all, although it was forbidden to drive a car while under the influence of alcohol, there was no law against parking by the roadside and quietly sleeping it off.

Clenin opened the car door and put a rousing hand on the stranger's shoulder. As he did so he realized that the man was dead—a bullet had passed through one temple and out the other. At the same time Clenin also noticed that the passenger door was unlatched. There was little blood in the car and the dead man's dark-gray coat was not even stained. The edge of a yellow wallet peeked out of the inside pocket, and Clenin drew it out. With no difficulty he established that the dead man was Ulrich Schmied, a lieutenant in the Berne police.

Clenin wondered what he should do next. As a village patrol-man, he had never encountered such a case of death. He paced up and down the roadside until the early morning sun, breaking suddenly through the fog, shone full on the corpse. This made Clenin uncomfortable. He went back to the car, picked up the gray felt hat that lay at the dead man's feet and pulled it so far down on the fellow's head that he could no longer see the wound. This made him feel a little better.

The officer crossed to the other side of the road that looks over Twann and wiped the sweat from his forehead. After some time he made a decision. Returning to the car, he shoved the dead man onto the passenger seat, gingerly raised it into an erect sitting position, and secured the lifeless body with a leather strap he found in the back of the car. Then he climbed in beside it and took the wheel.

The engine refused to start, but the car was standing on a steep incline and Clenin had no difficulty in coasting it down the hill into Twann and stopping outside the Bear. There he filled the tank without the attendant suspecting that the formal and motionless passenger was a corpse. That suited Clenin, who hated scandals, just fine, and he kept his silence.

As Clenin drove along the lakeside road towards the town of Biel, however, the fog thickened again and completely blotted out the sun. The morning grew as gray as Doomsday. After a time, Clenin found himself in a long line of cars, bumper to bumper, which for some mysterious reason seemed to move even more slowly than the poor visibility warranted. Like a funeral procession, Clenin thought involuntarily. The corpse sat motionless at his side, except that now and then, when they came to a bump in the road, it nodded its head like a wise old Chinaman, so that Clenin felt less and less inclined to overtake the cars in front of him. They reached Biel much later than he had expected.

While the main investigation of the Schmied case was entrusted to the Biel police, the sad remains were sent to Berne and given over to Inspector Barlach, who also had been the dead man's superior.

Barlach had spent much of his life abroad and had made a name for himself as an expert in the detection of crime, first in Constantinople and later in Germany, where he had been in charge of the criminal investigation department in Frankfurt-on-Main. He returned to his native Berne, however, in 1933. His reason was not so much a love for his birthplace, which he often described as his "golden grave," but the fact that he had slapped the face of a high official of what was then the new German government. His out-rageous act attracted a great deal of attention at the time in Frank-furt. In Berne it was assessed in accordance with the prevailing European political situation: first as disgraceful, later as regretta-ble but understandable, and finally (albeit in 1945) as the only possible thing a Swiss could have done.

Barlach's first action in the Schmied case was to order it to be kept secret, at least for a few days, and he had to exert all his authority to have the order observed. "We know too little," he insisted, "and in any case the newspapers are the most superfluous invention of the last two thousand years."

Barlach apparently expected a great deal from this approach, but his insistence on secrecy was not shared by his boss, Dr. Lucius Lutz, who also lectured on criminology at Berne University. This stuffy functionary, on whose mental outlook a childless but wealthy uncle in Basle had exercised a beneficent influence, had recently returned from a visit to the police departments of New York and Chicago. Greatly impressed by what he had seen there, he was now frankly horrified—as he admitted to Commissioner Frieber-ger as they rode home one evening on the tram—at the "prehis-toric state of crime prevention in the federal capital of Switzer-land."

The same morning, having had two telephone conversations with the Biel police, Barlach paid a visit to the Schönlers in Bantiger-strasse, where Schmied had lodged. As always he walked through the old city and over the Nydeck bridge, for in his opinion Berne was much too small for "trams and suchlike." It cost him some effort to climb the steep flight of steps that lay in his path—for he was over sixty and felt it at such times—but he eventually reached his destination and rang the bell.

The door was opened by Frau Schönler herself, a short, plump, not undistinguished woman who recognized Barlach and admitted him at once.

"Schmied had to go away on business last night," said Barlach. "He had to leave unexpectedly and asked me to send some things on to him. Kindly take me to his room, Frau Schönler."

The landlady nodded and led the way down the hall, passing a large picture in a heavy gilt frame. Barlach glanced at it; it was a painting of the Island of the Dead.

"Where did Herr Schmied go?" asked the plump woman as she opened the door of her lodger's room.

"Abroad," said Barlach, looking up at the ceiling.

The room was on the ground floor and looked out upon a small yard full of old brown fir trees, which must have been diseased, for the ground was covered thickly with needles. It was probably the best room in the house. Barlach went over to the desk and again took his bearings. One of the dead man's ties was lying on the sofa.

"He's gone to the tropics, hasn't he, Herr Barlach?" Frau Schönler was unable to hide her curiosity.

Barlach was a bit startled by the question. "No, he's not in the tropics, rather a bit higher."

Frau Schönler's eyes goggled and she raised her hands above her head. "My God! In the Himalayas?"

"Perhaps," Barlach agreed. "You've almost guessed it." He opened a briefcase that was lying on the desk and immediately tucked it under his arm.

"Have you found what you wanted to send to Herr Schmied?"

"Yes, I have."

He took another look around, but avoided a second glance at the tie on the sofa.

"He's the best lodger we've ever had," Frau Schönler assured him. "Never any trouble with ladies and suchlike."

Barlach went to the door. "I may send an officer around, or even look in now and then myself. Schmied has some other important documents here that he may need."

"Do you think I'll get a postcard from Herr Schmied while he's abroad?" Frau Schönler wanted to know. "My son collects stamps."

Barlach frowned and looked at Frau Schönler with a pensive glance. "Most unlikely," he said. "Police officers never send postcards when traveling on duty. It's forbidden."

Frau Schönler again raised her hands above her head, and cried protestingly, "Nowadays the police forbid everything!"

Barlach went out, glad to leave the house behind him.

Deep in thought, Barlach lunched in the Café du Théâtre instead of his usual restaurant, Schmidt's. As he ate, he leafed through the contents of the briefcase he had brought from Schmied's room, here and there pausing to read with great interest. Then he left the café and, after a short stroll along the Bundestrasse, returned to his office at two o'clock, where he heard that Schmied's body had been brought in from Biel. He decided not to pay a call on his deceased subordinate, for he had no liking for corpses and so as a rule preferred to leave them in peace.

He would also have preferred not to call on Lutz, but he had no choice in the matter and had to make the best of it. Without examining its contents any further, he carefully locked Schmied's briefcase in his desk, lit a cigar, and went into Lutz's office, well knowing that Lutz always resented the liberty he took by smoking cigars in his boss's room. Only once, some years before, had Lutz dared to object, but Barlach condescendingly waved his objections aside, saying that, among other things, he had served ten years in Turkey and had always smoked in his superior's office. It was a statement that was all the more exasperating to Lutz because it could not be disproved.

Dr. Lucius Lutz received Barlach with more than his usual irritation, for in his opinion nothing had yet been done in the Schmied case.

"Any news from Biel?" Barlach asked.

"Not yet," answered Lutz.

"That's strange," said Barlach, "especially since they're working like crazy."

He dropped into the comfortable armchair in front of Lutz's desk and threw a quick glance at the pictures by Traffelet that hung on the walls: tinted pen-and-ink drawings of soldiers, sometimes with a general, sometimes without, marching either from right to left or from left to right under a huge flowing banner.

"It causes me increasing anxiety," began Lutz, "that detective criminology in this country is still in its infancy. God knows I'm used to most of the ineptitudes that go on in this canton, but the procedure that seems to be regarded as right and proper in the case of the death of a police lieutenant throws so horrible a light on the professional competence of our rural local police that I am still appalled."

"Now, now, Dr. Lutz," Barlach soothed. "Our local officers are surely just as competent in their field as the Chicago police are in theirs. We'll find out who killed Schmied, take my word for it."

"Do you have a suspect, Inspector Barlach?"

Barlach looked reflectively at Lutz for some time. At last he said, "Yes, there is someone, Dr. Lutz."

"Who?"

"I can't tell you yet."

"Interesting, very interesting," said Lutz sarcastically. "I know you always prefer to follow your own line of investigation rather than take advantage of modern methods of detection, Inspector, but don't forget that time marches on and has no respect even for the most distinguished of reputations. I've seen crimes in New York and Chicago the likes of which you in Berne have absolutely no idea. But this time a police lieutenant has been murdered—a sure sign that there's trouble for us here at Headquarters. We've got to act ruthlessly."

Barlach replied that that was exactly what he was doing.

"I'm glad to hear it," said Lutz, and coughed.

A clock on the wall went on ticking.

Barlach placed his left hand gingerly on his stomach and with his right hand crushed out his cigar in the ashtray that Lutz had placed in front of him. He told Lutz that for some time now he had not been in the best of health and that his doctor at least was quite concerned. He had frequent attacks of stomach trouble, and would be grateful if Dr. Lutz would appoint someone to assist him in the Schmied case, someone who could undertake much of the active work. In this way, Barlach would be free to concentrate on the finer details of the case. Lutz agreed.

"Whom do you suggest as assistant?" he asked.

"Chance," Barlach replied. "I understand he's still vacationing in the Bernese Oberland, but we can recall him."

"Good idea," said Lutz. "Chance is a man who works hard to keep up to date as far as criminology is concerned."

He then turned his back on Barlach and stared out of the window at Orphans' Square, which was crowded with children.

He was suddenly conscious of an irresistible desire to quarrel with Barlach on the merits of modern scientific methods in criminal investigation. He spun around to face his visitor, but Barlach was no longer there.

Even though it was nearly five in the afternoon, Barlach decided to drive out to Twann to take a look at the scene of the crime. He was driven by a big, bloated officer named Blatter, who never spoke a word and for whom, therefore, Barlach had a warm affection. Clenin met them at Twann, looking a little sulky in anticipation of a reprimand. But the Inspector was all amiability, shook Clenin's hand and said he was pleased to meet a man who knew how to think for himself. Clenin brightened considerably when he heard this, even though he did not quite know exactly what the Inspector meant by it.

He led Barlach up the road to the scene of the crime, while Blatter trudged behind them, disgruntled at having to walk.

Barlach was curious as to the origin of the name Lamboing. "It's actually Lamlingen in German," explained Clenin.

"Oh, I see," said Barlach. "The German is prettier."

They quickly reached the scene of the crime, where the road was edged by a wall to their right and below which lay the village of Twann.

"Where was the car, Clenin?"

"Here," replied the officer, pointing to the spot, "almost in the middle of the road." Since Barlach scarcely glanced in the direction indicated, Clenin continued, "Maybe it would have been better if I had left the car here with the body inside."

"Why?" asked Barlach, looking up at the cliffs of Jura rock above them. "It's best to get dead bodies out of the way as soon as possible; they have nothing more to gain among us. You were quite right to drive Schmied back to Biel."

He crossed the road and looked down over Twann. There was nothing but vineyards between him and the ancient village. The sun had already set but he could still see the road winding like a snake between the houses, and a long freight train was standing in the station.

"Didn't anyone down there hear anything, Clenin?" he asked. "The village is not far away. Someone must have heard the shot."

"They heard nothing but the running of the engine. It ran most of the night, but they didn't think anything was wrong."

"Of course not. Why should they?"

His glance caught the vineyards again. "How is the wine this year, Clenin?"

"Good. We can try some if you like."

"Yes, I think I would like a glass of new wine."

His right foot struck against something hard, and Barlach bent down to pick it up. When he stood up again his lean fingers were holding a small, elongated piece of metal, crushed flat at one end. Clenin and Blatter looked at the object curiously.

"A pistol bullet," said Blatter.

Clenin was astonished. "How did you manage to find that, Inspector?"

"Just luck," said Barlach. And they set off down the hill for Twann.

The new wine did not seem to agree with Barlach, for next morning he declared that he had been vomiting all night. Lutz, who ran into the inspector on the stairs, was genuinely concerned about the state of his health and advised him to consult his doctor.

"All right, all right," growled Barlach, adding that he was even less fond of doctors than he was of modern criminology cranks. By the time he reached his office he felt better. He sat down at his desk, unlocked a drawer, and brought out the dead man's briefcase.

Barlach was still immersed in its contents when Chance came to see him at ten o'clock. The latter had just returned from his vacation late the previous night, and as he entered, Barlach gave a start. Chance was wearing the same overcoat as Schmied's and a felt hat very much like his as well. For a moment Barlach thought the dead man had entered the room. Only the face was different: it was round and good-natured.

"I'm glad you've come, Chance," said Barlach. "We have to talk about the Schmied case. You'll have to take over most of the hard work, I'm afraid. I'm not too well."

"Yes," said Chance, "so I've heard."

Chance drew up a chair and sat down, resting his left arm on Barlach's desk. Schmied's briefcase was lying open in front of them.

Barlach leaned back in his chair. "I don't mind telling you," he began, "that I've come across a thousand or so policemen, good and bad, between Constantinople and Berne. Many were no better than the poor devils who fill up all our prisons except that they happened to be on the other side of the law. But I never met one to compare with Schmied. He was the best. Most of us in comparison looked like pretty small stuff. He had a cool head that knew what it wanted and kept what it knew to itself. He never spoke except when it was necessary. We have to use him as an example, Chance. He had more on the ball than we do."

Chance had been looking out the window, and he now turned his head slowly back toward Barlach. "Possibly," he said, but Barlach saw by his expression that he was not convinced.

"We don't know much about how he died," the inspector continued. "All we've got to go on is this bullet." And he placed the bullet he had found at Twann on the desk. Chance picked it up and looked at it.

"It's from an army pistol," he said, putting it down again.

Barlach was closing the briefcase as he went on: "What we don't know is why Schmied was in Twann or Lamlingen in the first place. He was not on official business near the lake, for I would have known about it. We had absolutely no clue as to what might have motivated him to drive out there."

Chance was only half listening to what Barlach was saying. Crossing his legs, he remarked: "All we know is how Schmied was murdered."

"What makes you think we know that?" asked the inspector with some surprise after a brief pause.

"Schmied's car had a left-hand drive and you found the bullet on the left-hand side of the road when seen from the car. Also, the people in Twann heard the motor running all night. Schmied was stopped by the murderer as he was driving down from Lamboing to Twann. It's probable that he knew the man who shot him, otherwise he wouldn't have stopped. Schmied opened the passenger door to let the murderer in and sat back behind the wheel. That's when he was shot. Schmied cannot have had any idea that the man intended to kill him."

Barlach mulled over Chance's interpretation. "I think I'll have a cigar after all," he said, and only after he had lit it up did he continue: "You're right, Chance. That's probably what must have happened. I'd like to believe you. But it still doesn't explain what Schmied was doing on the road from Twann to Lamlingen."

Chance then pointed out that Schmied had had evening clothes on under his coat.

"I didn't know anything about that," said Barlach.

"But haven't you seen the body?"

168 · Friedrich Dürrenmatt

"No. I don't like corpses."

"It even said so in the official report."

"I like official reports even less."

Chance said nothing.

"If anything, that makes the case even more complex," Barlach said thoughtfully. "Why should Schmied be wearing tails in the Twann ravine?"

Chance replied that this fact might simplify rather than complicate the case. There couldn't be many residents in the area around Lamboing who would be likely to throw the sort of party for which the guests might wear tails. He produced a small pocket calendar from his pocket and explained that it had belonged to Schmied.

Barlach nodded. "I've seen it. There's nothing in it of any importance."

Chance was not so sure. "Against Wednesday, November 2," he pointed out, "Schmied has written the letter G. That is the day he was murdered—shortly before midnight, according to the medical examiner. There's another G on Wednesday, October 26, and again on Tuesday, October 18."

"G might mean anything," said Barlach. "A woman's name or something."

"Hardly a woman's name," Chance objected, "because his fiancé is called Anna, and Schmied was the steady sort."

"I didn't know anything about her, either," the inspector admitted, and, seeing that Chance was astonished at his ignorance, he added: "I'm only interested in Schmied's murderer, Chance."

"Of course," replied the latter politely. Then he shook his head and laughed. "What a man you are, Inspector Barlach."

"I'm a big, black tomcat"—Barlach spoke the words quite seriously—"and I have an appetite for mice."

Chance did not know what to say to that. Finally he remarked: "On the days marked G, Schmied always put on his tails and drove off in his Mercedes."

"And how do you know that?"

"From Frau Schönler."

"Ah-ha," said Barlach, and sat silent for a few moments. "Yes, those are facts."

Chance looked keenly into the inspector's face. He lit a cigarette and said with some hesitation: "Dr. Lutz told me you had a 'possible suspect' in mind."

"Yes, Chance I have."

"Now that I've been appointed to act as your assistant in this case, wouldn't it be better if you told me whom you suspect, Inspector Barlach?"

"Look here, Chance," answered Barlach slowly, weighing his words as carefully as Chance did. "What I have in mind is as yet completely without foundation in fact. I have no evidence to justify it. You've just seen how little I really know. All I've got is a hunch as to who the murderer might be, but the person I've in mind still has to produce the proof that will condemn him."

"What do you mean by that, Inspector?"

Barlach smiled. "Simply that I have to wait until I have the evidence that will justify his arrest."

"If I am to cooperate with you, I have to know who I am supposed to investigate," said Chance politely.

"The main thing is to remain objective. This holds for me and my suspicions as well as for you, who will conduct the main investigation. Whether my suspicion will be confirmed or not, I don't know. It depends upon your investigation. Your job is to find out who Schmied's murderer is, regardless of what my private suspicions may be. If my hunch is right, I'll end up with the same guy— although, in contrast to my own methods, you'll discover him by irreproachable scientific means. If I'm wrong, you will have found the real culprit without it ever having been necessary to divulge the name of the person I suspected so unjustly."

They sat in silence for a while, and then the older man asked: "Do you agree to our working on that basis?"

Chance hesitated for a moment before answering: "All right, I agree."

"So what do you want to do first, Chance?"

The detective walked over to the window. "Schmied marked a G against today. I want to drive out to Lamboing and see what I can find. I'll leave at seven o'clock, the same time Schmied always started out on these occasions."

He turned around and asked politely but half jestingly, "Would you care to come along, Inspector?"

"Yes, Chance, I'll come," was the unexpected reply.

"Right," said Chance, a little taken aback, for he had not reckoned on this. "At seven, then."

At the door he turned again. "I hear you went to see Frau Schönler, too, Inspector Barlach. Did you find anything there?" The old man did not answer right away, but instead locked the briefcase in a drawer of his desk and put the key in his pocket.

"No," he said at last. "I didn't find anything. I won't keep you any longer, Chance."

At seven o'clock, Chance drove to the house overlooking the river, where the inspector had lived since 1933. It was raining, and the speeding police car skidded as it turned by the bridge over the river. Chance quickly regained control and drove slowly along the Altenbergstrasse, for it was the first time he had been to Barlach's house, and he had to peer through the foggy windshield at the house numbers, which he had difficulty in deciphering. He finally found the one he was looking for, but repeated toots of the horn produced no sign of life from within. Chance got out of the car and ran through the rain to the front door. It was too dark to find the doorbell, and, after a moment's hesitation, he turned the knob. The door was unlocked, and Chance found himself in the vestibule. In front of him was a half-opened door, a ray of light shining through the crack. He knocked on this door, and, receiving no answer, pushed it wide open. In front of him was a large room whose walls were lined with books. Barlach was stretched out on the sofa. He was asleep, but he seemed to have prepared for the drive to Lake Biel, for he was wearing a heavy overcoat. He had a book in his hand. Listening to his quiet breathing, Chance felt uneasy and embarrassed. The sight of the sleeping man, surrounded by his shelves of books, was somehow oddly disconcerting. Chance looked cautiously around the room; it had no windows, but there was a door in each wall, leading no doubt to other rooms. A massive desk stood in the middle of the floor and on it lay a large brass snake. Chance recoiled as he caught sight of the reptile.

"I brought it back from Constantinople," said a quiet voice from the sofa, and Barlach sat up. "As you see, I already have my coat on, Chance. We can go."

"I apologize for breaking in," said Chance, a little taken aback. "You were asleep and didn't hear me. I couldn't find the bell on the front door."

"There is no bell. I don't need one. The door is never locked."

"Not even when you're out?"

"Not even when I'm out. It's always exciting to come home and see whether anything has been stolen."

Chance laughed and picked up the snake from Constantinople.

"I was nearly killed with that thing once," remarked the inspector somewhat mockingly, and Chance noticed for the first time that the snake's head formed a handle and its body the blade of a knife. Mystified, he stared at the strange decorations that shone on the terrible weapon. Barlach was standing beside him.

" 'Be ye therefore wise as serpents,' " he said and eyed Chance quizzically with a long, thoughtful look. Then he smiled. " 'And harmless as doves.' " He tapped Chance lightly on the shoulder. "I've had some sleep for the first time in days. It's this damned stomach of mine."

"It's as bad as that?"

"Yes, it's as bad as that," repeated the inspector coldly.

"You ought to stay home, Herr Barlach. It's cold and wet outside."

Barlach looked at Chance again and laughed. "Nonsense. We've got a murderer to hunt down. I think you would prefer it if I did stay at home, though," he added.

As they were driving across the Nydegg Bridge, Barlach asked, "Why aren't we going via the Aargauerstalden toward Zollikofen, Chance? It's quicker than driving through the town."

"Because I don't know to go through Zollikofen and Biel. The road through Kerzers and Erlach is better."

"It's an unusual route, Chance."

"It's not at all unusual, Inspector."

They lapsed into silence again. The lights of the town glided past them. As they approached Bethlehem hospital, Chance asked, "Did you ever drive with Schmied?"

"Yes, often. He was a careful driver." Barlach cast a critical glance at the speedometer, which pointed at nearly sixty-five.

Chance slowed down a little. "He drove me once—as slow as

hell, and I remember he had a strange sort of name for his car. He used it whenever he had to fill it up. It escapes me at the moment—do you remember it?"

"He called it 'Blue Charon,' " replied Barlach.

"That's it. Charon is the name of a character in Greek mythology, isn't it?"

"Charon ferried the dead across to the underworld, Chance."

"Schmied's parents were well off. They sent him to a good school. More than my people could affort for me. That's why he knew who Charon was, and why I didn't."

Barlach put his hands in his pockets and looked at the speedometer again. "Yes," he said. "Schmied was an educated man. He knew Greek and Latin. With his advantages he had a great future in front of him. Even so, that's no reason to drive more than sixty miles an hour."

The car pulled up sharply at a filling station a little beyond Gümmenen and a man came out to attend them.

"Police," announced Chance. "We need some information."

Indistinctly they saw an inquisitive and rather startled face framed in the car window.

"Did a man who called his car 'Blue Charon' stop here two days ago?"

The man shook his head in astonishment, and Chance drove on. "We'll try the next one."

The filling station attendant at Kerzers was equally unhelpful.

"What's the sense of all this?" growled Barlach.

But at Erlach Chance was lucky. Someone answering the description had been there on Wednesday evening.

"You see," said Chance triumphantly, as they joined the Neuchâtel-Biel road. "We now know that Schmied passed through Kerzers and Erlach last Wednesday night."

"Are you sure?" asked Barlach.

"Beyond a doubt."

"There's no holes in the proof, all right. But what good does it do you, Chance?" Barlach seemed quite curious.

"It's something, anyway. Every fact we know helps us along," was his answer.

"Right again," admitted the old man and looked through the window toward Lake Biel. The rain had stopped. Beyond Neuveville the lake came suddenly into sight through patches of mist. They passed through Ligerz. Chance drove slowly, looking out for the turning to Lamboing. They found the road and the car began to climb through the vineyards. Barlach opened the window and looked down at the lake. Several stars were shining above the island. Lights were mirrored in the water and a motorboat raced across the lake. Late for this time of year, thought Barlach. In the valley in front of them lay Twann, behind them Ligerz.

They found a bend in the road and drove toward the woods, which they could sense rather than see in the darkness ahead. Chance seemed a little uncertain and felt they might not be on the right road. He stopped. A man wearing a leather jacket was coming toward them. "Is this the way to Lamboing?"

"Straight ahead. Turn right into the forest when you come to a row of white houses along the edge," the man answered. He whistled to a small white dog with a black head that was dancing in the glare of the headlights. "Come on, Ping Ping."

They left the vineyards behind and were soon in the woods. The pines pressed in around them, an endless row of columns in the beam of headlights. The road was rough and narrow, so that now and then a branch would sweep along the windows of the car. To their right the land dropped away steeply. Chance drove so slowly that they could hear a stream gushing far below them.

"This is the Twann gorge," Chance explained. "The road into Twann lies on the other side."

To their left crags towered into the night, flashing white every once in a while. Otherwise all was dark, for it was the time of the new moon. The road leveled out and the stream they had heard earlier was now rushing beside them. They turned left and drove over a bridge. The road that lay before them was the road from Twann to Lamboing. Chance stopped the car.

He turned the headlights off and they were in complete darkness.

"Now what?" asked Barlach.

"Now we'll wait. It's twenty minutes to eight."

They sat waiting. When nothing had happened by eight o'clock, Barlach observed drily that it was about time Chance told him what he was up to.

"I've no definite plans, Inspector. I haven't gotten far enough in the case yet, and even you, despite your hunch, are still groping in the dark. Right now I'm staking everything on the chance that there'll be a party again tonight at the house Schmied visited on Wednesday. If so, some of the guests are almost certain to drive along this road. It's bound to be a fairly elaborate party if the guests wear evening clothes. Of course, it's only a guess, Inspector Barlach, but guesses are all we've got to go on in this business."

Interrupting his subordinate's train of thought, the inspector rather skeptically reminded him of the fact that the investigations of their colleagues in Biel, Neuveville, Twann, and Lamboing regarding Schmied's activities had so far produced precious little in the way of clues.

"That's simply because Schmied's murderer is a good deal cleverer than the police of Biel and Neuveville," returned Chance. Barlach muttered something regarding how he had reached that conclusion.

"I don't suspect anyone," said Chance, "but if one can use the word 'respect' in connection with a killer, I would use it of the man who murdered Schmied."

Barlach listened without moving, his shoulders hunched up. "And you're confident you'll catch this guy you respect so highly, Chance?"

"I hope to, Inspector."

Again they waited in silence. Suddenly a light shone through the trees from the direction of Twann, and a few moments later the headlights of a car flooded them with garish light. A limousine sped past them toward Lamboing and disappeared into the night. Chance started the motor and waited as two more cars passed by, large dark limousines full of people. Chance set out in hot pursuit.

The procession drove through the woods, passed a restaurant whose sign was illuminated by the light from an open doorway, and passed a cluster of farmhouses, each driver intent upon the rear lights of the car in front.

They reached the broad plateau of the Tessenberg. The sky was swept clean, the setting Vega, the rising Capella, Aldebaran, and flaming Jupiter burned in the heavens. The road turned northward, and ahead of them stood the dark outlines of mountain peaks at whose feet lay the few flickering lights of the villages of Lamboing, Diesse, and Nods.

Suddenly the cars ahead turned left onto a dirt road, and Chance stopped the car. He rolled down the window and stuck his head out. Across the field they could see the indistinct mass of a house surrounded by poplars. Its front door was illuminated and the cars they had been following were pulling up in front of it. The sound of voices drifted across to them as the new arrivals got out and streamed into the house. Then the light in the doorway went out and all was still. "They don't expect anyone else," Chance said.

Barlach got out and inhaled the cold night air. He felt the better for it and watched while Chance parked the car on the right shoulder of the road, for the route to Lamboing was a narrow one. Then Chance got out and walked across to the inspector. Together they went down the dirt track toward the house. The ground was muddy, and there were puddles everywhere, reminders of the recent rain.

They soon came to a low wall with a closed gate. The two policemen peered at the house through the rusty iron bars that rose high above the top of the wall. The garden was bare and the limousines lay like great beasts among the poplars. Not a light could be seen. Everything looked deserted and desolate.

Despite the darkness they managed to make out a nameplate that was attached to the center bars of the gate. One of the screws must have come loose, for the plate was hanging sideways. Chance switched on the flashlight he had brought from the car: the only letter on the plate was a capital G.

Standing in the dark again, Chance said, "You see, my hunch was right. A chance shot that hit the bull'seye," and then, "Give me a cigar, Inspector. I deserve it," he added complacently.

Barlach offered him one. "The next step is to find out what G stands for."

"That's no problem," said Chance. "It stands for Gastmann."

"How do you know?"

"I looked it up in the telephone book. There are only two G's in Lamboing."

Barlach laughed in surprise, but then he said, "Couldn't it also be the other G?"

"No, that's the gendarmerie. Unless you think a gendarme had something to do with the murder?"

"Anything's possible, Chance," was the old man's reply.

Chance lit a match, but a strong breeze had sprung up and was shaking the poplars in fury. He found it difficult to light his cigar.

Barlach could not for the life of him understand why the police of Lamboing and environs had managed to overlook this Gastmann, for his house lay in open country, easily visible from Lamboing; moreover, it would be difficult, if not impossible, to give a party there without it being seen and noted by everybody in the village. As a matter of fact, such an event would be most conspicuous. He mentioned these points to Chance, but his subordinate had no explanation to offer either.

They then decided to circle the house, going separately in opposite directions. Chance disappeared in the darkness, and Barlach was left alone. He turned his coat collar up, for he was shivering and was again tormented by the pressure and stabbing pain in his stomach that brought a cold sweat to his forehead. He walked along the wall, following it closely as it bent to the right. The house still lay in utter darkness.

After a while he stopped and leaned against the wall. He could see the lights of Lamboing coming down to the edge of the wood. He walked toward them. The wall changed its direction again, this time toward the west. The back of the house came into view, ablaze with light, and an especially bright light poured from a row of windows on the second floor. He stopped as he heard the notes of a piano; listening intently, he realized that someone was playing Bach.

He walked on. According to his reckoning he should soon be meeting Chance again, and he strained his eyes to see across the light-flooded stretch of lawn. He noticed too late that a huge dog was standing only a few steps from him. Barlach knew a good deal about dogs, but he had never seen a creature as big as this. He could not distinguish its breed; all he could see was a silhouette that stood out against the lighter surface of the ground. Yet this was enough to show that the beast was so big and threatening that Barlach could not stir. He saw the brute slowly turn its head, almost as if coincidentally, and stare at him. Its round eyes were bright, blank orbs.

The suddenness of the encounter, the huge size of the animal, and the strangeness of its appearance seemed to paralyze Barlach. Although he did not lose his head, he did forget the need for action, and simply stared at the beast, unafraid but spellbound. Evil had always had this kind of fascination for him; it was a huge riddle he was repeatedly tempted to solve.

Suddenly the dog leaped at him. Its gigantic shadowy bulk hurtled through the air, an unleashed mass of bloodthirsty power. Barlach hardly had time to raise his left arm to protect his throat before the weight of the raving beast threw him to the ground. It all seemed so natural and so in keeping with the laws of this world that the inspector was not even surprised at his inability to utter the slightest sound. The beast was now on top of him, with its jaws about his forearm, when Barlach heard the whipcrack of a shot. A sudden convulsion ran through the dog's massive body and Barlach felt its warm blood oozing over his hand. The hound was dead.

The weight of the beast lay heavy upon him. Barlach passed his hand over its smooth, sweaty fell; trembling and with some effort, he rose to his feet and wiped his hand in the thin grass. Chance was at his side, concealing his revolver in his coat pocket as he came up.

"Are you all right, Inspector?" he asked, looking with concern at Barlach's torn sleeve.

"Perfectly. The brute's teeth didn't reach my arm."

Chance bent down and turned the creature's head: the light fell dully on its lifeless eyes.

"Teeth like a wolf's," he said with a shudder. "The beast would have torn you to pieces, Inspector."

"You saved my life, Chance."

"Don't you ever carry a gun?" Chance wanted to know.

Barlach prodded the motionless mass with his toe. "Not very often," he answered, and the two fell silent.

The dead hound lay on the bare, muddy ground, and both men looked down at it. The blood that had welled from the creature's throat like a dark lava stream had spread out to form a black pool at their feet.

When they looked up again the scene at the house had changed. The music had stopped, the lighted windows had been thrown open and men and women in evening clothes were leaning out. Barlach and Chance looked at each other, rather embarrassed at standing in front of a tribunal, as it were, and that in the middle of nowhere—where the birds and the bees bid each other good night, the inspector thought grimly.

In the mid-most of the five windows was standing a solitary man, apparently isolated from the rest. In a distinguished, clear voice he demanded to know who they were and what they were doing.

"Police officers," answered Barlach calmly, adding that they had come to speak to the host, Herr Gastmann. The man replied to the effect that he found it extraordinary that they should need to shoot a dog in order to speak to Herr Gastmann. Moreover, his desire right then was to listen to Bach. With that, he closed the window, giving the action a quality of unhurried finality, as unemotional and indifferent to outside disturbances as the tone of his voice.

From the other windows came a babel of exclamations: "Disgraceful!" "Scandalous!" "What boors these policemen are!" Then the heads withdrew, the windows closed one by one, and all was silent again.

The two policemen had no choice but to retrace their steps. At the main gate in front of the house, a solitary figure was waiting for them, pacing nervously up and down.

"Quick, flash your light on him," whispered Barlach. The sudden beam of Chance's flashlight revealed above the starched collar and white tie a square, bloated face, not undistinguished yet of limited intelligence. A large stone sparkled on the finger of one hand. At Barlach's whisper the light was switched off again.

"Who the devil are you?" growled the stout man.

"Inspector Barlach. Are you Herr Gastmann?"

"Colonel von Schwendi, member of the National Council. Good God in heaven, man, what do you think you're doing with all this shooting?"

"We're making some inquiries and have to speak to Herr Gastmann, Councillor," answered Barlach, quite unperturbed.

The Councillor was not to be easily mollified. "A Separatist, eh?" he thundered.

Barlach decided to address him by his alternative title. "You're mistaken, Colonel," he answered warily. "We're not interested in the political affairs of—"

But before Barlach could go on, the Colonel had become even more furious than the Councillor had been. "A Communist!" he roared. "Hell and damnation! As an officer and a gentleman I will not have target practice in the middle of a private concert! I will not allow any demonstration against Western civilization! I'll summon the Swiss army if need be to restore order!"

The Councillor was obviously beside himself. Barlach saw that it was time to take the situation firmly in hand.

"Don't put the Councillor's remarks in your report, Chance," he said in official tones.

The Councillor immediately regained a modicum of composure. "What report, man?" he demanded.

As an inspector in the Criminal Investigation Department of the Berne Police, Barlach explained, he was condicting an official investigation into the murder of police lieutenant Schmied. It was his duty, he continued, to include in his report anything and everything that certain persons, whom it was found necessary to question, might say. But since—and he hesitated for a moment about which title he should use this time—since the Colonel had evidently misjudged the situation, he would not record the Councillor's words in his report.

The Colonel was confused.

"So, you're from the police," he said. "That's different." He begged their pardon and was sure they would understand his outburst; after all, he had attended a special meeting of his political party that morning, had lunched at the Turkish Embassy shortly thereafter, and from there had gone to a meeting of an association of army officers (The Swiss Swords), of which he had been elected president. Afterward, he had celebrated his election with a glass or two at his club, and finally he had come to this reception of Gastmann's in honor of a world-famous pianist. He was dead tired.

When he had finished, Barlach again patiently inquired whether he might speak to Herr Gastmann.

"Just what do you want with him?" demanded von Schwendi. "What does Gastmann have to do with a murdered police lieutenant?"

"The lieutenant was a guest at Gastmann's party last Wednesday night and was murdered in Twann on his way home."

"Just goes to show," sneered the Councillor. "Gastmann invites anyone and everyone to his soirées—an incident was bound to happen sooner or later."

He stood in silence, apparently lost in thought.

"I'm Gastmann's lawyer," he went on at last. "Why did you have to choose tonight of all nights to call on him unannounced? You could at least have telephoned."

Barlach explained that they had only just discovered that Schmied and Gastmann had been acquainted.

The Colonel was still not satisfied. "What about the dog? What am I supposed to say about that?"

"The dog attacked me, and Chance had to shoot."

"All right, then," said von Schwendi in a more amicable tone. "There's no way you can see Gastmann tonight. Even the police occasionally have to make some exception for social obligations. I'll have a word with Gastmann later on and will come to your office in the morning. By the way, do you fellows happen to have a picture of this Schmied?"

Barlach took a photograph from his wallet and gave it to him.

"Thank you," said the Councillor. Then with a nod he went into the house.

Barlach and Chance found themselves once more in front of the rusty bars of the gate. The front of the house was as dark as it had been before.

"There's not much you can do with a member of the National Council," said Barlach, "and when he's a colonel and a lawyer to boot, you have three kinds of devil to deal with at once. So here we are with a murder on our hands and nothing we can do about it."

Chance was silent and seemingly deep in thought. "It's nine o'clock, Inspector," he announced at last. "I think the best thing we can do is drive to Lamboing and find out what the officer there can tell us about this Gastmann."

"Right," answered Barlach. "You go and talk to him. Find out why no one in Lamboing knows anything about Schmied's visits to Gastmann. I'm going to that little restaurant at the entrance to the gorge. I have to do something about my stomach. I'll wait for you there."

They walked back along the path to the car and Chance drove off. It only took him a few minutes to reach Lamboing.

He found the policeman with Clenin, who had walked over from Twann, sitting at a table in the inn. The Lamboing constable was short, fat, and red-haired. His name was Jean Pierre Charnel. They sat apart from the farmers, importantly aware of having official business to discuss.

Chance joined them and soon managed to dispel the suspicion they felt for their colleague from Berne. But Charnel was still uncomfortable, because he realized he now had to speak German instead of his customary French and it was a language he had never properly mastered. They drank white wine and Chance ate bread and cheese with it. He made no mention of the fact that he had just come from Gastmann's. Instead, he asked whether they had any new clues.

"Non," said Charnel. "No sign of the assassin. On n'a rien trouvé. Nothing." He then went on to say that there was only one person in the district about whom the authorities knew very little—Herr Gastmann. He had bought a place called the Maison Rollier and he entertained there on a big scale. In fact, he had given a large party only the previous Wednesday, but Schmied had not been present. Gastmann knew absolutely nothing, hadn't even recognized Schmied's name. "Schmied n'était pas chez Gastmann—absolutely impossible."

Chance listened to Charnel's pidgeon German and suggested he interrogate others who happened to have been present at Gastmann's house that night.

"I've done that," Clenin announced. "There's a writer who lives at Schernelz near Ligerz. He knows Gastmann well and often goes to his house. He was there last Wednesday. But he'd never heard of Schmied, either, didn't know the name, and said he didn't believe Gastmann had ever had a policeman in his house."

"A writer, you say?" repeated Chance and frowned. "I'll probably have to confront this oddball myself some time. Writers are always shady characters, but I know how to handle these smart alecs. Meanwhile, what sort of person is this Gastmann, Charnel?"

"Très riche," Charnel answered enthusiastically. "Spends money like water, and très noble. He give my fiancée tips"—and he pointed proudly to the waitress—"comme un roi, but he no want anything from her. Jamais."

"What's his business?"

"Philosophe."

"What do you mean by that, Charnel?"

"A man who think much but do nothing."

"How does he make a living?"

Charnel shook his head. "He earn no money, he got money. He pay taxes for all in the village Lamboing. It's enough for us that Gastmann the best man in the whole canton is."

"Even so," Chance replied, "it may be necessary to ask some pretty searching questions of Herr Gastmann. I'll come out tomorrow and have a talk with him."

"Then watch out for his dog," warned Charnel. "Un chien très dangereux."

Chance stood up and patted the Lamboing police officer reassuringly on the shoulder. "Don't worry, I'll take care of his dog."

It was ten o'clock when Chance left Clenin and Charnel to drive to the restaurant where Barlach was waiting. Nevertheless, he stopped the car when he reached the spot where the dirt road branched off to Gastmann's house. He got out and walked slowly to the front gate and then along the wall. The house was just as it had been earlier, dark and solitary, surrounded by huge poplars swaying in the wind. The limousines were still parked outside. Chance did not go all the way around the house, but rather stopped at a corner from which he could survey the lighted rear windows. From time to time the figures of men and women were silhouetted against the yellow panes. Keeping close to the wall to avoid being seen, Chance looked across the grass to where the hound had been lying on the bare ground. Someone must have taken the body away, for there was no sign of it now except the pool of blood, which still gleamed dark in the light of the windows. Chance returned to the car.

Barlach was not in the restaurant when he got there. The waitress said that he had left for Twann about half an hour ago, after he had finished his brandy. He hadn't been in the restaurant more than five minutes, she assured him.

As he drove off, Chance wondered what the old man was up to, but he gave up his speculations when the narrow road demanded his full attention. He drove past the bridge where they had waited and down into the woods. He gradually became aware of a strange and uncanny feeling, which left him in a pensive mood. He had been driving quickly, and suddenly caught sight of the lake gleaming below him, a nocturnal mirror edged by white crags. With something of a shock he realized he had reached the scene of the murder. A dark figure detached itself from the wall of rock and clearly signaled the car to stop.

Without knowing why he did so, Chance pulled up and opened the passenger door. He regretted his action almost immediately as he remembered in a flash that this was precisely what Schmied had done a few seconds before he was shot. Chance's hand flew to his coat pocket and his fingers closed round the revolver. Its cold metal reassured him. The figure came closer, and Chance realized that it was Barlach. Even so his tension did not immediately relax; he was pale with an uncanny horror which he was unable to explain even to himself. Barlach leaned forward and they looked into each other's faces. Those few seconds seemed like hours. Neither spoke a word and their eyes were like stones. Then Barlach got into the car, and Chance's fingers released their grip on the hidden revolver.

"Drive on, Walter," said Barlach in an unfeeling tone. Chance winced at the sound of his first name, for the old man had never used it before. The inspector, however, continued to address him in this more intimate manner from now on.

They had passed through Biel before Barlach broke the silence, asking what information Chance had managed to gather in Lamboing, "since we now probably have to call the place by its French name." Chance reported that both Charnel and Clenin thought it quite impossible that Schmied could have been a guest at Gastmann's. Barlach said nothing to this, but when Chance mentioned the author who lived in Schernelz, the inspector said he would interview the fellow himself.

Chance spoke with more animation than usual, relieved that

184 · Friedrich Dürrenmatt

they were at least talking again. But he also had another reason: he was trying to conceal the strange fear he had felt. Despite his efforts, however, they had again relapsed into silence even before they reached Schüpfen.

Shortly after eleven the car drew up in front of Barlach's house in Altenberg and the inspector got out.

"Thanks again, Walter," he said, and shook his hand. "I don't mean to embarrass you by mentioning it again, but you did save my life."

He stood on the pavement and watched the car drive rapidly away till the rear light was lost in the distance. "Now he can drive as fast as he likes," he said to himself.

He entered his house by the unlocked door. Standing in the book-lined study, he put his hand in his coat pocket and took out a weapon, which he carefully placed on the desk beside the brass snake. It was a large, heavy revolver.

Then he slowly removed his overcoat, revealing his left arm thickly wrapped in bandages. The bandages were loosely wound and bulky, the kind men use to protect themselves when training dogs to attack intruders.

The inspector knew from experience that some unpleasantness (for so he described the ever-present friction between himself and Lutz) was to be expected next morning. "All Saturdays are the same," he said to himself, as he walked across the Altenberg Bridge. "These functionaries bare their teeth out of a guilty conscience because they've done nothing sensible all week long." He was wearing formal black for Schmied's funeral, which was to take place at ten o'clock. There was no way he could avoid attending, and this was the real cause of his irritability.

Von Schwendi called at police headquarters shortly after eight that morning. He bypassed Barlach and asked to see Lutz, to whom Chance had just reported the happenings of the previous night.

Von Schwendi belonged to the same political party as Lutz, the Liberal-Conservative Socialist Association of Independents, and had played some part in Lutz's advancement. Ever since the last party dinner, which had followed a meeting of the central committee, they were on a first-name basis, despite the fact that Lutz had not been elected to the local parliament seat. Von Schwendi explained

Lutz's nonelection by the fact that it was a sheer impossibility in Berne for anyone with the name of Lucius to become a local representative.

"You'd never believe, my dear Lucius," he began, almost before his stout figure was visible in the doorway of Lutz's office, "how these Berne policemen of yours behave. Shoot my client Gastmann's dog to shreds, a rare breed from South America, and violate culture, Anatol Kraushaar-Raffaeli's piano recital. A Swiss has no manners, no breadth of vision, and not the slightest trace of European culture. Three years of compulsory military training would do them all a world of good."

Lutz, who found the visit of his political colleague embarrassing and was apprehensive lest he embark on one of his usual endless tirades, offered von Schwendi a chair.

"You must understand," he began, intimidated despite himself, "that we are involved in a very tricky investigation. The young police officer who is mainly responsible for its conduct is, by Swiss standards at least, an able man. The old inspector who was with him last night is, I must admit, more than ready for the junk heap. I deeply regret the death of such a rare South American hound, particularly since I myself own a dog and love animals. But you can trust me to have this incident properly investigated."

"The trouble is," he went on, "our men haven't the foggiest notion of modern methods of criminal detection. When I recall what I saw in Chicago, I am forced to admit our present organization is absolutely hopeless."

He paused for a moment, embarrassed by von Schwendi's silence and by the unblinking stare the latter had fixed on him. His self-assurance was visibly oozing away and in an effort to conceal his consternation he asked whether the murdered Schmied had been a guest of his client Gastmann Wednesday night, for the police had some reason to believe he was.

"My dear Lucius," interjected the Colonel. "Let's ditch this nonsense. The police knew all about Schmied's visits to Gastmann, you can't fool me."

"What do you mean by that, Councillor?" Lutz demanded, bewilderment making him involuntarily relapse into formality. Actually, he never found it easy to call von Schwendi by his first name.

186 · *Friedrich Dürrenmatt*

The councillor leaned back and folded his hands across his chest. He bared his teeth in a grimace that he felt was particularly appropriate to his role as colonel and councillor. "Doc," he said, "I'd give a lot to know why you're trying to dump this Schmied affair on my friend Gastmann's shoulders. The police shouldn't give a damn about what goes on in the mountains—we're a far cry from the Gestapo, you know."

By now Lutz was utterly dumbfounded. "Why should you say we are trying to connect Schmied's murder with Gastmann?" he asked helplessly. "And why shouldn't we give a damn about a murder?"

"If you mean to tell me," von Schwendi persisted, "that you did not know that Schmied attended Gastmann's parties in Lamboing under the name of Dr. Prattl, lecturer in American Cultural History at the University of Munich, then you and the whole police force should resign on the grounds of abysmal criminal incompetence." Von Schwendi drummed impatiently on Lutz's desk with the fingers of his right hand.

"My dear Oscar, we knew absolutely nothing about that," said Lutz, relieved at having at last remembered the councillor's first name. "I am consumed by curiosity."

"Ah!" von Schwendi exclaimed drily.

In the moments of silence that followed Lutz became more and more uncomfortably conscious of a growing sense of inferiority. He knew that he would have to give way to the colonel step by step at every point. To cover his discomfort, he stared desperately at the Traffellets on the wall, at the marching soldiers and their waving Swiss flags, the general sitting on his horse. The councillor noted the magistrate's embarrassment with a certain satisfaction.

"So it's news to the police, is it?" he said, rubbing it in. "Once again they know less than the man on the street."

Unpleasant as the admission was, and intolerable as von Schwendi's overbearing behavior was, the police official had no choice but to admit that Schmied's visits to Gastmann had nothing to do with official business, and his repeated presence in Lamboing had been unknown to the police. He blustered a little when he pointed out that Schmied, when off duty, was entitled to behave in a private capacity as he thought fit, though it was a complete mystery why he should have chosen to assume a false name.

Von Schwendi leaned forward and gazed intently at Lutz with heavy, bloodshot eyes. "That explains it, then," he said. "Schmied was spying for a foreign power."

"What are you saying?" Lutz was at an absolute loss for words.

"From now on," the councillor persisted, "the primary duty of the police is to find out Schmied's reason for going to Gastmann's."

"In that case the police must first know a great deal more about Gastmann, my dear Oscar," Lutz pointed out.

"Gastmann is no threat to the police," von Schwendi replied, "and I don't want you or any other police officer to concern themselves with him. That's his wish, he's my client, and it's my job to see that his wishes are respected."

Lutz was so nonplussed by this impertinent reply that at first he could find nothing to say. He lit a cigarette, forgetting in his confusion to offer one to von Schwendi. Then he sat back in his chair and reminded his visitor: "Unfortunately, the fact that Schmied went to Gastmann's compels us to give your client a measure of our attention, my dear Oscar."

Von Schwendi was not to be diverted. "It also compels you to give me a little of your attention, for I am Gastmann's attorney," he said. "You can be glad, Lutz, that you have me to deal with. I'm not here merely to help Gastmann—I'm ready to help you, too. Admittedly, the whole case is unpleasant for my client, but I think it must be even more embarrassing for you because the police have not advanced very far, have they, and it seems unlikely they will ever get any further."

"The police," answered Lutz, "have solved just about every murder case, a fact that can be proven by statistics. I admit that we have encountered unforeseen difficulties in the present instance, but we have also"—he hesitated a second—"made substantial progress. How else do you think we got on the trail of Gastmann in the first place? And aren't we the reason why Gastmann sent you here? It's Gastmann who faces embarrassment, not us, and it's up to him to put his cards on the table. Schmied was a visitor at his house, even if under a false identity, and that fact alone compels the police to investigate him, for the unusual behavior of the deceased probably has a lot to do with Gastmann himself. Gastmann must be made to talk, either personally or

188 · *Friedrich Dürrenmatt*

through you. Are you prepared to tell us honestly and completely why Schmied went to Gastmann's house under a false name, not once but on several different occasions, as we have discovered?"

"Very well," said von Schwendi. "Let's clear the air. You'll soon see that it's not so much a question of my explaining Gastmann as of you explaining Schmied. It's you, my dear Lucius, who are in the dock here, not we."

With these words he produced a large white sheet of paper, which he unfolded and placed on Lutz's desk. "Here are the names of the persons who have been guests at Gastmann's house," he said. "The list is complete. I have divided it into three sections. The first section we can ignore—it's of no interest because it consists only of artists. It comprises the names of only small-time home-bred artists—the sort that write plays about the Battle of Morgarten or paint pictures of mountains. It does not, of course, include the names of such great performers as Kraushaar-Raffaeli, who, anyway, are foreigners. The second section consists of industrialists; you'll recognize their names: they're men of rank, men whom I regard as the cream of Swiss society. I say this quite openly, even though I myself come from peasant stock on my maternal grandmother's side."

"And the third group?" asked Lutz, when the councillor suddenly stopped speaking. Von Schwendi's calm gaze only increased Lutz's nervousness, which, of course, was his intention.

"The third section," he continued at last, "represents the major complication of the Schmied case. It makes the whole incident unpleasant for you and for the industrialists, as I freely admit. It compels me to speak of matters that should actually remain secret even from the police. But since your Berne flunkies could not resist searching out Gastmann, and since, unfortunately, it has come to light that Schmied was in Lamboing, the industrialists see no alternative but to have me give the police only as much information as pertains to the case. It is a matter of some embarrassment to us, since it means we shall have to reveal important political activities we should have preferred to keep secret. But it may well be embarrassing to you, too, because the people named in the third list are people over whom you, as policemen, have no authority or jurisdiction."

"I don't understand a word you are saying," Lutz interjected.

"That's because you have never understood politics, my dear Lucius," was von Schwendi's reply. "The third section contains the names of members of the staff of a foreign embassy, and the embassy concerned considers it desirable that its staff should not be associated in the public mind with certain of the industrialists whose names appear on my list."

At last Lutz began to understand the councillor, and a long silence descended over the magistrate's office. The telephone rang and Lutz took up the receiver merely to snap into it, "In conference," whereupon the silence was reestablished. At last he said, "As far as I understand, official negotiations are currently underway with this power for a new trade agreement."

"Precisely. Negotiations are being conducted officially and at high levels; after all, diplomats have to have something to do. But there are also unofficial negotiations, and in Lamboing the talks are private and off the record. In modern industry there are some affairs in which the State may not interfere, my dear magistrate."

"Of course," agreed Lutz, totally intimidated by the colonel's words and manners.

"Of course," repeated von Schwendi. "And unfortunately, your deceased subordinate, Lieutenant Schmied, insinuated himself into these secret negotiations under a false name."

Von Schwendi saw by the awkward silence which again intervened that he had calculated rightly. Lutz was now so utterly at a loss that the councillor could do whatever he wanted with him. As is frequently the case with somewhat simple natures, the policeman was so put out by the unexpected developments in the Schmied case that he was ready to be driven to almost any concession, even though it might seriously prejudice further legitimate investigation. Nevertheless, Lutz made yet another effort to pretend he had the situation under control.

"My dear Oscar," he said, "aren't we taking all this a bit too seriously? Naturally our Swiss industrialists have every right to negotiate privately with whomever they like, including foreign governments. I don't dispute it, and the police don't interfere in such matters. But I must repeat that Schmied went to Gastmann's as a private individual, and I am therefore prepared to offer an official apology, for it certainly was wrong of him to masquerade under a false name and a false occupation. Still, if you're a police-man, you sometimes have certain inhibitions. But he wasn't there alone; there were all those artists you talked about, too."

"The necessary framework to cloak our affairs. We live in a cultured society, Lutz, and the word has to get around. The ne-gotiations had to be kept secret and secrets are safest in a crowd of artists. All dine together, good food, wine, cigars, women, con-versation. Then the artistic ones get bored, gather in little groups, drink, and fail to notice that the capitalists and the foreign repre-sentatives have also drifted together. They don't notice it because it doesn't interest them. Artists are only interested in art. But a policeman who happens to be there, too, can learn an awful lot. No, Lutz, the Schmied case is a serious matter."

"I can only repeat," answered Lutz, "that we have no knowl-edge of why Schmied visited Gastmann."

"If the police did not send him there, someone else did," re-turned von Schwendi. "Other governments, my dear Lucius, are deeply interested in what has been going on at Lamboing. It's called global policy."

"Schmied was not a spy."

"We have every reason to assume that he was. It would be bet-ter for the honor of Switzerland that he should have been spying for a foreign power than as a squealer for the Swiss police."

"Well, he's dead now," sighed Lutz, who would have given any-thing at that moment to be able to put a few questions to Schmied himself.

"That's not our concern," said the colonel. "I don't want to make any accusations, but it is a fact that the people who insisted on the secrecy of the negotiations at Lamboing were the represen-tatives of the foreign power concerned. As far as we're concerned, it's a matter of money; with them it's a matter of national policy. Let's face it. If these people are behind Schmied's death, it's going to be very difficult for you fellows to take positive action."

Lutz rose from his chair and walked over to the window. "I still don't see where your client Gastmann comes into the picture," he said slowly.

Von Schwendi fanned himself with the sheet of paper. "Gast-mann put his house at the disposal of the parties concerned. That's all."

"But why Gastmann?"

His highly respected client, growled the colonel, happened to be the only man with the necessary background and qualifications. As a former Argentine ambassador to China, he enjoyed the trust of the foreign power, and as a former executive of the Tin Trust he had the confidence of the industrialists. Besides that, he happened to live in Lamboing.

"What difference does that make, Oskar?"

Von Schwendi smiled patronizingly. "Had you ever heard of Lamboing before Schmied was murdered?"

"No."

"That's just it, because nobody has ever heard of the place. We needed an obscure site for our meetings. That's all there is to it, so you can leave Gastmann in peace. You can understand that he wants no dealings with the police and doesn't want them sniffing around with their everlasting questions and investigations. That technique is all very well when you are dealing with crooks and criminals who've gotten themselves into a mess, but not for a man who once refused election to the French Academy. Besides, your policemen really behave very badly—nobody shoots a dog in the middle of a Bach recital. Not that Gastmann feels offended—he really doesn't give a damn. You could shoot his house to pieces and he wouldn't bat an eyelash. It's just that it doesn't make any sense to pester him any more, especially since there are forces behind this murder that have nothing to do with our worthy Swiss industrialists or with Gastmann."

Lutz paced back and forth in front of the window. "We shall have to concentrate our efforts on probing into Schmied's private life," he observed. "As for the foreign power of which you speak, that is a matter for the federal attorney. To what extent he will want to take up the case, I cannot yet say. But he will hand over most of the work to us, you can be sure of that. Meanwhile, you can count on our sparing Gastmann as much as possible. Naturally, we will also dispense with searching his house. Should it become necessary to question him later, I will ask you to arrange the meeting and will invite you to be present. In this way we may be able to dispose of the formalities in an informal way. It's thus not so much an investigation as it is a mere formality within the investigation. Circumstances may dictate that Gastmann be interrogated, even if there is no purpose to it. The important thing is that the investigation is complete. We'll talk about art in order to make the interview as innocuous as possible, and I won't ask any questions. If that should become necessary, purely pro forma, you understand, I'll let you know ahead of time."

By this time the councillor had also risen to his feet and the two men stood facing each other. Von Schwendi patted Lutz on the shoulder.

"So that's agreed," he said. "You'll leave Gastmann alone, Lutzi—I have your word for it. I'll leave this paper; the list is accurate and complete. Its compilation meant telephoning most of the night, and there is great concern about it. The important speculation now is whether our foreign friends will want to pursue negotiations when they find out about the Schmied murder. Millions are at stake, Doc, millions! I wish you luck with your inquiries. You'll need it."

With these words von Schwendi barged out of the room.

Lutz had just had time to glance through the councillor's list and note with a groan the celebrity of many of the names it contained—How did I ever get involved in such an unholy mess? he thought to himself—when Barlach came in. He entered, as usual, without knocking. The old man had come to ask for authority to visit Gastmann of Lamboing, but Lutz put off the discussion till the afternoon. It was time to go to the funeral, he said, as he stood up.

Barlach raised no objection and the two men left the room together. With each passing moment Lutz became more aware of the foolishness of his promise to leave Gastmann in peace, and he feared Barlach's justified and sharp opposition. They reached the street in silence, both in black coats. They turned up their collars. It was raining, but it was not worthwhile to open their umbrellas for the few steps to the car. Blatter drove. The rain was pouring down, lashing slantwise against the windows. Lutz and Barlach sat motionless, each in his own corner. I must tell him soon, thought Lutz, and looked at Barlach's calm profile. Barlach put his hand to his stomach as he had done so often in recent months.

"Are you in pain?" asked Lutz.

"Always," answered Barlach.

They fell silent again, and Lutz thought, I'll tell him this afternoon. Blatter drove slowly. The surrounding buildings disappeared behind an opaque veil, the rain was so heavy. Trams and automobiles somehow managed to swim through the monstrous oceans of descending water. Lutz did not know where they were; the dripping windowpanes defeated all efforts to see through them. Inside the car it grew darker and darker. Lutz lit a cigarette, exhaled, and determined to avoid any discussion with Barlach concerning the Gastmann case. He said, "The newspapers will report about the murder. We couldn't hold it back any longer."

"There's no need to any more," answered Barlach. "We're on the track of something now."

"There never was any need," said Lutz, crushing out his cigarette.

Barlach did not reply. Lutz would have liked to quarrel with him, but peered through the window instead. The rain began to subside a little. They had already reached the avenue leading to the Schlosshalden Cemetery, which now came toward them between the steaming treetrunks as a dripping gray mass of masonry. Blatter drove into the courtyard and stopped. They got out, opened their umbrellas, and set off on foot between the rows of tombstones. They did not have to look for long. The gravestones and crosses receded, and it seemed to the two men that they had stumbled across a construction site. The ground was dotted with freshly dug graves that had been covered with planks. The moisture from the wet grass penetrated their shoes and the muddy earth clung to them. In the middle of this open space, among these still unoccupied graves in the depths of which the rain had collected in dirty pools, between a forest of provisional wooden crosses and mounds of earth thickly covered with rotting flowers and wreaths, a group of people was standing around a gaping hole.

Schmied's coffin had not yet been lowered. The priest was reading from the Bible and beside him, holding an umbrella over both their heads, the gravedigger, wearing a ridiculous work suit that resembled a frock coat, and shifting his weight from one frozen foot to the other. Barlach and Lutz stopped at the graveside. Someone was crying. It was Frau Schönler, round and shapeless under the unceasing rain. At her side was Chance; he had no umbrella, but the collar of his raincoat was turned up and the belt dangled loosely at his side. He was wearing a black bowler hat. Beside him was a girl, pale, hatless, her blond hair hanging down in dripping strands—Anna, thought Barlach involuntarily. Chance bowed to them; Lutz nodded in return, but the inspector gave no sign of recognition. He looked across at the other figures around the grave—all policemen, all out of uniform, all with the same raincoats, the same black bowler hats, holding their umbrellas like sabers: fantastic mourners blown in from God knows where, unreal in their ingenuousness.

Behind them in orderly ranks stood the municipal band in their black and red uniforms, hastily summoned and desperately trying to protect their brass instruments under their coats. Such was the group around the coffin, a wooden box without a wreath, without flowers, and yet it was somehow the only warm, homely thing in this ceaseless rain that continued to fall in torrents.

The priest had stopped speaking some time ago. No one noticed. All that mattered was the rain, and they heard nothing else. The priest coughed. Once. Then several times. Suddenly there was a blare of trombones, French horns, cornets, and bassoons, the instruments proud and ceremonious like yellow lightning flashes in the floods of rain. Then they, too, subsided, faded away, gave up. Everyone crawled under their umbrellas and raincoats. The storm grew more violent, shoes sank into the mud, water streamed into the empty grave. Lutz bowed and stepped forward. He looked down at the wet coffin and bowed again.

"Men"—his voice was almost inaudible through the sheets of rain—"men, our comrade Schmied is no more." Suddenly his graveside oration was interrupted by the raucous bawling of a song:

> "The devil goes round,
> The devil goes round,
> And beats us all into the ground!"

Two men in black frock coats came staggering across the cemetery. Without overcoats or umbrellas, they were totally at the mercy of the rain. Their clothes clung to their limbs. Both wore top hats on their heads, from which the water streamed over their faces. Between them they carried a huge laurel wreath whose ribbon hung down and trailed along the ground. Two huge bruisers, butchers in tails, so drunk that they were always on the verge of falling, but since neither of them stumbled at the same time, they managed to steady themselves by clutching on the laurel wreath, which foundered like a ship in distress. Suddenly they struck up a fresh song:

> "The miller's wife, her husband's dead,
> But she's alive, alive-o!
> She sells herself to earn her bread,
> And she's alive, alive-o!"

They ran up to the group of mourners and plunged right through them between Frau Schönler and Chance. No one hindered them, for everyone was watching as if petrified. The two then stumbled away through the wet grass, each holding the other up, clinging to each other, falling over graves and overthrowing crosses in their drunken oblivion. Their song died away in the rain, and the last glimpse of them soon disappeared in the fog.

> "Everything passes over,
> Everything passes by . . ."

was the last that was heard of them. Only the wreath remained, carelessly tossed onto the coffin, bearing the words in smeared ink on the muddy ribbon: "To our dear Dr. Prattl."

By the time the people around the grave had recovered their composure and were beginning to express their outrage at what had happened, and the Municipal Band was desperately trying to retrieve the situation, the storm suddenly increased to such fury that everyone was forced to run for shelter. Only the gravediggers, black scarecrows in the howling wind and drenching downpour, were left to lower the coffin into the ground at last.

As Barlach and Lutz were back in the car and Blatter was driving along an avenue overrun by fleeing police and municipal bandsmen, Lutz finally gave vent to his indignation.

"What an intolerable man that Gastmann is!" he cried.

"Why do you say that?" asked Barlach.

"Schmied went to Gastmann's parties under the name of Prattl."

"Then that little exhibition was meant as a warning," returned Barlach, but without asking for further information.

They drove toward the quarter where Lutz lived. Now was the moment, thought Lutz, to speak to the old man about Gastmann and tell him he was to be left alone. But again he said nothing. At the Burgernziel he got out of the car, leaving Barlach alone.

"Shall I take you into town, Inspector?" asked the officer at the wheel.

"No, take me home, Blatter."

Blatter sped along. It was raining less heavily now, so that when they reached the Muristalden, Barlach was bathed for a few seconds in dazzling light as the sun burst through the clouds, vanished once again, and came back a second time—all part of the wild game of the elements. Monster clouds came hurtling from the west, banked up against the mountain sides, throwing fantastic shadows across the town that lay by the river like a submissive body between forest and hills. Barlach passed a weary hand over his wet overcoat; his narrow eyes sparkled as he avidly drank in the spectacle. The world was beautiful. Blatter stopped. Barlach thanked him and got out. Even though the rain had ceased, the wind was still high, a wet, cold wind. The old man stood waiting while Blatter turned the big car, then he waved once more as the officer drove off. He walked across to the river bank. The water was high and dirty brown. An old rusty baby carriage floated by, branches of trees, a young pine; then a little paper boat came dancing along. Barlach stood for some time looking at his beloved Aare. Then he walked through his garden to the house.

Barlach removed his wet shoes before entering the house. At the doorway to his study he stopped short. A man was sitting at his desk and rummaging through Schmied's briefcase. With his right hand he was toying with Barlach's Turkish knife.

"So it's you," said the old man.

"Yes, it's me," said the other.

Barlach closed the door and sat down in his armchair, facing the desk. He watched in silence as the other went on calmly turning over the papers from Schmied's briefcase, an almost rustic figure, calm and reserved, with short hair and deep-set eyes in a full, large-boned face.

"So you call yourself Gastmann now," said the old man at last.

The other took out his pipe and filled it, keeping his eyes all the time on Barlach. He lit his pipe and then tapped Schmied's brief case with his forefinger: "You've known that for some time. You set that young fellow on my track. These notes are yours."

He shut the briefcase. Barlach glanced at his desk and saw that his revolver was still there with the butt turned toward him. He had only to put out his hand. He said: "I'll never stop hunting you down. One day I'll even provide proof of your crimes."

"You'll have to hurry, Barlach," answered the other. "You don't have much time left. The doctors give you one more year and that only if you let them operate at once."

"True," said the old man. "One more year. But I can't let them operate now. I have to act—it's my last chance."

"Your last," confirmed the other. Then they fell silent again, sitting there as though they would never move or speak again.

"It's over forty years," began the other at last, "since we first met in the decaying Jewish wine shop in the Bosporus. A moon like a slice of Gruyère cheese hung between the clouds, and its light fell on our heads through the rotting rafters. I remember it very well. At the time, Barlach, you were still a young Swiss policeman working for the Turks, who had come to the Bosporus to institute some sort of reform, and I—I was a footloose adventurer, as I still am, voraciously trying to find out the meaning of my own unique existence, and that of this mysterious world. We loved each other at first sight, sitting opposite each other among Jews in caftans and unwashed Greeks. But then that infernal local schnapps that we used to drink, made of fermented dates and fiery potions from the cornfields of Odessa, began to work on us. Our eyes shone like red-hot coals in the Turkish night and our conversation became heated and impetuous. Oh, I love to think of that hour—it determined the course of your life as well as mine."

He laughed.

The old man just sat there and gazed at him in silence.

"You have one more year to live," the other continued. "And you've spent forty stubbornly tracking me down. That's how the account stands. Do you remember what we talked about that night, Barlach, in that stinking wine shop outside Tophane with its air thick with clouds of Turkish cigarette smoke? Your theory was that human imperfection, the fact that we can never predict with any degree of certainty the way others will act, and that we will never be able to calculate exactly and on every occasion the ever-present element of chance, was the reason why most crimes would necessarily have to be solvable. You considered committing a crime a stupidity, because it was impossible to deal with people as if they were chessmen. I, on the other hand, maintained—more for the sake of argument than because I believed it at the time—that it is just this chaos in human relationships that makes it possible to commit a crime that could not be discovered. It was because of this that the majority of crimes were not only not solved but were incapable of solution because the world never even knew they had been committed. So we went on arguing, seduced by the infernal burning of the schnapps the Jewish innkeeper brought us and even more by the ardor of youth. Much later that night, just as the moon was sinking in the east, we made a wager, a bet with the satanic appeal of an impious joke that blasphemes the divinity. And we did it only because it intrigued us like the devil's own temptation of the spirit through itself."

"That's right," said Barlach quietly. "That's when we made that wager."

"But you never thought," laughed the other, "when we woke with a hangover in that filthy wine shop next morning—you on a rotting bench and I under a table still wet with schnapps—you never thought I would see it through."

"I never thought it possible that any man would even try." They fell silent.

" 'Lead us not into temptation,' " resumed the other. "Your innocence was never in danger of succumbing to temptation, but it was your innocence that tempted me. I accepted it boldly and proved, as I promised, that I could actually commit a major crime in your presence without your being able to convict me of it."

"Three days later," said Barlach softly, immersed in his memories, "we were walking across the Mahmud Bridge with a German shopkeeper and you pushed him into the water right in front of my eyes."

"The poor devil couldn't swim, and you weren't much of a swimmer yourself, for when you tried to save him they had to drag you half drowned out of the muddy waters of the Golden Horns," continued the other, unmoved. "The murder was com-

mitted on a fine Turkish summer day with a pleasant breeze from
the sea on a bridge crowded with courting couples from the European colony, Moslems, and local beggars. And yet you still
couldn't prove I murdered him. You had me arrested, had me put
through hours of cross examination, but all in vain and to no
purpose. The court accepted my version that the German committed suicide."

"You won because you proved that the German was on the
point of bankruptcy and had tried unsuccessfully to save the situation by defrauding his creditors," said Barlach, bitterly, paler than
usual.

"Naturally, I chose my victim carefully, my friend," laughed the
other.

"And that's how you first became a criminal," said the inspector.

The other played absentmindedly with the Turkish knife.

"I can't deny," he said at last in a casual tone, "that I am somewhat of a criminal. As the years went by I grew to be a better and
better criminal and you became a better and better detective. But
I was always one step ahead of you, and you've never been able
to catch up. I've crossed your path again and again, like a gray
spectre, committing crimes under your very nose, bolder, madder,
more heinous crimes, and each time you have failed to convict me.
You've triumphed over fools, but I have triumphed over you."

His expression as he smiled at Barlach was a mixture of contempt and amusement. "So we have lived our lives—you at the
beck and call of superior officers, working in police stations and
musty offices, a worthy fellow, climbing up the ladder of modest
success rung by rung, and pitting yourself against thieves, forgers,
miserable little crooks, and if you were lucky a pathetic murderer
now and then, all of them poor slobs who never really made a go
of life. How different my life has been. Sometimes underground in
the jungles of great cities, sometimes in the splendor of high positions with a breastful of decorations. Sometimes when I was in the
mood practicing virtue for the fun of it and sometimes, when the
mood changed, loving evil. What an adventure. You yearned to
destroy me, and I to exist in spite of you. That one night on the
Bosporus literally chained us to each other for ever!"

The man behind Barlach's desk clapped his hands in a single, violent concussion. "Now we're reaching the end of our careers," he said. "You've come back to Berne, a semifailure in a pleasant, sleepy town where no one can really distinguish between what is still living and what is already dead. And I've come back to Lamboing simply as a matter of caprice. It's nice to round things off: I was born in that Godforsaken village. A woman, long since dead, bore me without thought or purpose. Then, one rainy night when I was thirteen, I ran away. And now, after all the years between, we're both back where we started from. Give it up, my friend, it doesn't make any sense. Death doesn't wait."

With a movement so fast it was almost imperceptible, he threw the knife he had been playing with, hard and accurately. It grazed Barlach's cheek and buried its point deep in the back of the chair. The old man did not flinch; the other laughed.

"So you think I'm the one who killed Schmied?"

"My job is to investigate the case," answered the inspector.

The other stood up, the briefcase in his hand. "I'll take this with me."

"Someday I'll prove your crimes," said Barlach for the second time. "And this is my last chance."

"This briefcase contains the only evidence—and not much of it—that Schmied collected for you in Lamboing. You're lost without it. I know you well enough to know you have no copies or photostats."

"No," admitted the inspector. "I have nothing of the kind."

"Why don't you stop me with that revolver?" Gastmann asked with a sneer.

"Because you've taken the cartridges out," answered Barlach, unmoving.

"Exactly," said the other. He patted Barlach on the shoulder and walked past him. The door opened and closed. Outside, a second door opened and closed. Barlach remained in his armchair, the steel blade of the knife cold against his cheek. Suddenly he picked up the revolver and opened it. It was still loaded. Pistol in hand he jumped up, ran into the vestibule and tore open the front door.

The street was empty.

Then came the pain, the raging, throbbing, stabbing pain, like a sun rising inside him. It threw him on the sofa and convulsed him, scalding him with feverish heat. For some minutes he crawled around the floor on his hands and knees like an animal; then he threw himself full length across the rug and lay still somewhere in his study between the chairs, bathed in a cold sweat. "What is man?" he moaned softly, "What is man?"

Things gradually began to pick up again. Barlach actually felt better after the attack because he was at least and at long last free of pain. He ate little and drank mulled wine in little cautious sips. Even so, he did not fail to take his usual walk through the town and along the Bundestrasse. Though utterly exhausted, every step in the rain-washed air did him good.

He soon found himself in his superior's office, sitting face to face with Lutz, who gave no indication that he noticed anything amiss. Perhaps Lutz was too occupied with his own guilty conscience to be able to notice anything. He decided he would tell Barlach of his talk with von Schwendi before the afternoon was out rather than wait for the evening as he originally planned. He settled himself in his chair, assuming a cold impersonal attitude with his chest held high like the general in Traffelet's picture on the wall above him, and addressed the inspector in abrupt phrases, telegram-style. To his immeasurable surprise, however, the inspector raised no objection; he approved of everything; he agreed that it was better to wait for government instructions and to concentrate the investigations on Schmied's private life. Lutz was so surprised that he dropped his pose and became downright cheerful and talkative.

"Of course, I've found out a good deal about Gastmann," he said, "and I know enough about him to be sure that he could not possibly be regarded as a suspect."

"Of course," agreed the old man.

Lutz, who had received some odd bits of information from Biel during the lunch hour, assumed an air of self importance. "Born at Pockau in Saxony, son of a wholesale dealer in leather goods, he first appears as an Argentinian—was once Aregentine ambassador to China. Must have emigrated to South America as a young man. He turns up next as a Frenchman, usually on extended travels. He wears the cross of the Legion of Honor, and is well known as the author of several publications on biology. Characteristic of the man is the fact that he refused to be elected to the French Academy. I find that impressive."

"An interesting trait," agreed Barlach.

"We're still making inquiries about his two manservants. They have French passports but appear to come from Emmental. They were the ones who behaved so disgracefully at the funeral. A joke in the worst possible taste."

"Gastmann seems to be in the habit of making such jokes," observed the inspector.

"Perhaps he was upset over the death of his dog. We've got to be careful how we handle the Schmied case. Right now we're standing in a very bad light. It's lucky I happen to be a friend of von Schwendi's. Gastmann's a sophisticated cosmopolitan who enjoys the full confidence of Swiss industrialists."

"Then he has to be all right," said Barlach.

"Quite beyond suspicion."

"Definitely," the old man nodded.

"Unfortunately, we can't say the same about Schmied," added Lutz. He picked up the telephone and asked the switchboard operator to connect him with a government department.

As Lutz sat waiting for the call, the inspector, who had gotten up to leave, suddenly said: "I have to ask you for a week's sick leave, Dr. Lutz."

"Very well," answered Lutz, has hand over the receiver, for the call had just come through. "No need to come in on Monday."

Chance was waiting in Barlach's office. He got up when the old man came in. He looked calm, but the inspector sensed his underlying nervousness.

"Let's drive out to Gastmann's," said Chance. "It's getting late."

"We'll go to the writer instead," answered Barlach, putting on his overcoat.

"Detours, always detours," protested Chance as he followed Barlach down the stairs. The inspector stopped as they reached the door. "There's Schmied's blue Mercedes!"

Chance explained that it was now his, he had bought it and was paying for it in installments—after all, it had to belong to someone. He got into the driver's seat. Barlach took the seat beside him and they drove across the Bahnhofplatz toward the hospital.

"You're going via Ins again," grumbled Barlach.

"I like that route."

Barlach looked across the rain-washed fields. Everything was bathed in bright, tranquil light. A warm, mild sun hung in the sky and was already beginning to sink in the west. The two men were silent and only once, when they were between Kerzers and Müntschemier, did Chance speak. "Frau Schönler tells me you took a briefcase from Schmied's room," he said.

"Nothing official, Chance. Just private papers."

Chance made no reply and asked no more questions. When the speedometer needle pointed to eighty, Barlach felt obliged to tap its glass face. "Not so fast, Chance, not so fast! Not that I'm afraid; it's just that my stomach is jumpy. I'm an old man, you know."

The author received them in his study. It was an old, low room, and both visitors had to stoop to enter, as if passing under the yoke. A little white dog with a black head was still barking outside, and somewhere in the house a child was crying. The writer, dressed in jeans and a brown leather jacket, was sitting by the Gothic window. Without rising from his paper-strewn desk, he turned sideways in his chair to face his visitors. He dismissed all amenities and demanded to know what the police wanted of him.

He has no manners, thought Barlach. And he doesn't like the police. Writers never do like the police. He resolved to proceed cautiously, and even Chance felt uncomfortable with the whole situation. We mustn't let him study us, they both thought to themselves, or we'll end up in some book. Their offhand host gestured to two soft armchairs, and when they were seated they found to their annoyance that they were basking in the full light of the window. They themselves could hardly see his face, so confusing was the reflected light in this little green room with its rows of books.

"We're investigating the death of a police lieutenant Schmied," began the inspector. "He was the man who was found dead on the hill above Twann."

"I know. Dr. Prattl, the man who was spying on Gastmann," said the indistinct mass between them and the window. "Gastmann told me about it." He lit a cigarette, and for a few seconds his face was fully visible.

The two policemen saw it twist into a grin. "Do you want my alibi?"

"No," said Barlach.

"You don't think me capable of murder?" asked the novelist, visibly disappointed.

"No," answered Barlach, drily. "Not you."

The writer moaned. "There you have it, writers are shockingly underestimated in Switzerland."

Barlach laughed. "If you really want to know, we've already got your alibi. At half past twelve on the night of the murder you met a forester between Lamlingen and Schernelz and the two of you walked home together. The forester said you were quite jolly."

"I know. The local officer from Twann has already questioned the forester twice about me. And most of the other people around here, too. Even my mother-in-law. At least it indicates you did suspect me—success of a sort, I suppose."

Barlach thought, it's just a sign of this writer's vanity that he wants to be taken seriously. All three fell silent. Chance tried hard to catch a clear glimpse of the writer's face, but it was impossible in that light.

"What else do you want?" hissed the novelist at last.

"How often do you go to Gastmann's?"

"If this is to be a cross examination," the man said, edging farther into the shadow, "I'm busy."

"Come on, don't be so hard," said the inspector. "We just want to talk a little." The writer grunted, and Barlach began again. "How often do you go to Gastmann's?"

"Occasionally."

"Why?"

The old man was expecting another gruding answer, but the writer laughed, blew a thick cloud of smoke in their faces and said, "An interesting man, Gastmann. A man of his kind attracts a novelist as honey does bees. And he's a magnificent cook. Did you know that?"

He began to expound upon Gastmann's culinary skill, describing one dish after another. The two policemen listened for five minutes, then another five minutes. After their host devoted a solid quarter of an hour exclusively to Gastmann's cooking, Chance got up. "I'm sorry," he said, "but we didn't come here to discuss gastronomy."

But Barlach, invigorated by the talk, contradicted him, professing profound interest. He took up the theme himself, waxing enthusiastic as he talked of the culinary masterpieces of the Turks, Rumanians, Bulgarians, Yugoslavs, Czechs. He and the writer volleyed dishes at each other like tennis balls. Chance became increasingly nervous and cursed inwardly, but nothing could distract the other two men from their subject. Three-quarters of an hour had passed before they finally stopped, as replete as if they had partaken of a gargantuan meal. There was silence. The author lit a cigar. In the next room the child began to cry again and the dog barked outside. Chance took the opportunity to snap out the words: "Did Gastmann kill Schmied?"

The crudity of the question made Barlach shake his head. The dark figure in front of them replied, "You don't beat about the bush, do you?"

"I demand an answer," said Chance stolidly. He leaned forward to see the novelist's face, but the features were indistinguishable.

Barlach waited, curious to see how their man would react. The writer remained unruffled. "At what time was the policeman killed?" he asked.

Shortly after midnight, was Chance's reply.

"Of course I have no way of knowing whether the rules of logic are also valid for the police," the writer said. "Personally I doubt it very much. But since the local police have already ascertained with great ingenuity that I met the forester on the Schernelz road at half past twelve, which means that I must have left Gastmann not earlier than twenty past, Gastmann obviously could not have committed the murder."

Chance wanted to know whether any other guests had remained at Gastmann's after the writer had left. The author answered in the negative.

"Schmied left with the others?"

"Dr. Prattl was invariably the next to last to leave," answered the writer in a faintly mocking tone.

"Who was the last?"

"I."

Chance did not let up. "Were the servants present?"

"I don't know."

"Why can't you give a straight answer?" Chance demanded abruptly.

"I thought I had," snapped the novelist. "I don't generally concern myself with what other people's servants are doing."

With a degree of desperation and lack of restraint that caused the inspector some embarrassment, Chance boldly demanded to know their host's opinion of Gastmann: was he an honest man or a crook? Only a major miracle can prevent him from putting us in his next novel, Barlach thought with amusement.

In reply the author blew such a cloud of smoke into Chance's face that the officer began to cough. Then followed a long silence throughout the house; even the child had stopped crying.

"Gastmann is a bad man," the writer volunteered at last.

"And yet you continue to visit him often, presumably just because he cooks well?" sneered Chance, disbelieving, after a fresh fit of coughing.

"Precisely."

"I don't understand that."

The novelist laughed. "I'm a kind of policeman, too," he said, "even though I have no authority or state, no law or prison system behind me. It's my job as much as it is yours to keep a sharp eye on people."

His answer left Chance confused and at a loss for words. Barlach took up the thread. "Of course. We understand that," he said. The streaming sunlight suddenly faded from the window as he spoke. "I'm afraid that, in his unbridled zeal, my subordinate Chance has driven us into a bottleneck, and we'll be lucky to get out unscathed. But there is something to be said for the brashness of youth, and it seems that in this instance the ox in his impulsiveness has trampled a path for us." (At these words Chance turned red with fury.) "So let's stay with the questions he put and the answers you gave, and take the bull by the horns, as it were. What do you think of the whole affair, Sir? Is Gastmann capable of committing murder?"

It had suddenly become very dark in the room, but it never dawned on the writer to switch on the light. Instead he crossed to the window seat and faced the police officers, who looked back at him like two prisoners in a cell.

"I would say that Gastmann is capable of any crime under the sun." His voice was brutal in its judgment, with a hint of malice in it. "But I am also convinced that he did not murder Schmied."

"You know Gastmann pretty well then?"

"I've a good idea of the type of man he is."

"But it's *your* idea," corrected the old man coolly, speaking straight at the indistinct mass silhouetted in the window frame.

"What fascinates me about him," said the writer, "is not so much his cooking—though these days I find it difficult to raise much enthusiasm for anything else—but that here is a man who is a genuine nihilist. It always gives me a thrill to meet a cliché in the flesh."

"I'd say it was always a thrill to listen to a novelist," was the inspector's dry retort.

"Yet, for all I know, Gastmann may have done more good in his life than the three of us put together," the author continued. "When I say he's bad, I mean that if he ever does good, it is out of pure caprice, on the spur of the moment, in the same way that I am sure he would commit any of the crimes of which I believe him capable. He is not the man to do evil for the sake of gain, as other people commit crimes, for money, women, or power. He will do it for no reason at all, perhaps because for him two things are always possible, good and evil, and chance is what decides it."

"You deduce all of this as if it were mathematics," the old man remarked.

"It is mathematics," the writer returned. "You could construct his opposite in evil just as you can construct a geometric figure as the mirror image of another one, and I am sure that such a man exists—somewhere—and you may even meet him. If you meet the one, you will meet the other."

"It all sounds so programmed," said the old man.

"It is, and why shouldn't it be?" said the writer. "I imagine the mirror image of Gastmann as a man who would be a criminal simply because evil represents his moral system, his philosophy, and that he would pursue his calling just as fanatically as another would pursue the good."

"Well, that may be," remarked the inspector. "But perhaps we had better get back to Gastmann. He's more important to me at the moment."

"As you wish," said the novelist. "Gastmann, Inspector, represents the negative pole of evil. For him evil is not the expression of a philosophy or an instinct, but of his freedom, the freedom of the nihilist."

"I wouldn't give a hoot for such freedom," answered the old man.

"And you shouldn't either," returned the other. "But one could devote one's life to the study of such a man and his idea of freedom."

"The whole of one's life," the old man agreed.

The novelist was silent. He didn't appear to want to continue the conversation.

"Meanwhile, I have to deal with Gastmann as he is," said Barlach at last. "With the man who lives near Lamlingen, and gives parties, one of which cost a police lieutenant his life. I want to know whether the person you have described to me is the real Gastmann or a figment of your imagination."

"*Our* imaginations," corrected the writer.

The inspector said nothing.

"I don't know," said the other abruptly, and came forward to show them out. He offered his hand to Barlach, but not to Chance.

"I never bother about such things. After all, its the policeman's job to investigate these matters."

The two policemen went back to the car, the little white dog following at their heels, barking furiously. Chance took the wheel.

"I don't like that fellow," he said. Barlach buttoned his coat before he got in. The dog jumped up on a wall and continued to bark.

"Now to Gastmann," said Chance as he started the engine. But Barlach shook his head.

"Back to Berne."

As they drove toward Ligerz the landscape opened out in vast depths ahead of them. There, unfolded before them, lay the elements—stone, earth, and water. The road was in shadow, for the sun had sunk behind the Tessenberg, but it was still shining on the lake, the island, the hills, the foothills of the mountains, the glaciers on the horizon and the cloud monsters piled in tiers and floating away in the blue oceans of the sky. The old man gazed imperturbably into the constant changes of the late autumn weather. It's always the same, he thought, no matter how much it changes, it's always the same. At a sharp turn of the road the convex shield of the lake appeared perpendicularly below them. Chance stopped the car.

"I have to talk to you, Inspector," he said in a nervous voice.

"What about, Walter?" asked Barlach, staring down at the rocky cliffs.

"We have to see Gastman; it's the only way to make any progress. It's just logical. And we have to question those servants of his especially."

Barlach leaned back in his seat, a gray-haired, well-groomed figure. His eyes narrowed to cold slits as he calmly observed the young man at his side.

"My God, Chance, we can't always do the logical thing. Lutz insists that we leave Gastmann alone. And it's not unreasonable now that he's had to surrender the case to government ruling. We have to wait for their instructions. That's what happens when you're up against a bunch of tricky foreigners." Barlach's casual attitude enraged Chance.

"That's nonsense," he shouted. "Lutz is sabotaging the case for political reasons. He's a friend of von Schwendi, Gastmann's lawyer. Can't you see what he's up to?"

Barlach's expression did not change. "It's a good thing we're alone, Chance. Lutz may have acted a bit hastily, but he had sound reasons. Schmied is our problem, not Gastmann."

But Chance was not to be put off. "All we want is to learn the truth," he contradicted, desperately flinging the words into the swelling clouds that were drifting toward them. "The truth and nothing but the truth! We want the man who murdered Schmied!"

"You're right," agreed Barlach, coldly and unemotionally. "The truth—the man who murdered Schmied."

The young officer put his hand on the old man's left shoulder and peered into his impenetrable face. "That's why we have to make use of every means in our power against Gastmann. The investigation has to be complete. You say we can't always do the logical thing, but in this case we have to do it. We can't overlook Gastmann."

"Gastmann is not the murderer," said Barlach, drily.

"But there is a possibility that Gastmann arranged it. We have to interrogate his servants," returned Chance.

"I can't see the slightest reason why Gastmann should have wished to have Schmied killed," said the old man. "We have to look for a man who had some motive for killing Schmied, and that is where the government sources come in."

"Even that author thinks Gastmann is the murderer," cried Chance.

"And you think so, too?" asked Barlach warily.

"Yes, I do, Inspector."

"Then you're the only one who does. That novelist only regards him as being capable of any crime whatsoever, and that is something quite different. He told us nothing of what Gastmann had done, only of what he's capable of doing."

His companion suddenly lost patience. He gripped the older man by the shoulders and almost gasped his words: "I've been in the background for years, Inspector. I've always been passed over, looked down upon, kicked around and treated like some sort of postman!"

"I don't deny it, Chance," said Barlach, looking unmoved into the young man's contorted face. "For years you've played second fiddle to the man who has now been murdered."

"Simply because he'd had a better education. Simply because he knew Latin and things like that."

"You're not being fair to him," answered Barlach. "Schmied was the best detective I have ever known."

"And now," cried Chance, "now that I at last have a chance of promotion it's to be snatched away from me and lost because of some idiotic game of diplomacy. You're the only one who can change that, Inspector. Speak to Lutz. You're the only one who can persuade him to let me go to Gastmann."

"No, Chance, I can't," said Barlach.

The other man shook him as though he were a child, held him between clenched hands and shouted: "Speak to Lutz! You must speak to Lutz!"

The old man, however, was not to be bullied. "It's no good, Chance," he said. "I can't be used for these things any more. I'm old and sick, and I need peace. You have to look after yourself."

"Very well," said Chance. He released Barlach suddenly and took hold of the wheel, though he was still trembling and deathly pale. "Then don't. You can't help me."

They continued their journey toward Ligerz. The old man was the first to break the silence. "You spent your vacation in Grindelwald, didn't you, Walter? In the Eiger Pension?"

"Yes."

"Quiet and not too expensive?"

"Yes."

"Good, Chance. I'll go there tomorrow for a rest. I have to get back on my feet—I've been given a week's sick leave."

Chance did not reply immediately. Finally, as they were turning into Biel-Neuenburg-Strasse, he said, in his usual tone of voice, "Altitude doesn't always help, Inspector."

That evening Barlach went to see his internist, Dr. Samuel Hungertobel, who lived at Bärenplatz. The streetlights were already lit and night was rapidly falling. Barlach looked down from Hungertobel's window onto the surging crowds of people in the square while the physician packed up his instruments. The two men had known each other most of their lives; they had been at school together.

"Your heart is sound, thank goodness," said Hungertobel.

"Have you kept notes on my case?" Barlach wanted to know.

"Naturally. A whole folder full of them," answered the doctor, pointing to a pile of papers on his desk. "That's all about you."

"You've never talked to anyone about it, have you, Hungertobel?" inquired the old man.

"My dear Hans," returned the other, shocked. "There is such a thing as professional secrecy."

Out in the square a blue Mercedes drove up and stopped between other parked cars. Barlach's glance became more intent. Chance got out of the car, followed by a young woman in a white raincoat; her hair flowed down to her shoulders in a blond cascade.

"Ever had burglars, Fritz?" asked the inspector.

"What makes you ask that?"

"I just wondered."

"Not burglars, but I noticed my desk had been ransacked once," admitted the physician, "and your case history was left lying on top. No money was taken, even though there was a substantial sum in the desk."

"Why didn't you report it to the police?"

The doctor scratched his head. "As I said, no money was taken. Even so, I did intend to report it. I suppose I forgot all about it."

"I see," said Barlach. "You forgot. Burglars evidently have an easy time with you." So that, he thought, is how Gastmann found out about me. He looked down into the square again. Chance and the young woman were just entering an Italian restaurant.

On the day of Schmied's funeral, thought Barlach, and turned his back to the window. He watched Hungertobel, who was sitting at his desk, writing.

"Well, what's the verdict?"

"Do you have much pain?"

Barlach told him of his recent seizure.

"That's bad, Hans," said Hungertobel. "We'll have to operate within three days. There's no other way."

"But I feel better than ever right now,"

"In four days you'll have another attack, Hans," said the doctor, "and you won't survive it."

"Well, I still have at least two days left. Two days. You can operate on the morning of the third, Fritz, on Tuesday morning."

"On Tuesday morning," repeated Hungertobel.

"After that I'll have one more year to live, right, Fritz?" said Barlach, looking with his usual air of inscrutability at his school friend. The latter got up quickly and paced across the room.

"Who told you that nonsense?"

"The man who read my case history."

"Did you break in here yourself?" demanded the doctor angrily.

Barlach shook his head. "No, not I. But it's true, Fritz, isn't it? Twelve more months."

"Yes, it's true," Hungertobel admitted. He sat down on a chair by the wall and looked helplessly at Barlach, who was standing in the middle of the room. There was something cold, remote, and solitary about him, something humble and yet immovable, and the physician averted his eyes from the forlorn look in his friend's face.

It was almost two o'clock in the morning when Barlach suddenly woke up. On his physician's advice he had gone to bed early and taken a sleeping pill. It was the first time he had done so, and for a moment he attributed his sudden waking to this unaccustomed measure. Then he realized that he had been awakened by a strange noise. His sight and hearing were abnormally clear, as often happens when one wakes with a start. Nevertheless, it still took him some time to get his bearings, and only after a few seconds—which always seem like an eternity—did he realize where he was. He was not in the room where he usually slept, but rather in his library. Expecting a bad night, he had intended—he remembered it now—to read, but he must have fallen into a sudden, profound sleep. He passed his hands over his body and found he was still in his day clothes and had merely covered himself with a woolen blanket. He listened. Something fell to the floor—it was the book he had begun to read. The blackness of the windowless room was profound but not complete: a faint light came through the open door of the bedroom; it was the gray shimmer of the stormy night. He heard the wind howling in the distance. Through the gloom he gradually managed to make out a bookcase, a chair, then the edge of the table, on which, he wearily recalled, his revolver was lying. Suddenly he was conscious of a draft of air; a window rattled in the bedroom, then the door shut with a loud bang. Immediately afterward the old man heard a soft sound in the hallway. Now he knew. Someone had opened the front door and entered the hall, forgetting that by doing so he would cause a draft of air. Barlach rose to his feet and switched on the floor lamp. He snatched up the revolver and released the safety catch. The intruder in the hallway also turned on the light, so that Barlach could see the shining bulb through the half-open door. This action of his unknown visitor surprised Barlach, for he could see no sense in it. He understood when it was too late. He saw the silhouette of an arm and hand as it reached toward the bulb. Then a blue flame blazed out and everything was darkness. The unknown intruder had torn out the bulb and blown the fuse. Barlach stood in complete darkness. The intruder had taken up the challenge and determined the conditions. Barlach was to fight in the dark. Gripping his gun, the old man cautiously opened the door to the bedroom and went in. A dim light seeped through the window, hardly perceptible at first, though it grew stronger as his eyes became accustomed to it. Barlach leaned against the wall between the bed and the window that faced onto the river. The other window was to his right and over- looked the neighbor's house. Thus he stood in impenetrable shadow. The only disadvantage of his position was the impossi- bility of retreat, but he hoped that his invisibility would outweigh it. The library door was faintly lighted by the windows. He would be bound to see the outline of anyone coming through the door. Suddenly he saw the thin beam of a flashlight in the library. It glided searchingly over the books, across the floor, over the arm- chair, and finally reached the desk. Its ray lit up the snake knife. Again Barlach saw the hand through the open door in front of him. It was covered by a brown leather glove; it groped across the desk and closed round the handle of the snake knife. Barlach raised his pistol and took aim. The flashlight went out. The old man lowered his weapon without firing and waited. From where he stood he could look out through the window at the dark mass of the unresting river, the piled-up town beyond, the cathedral stab- bing the sky with its arrowlike spire, and over all the drifting clouds. He stood motionless, waiting for the enemy who had come to kill him. His eyes bored into the vague opening of the door. He waited. All was still and lifeless. Then the clock struck in the hall— three. He listened. In the distance he could hear the soft tick of the clock. Not far away a car honked and then drove by. People coming home from a nightclub. Once he thought he heard breath- ing, but decided he must have imagined it. So he waited, and somewhere in his house the other one was waiting, too, and be- tween them was the night, this patient, cruel night, that hid be- neath its black mantle the deadly snake, the knife that sought his heart. The old man hardly breathed. He stood clasping his gun, scarcely aware of the cold sweat that ran down the back of his neck. He thought of nothing—not of Gastmann, not of Lutz, not even of the disease that gnawed at him hour by hour, that was about to destroy the life he was defending, defending with such lust just to live. His whole being was focused in his eye, the eye that searched the night, in an ear that examined the faintest sound, in a hand closed around the cool steel of a revolver. When at last he became conscious of the approaching attacker it was in an unexpected way: he felt a vague chill on his cheek, a slight change in the air. It was a long time before he could explain it, then he guessed that the door between the bedroom and the dining room had been opened. Again the stranger acted contrary to Barlach's expectations: he had reached the bedroom by a roundabout route, remaining invisible, inaudible, irresistible, with the snake knife in his hand. Barlach now knew that he would have to be the first to act, that he must take the initiative and begin the fight. He, an old and mortally sick man, would have to begin the battle for a life that at best could only last a year, and even that only if Hungertobel used his knife skillfully. Barlach aimed at the window overlooking the river. He fired, fired again, three times in rapid succession, through the splintering glass out toward the river. Then he dropped to the floor and as he did so something hissed above his head. It was the knife, which implanted itself quivering in the wall. But the old man had accomplished his goal: the lights were turned on behind the neighboring windows. The people in the next house were leaning from their open windows, staring, startled and confused, into the night. Barlach rose to his feet. The light from the next house flooded his bedroom: he caught a vague glimpse of a figure in the dining room doorway, then the front door slammed shut, and almost immediately after it the library door slammed shut in the sudden draft of air, then the dining room door—crash after crash. The window slammed down, and all finally settled into silence. The occupants of the neighboring house were still staring out into the darkness. The old man stood there by the wall, his hand still holding his gun. He stayed there, unmoving, as though he had lost count of time. The neighbors withdrew, the lights went out. Barlach stood by the wall in the darkness, at one with it, alone in the house.

Half an hour passed before he went into the hall and looked for his flashlight. He telephoned Chance and asked him to come around. Then he changed the blown fuse for a new one, and the lights went on again. Barlach sank into his armchair and listened to the sounds of the night. Outside a car drove up and braked sharply. The front door opened again, and again he heard a step. Chance entered the room.

"Someone has tried to kill me," said the inspector. Chance was pale. He had forgotten his hat, his hair hung in disorder over his forehead, and his pajamas showed under his overcoat. Together they went into the bedroom. Chance pulled the knife out of the wall. It cost him some effort, for it had buried itself deep in the paneling.

"With this?" he asked.

"With that, Chance."

The young policeman looked at the splintered window pane. "Did you fire through the window, Inspector?" he asked in surprise.

Barlach told him the whole story.

"It's the best thing you could have done," the other mumbled.

They went into the hall and Chance picked up the bulb from the floor.

"Pretty clever," he said, not without admiration, and laid it down again. Then he went back into the library. Barlach lay down on the sofa and pulled the blanket over him. He lay there, helpless, and suddenly very old and frail. Chance still had the snake knife in his hand.

"You couldn't see who it was?"

"No. He was cautious and kept in the darkest shadows. All I saw was that he was wearing brown leather gloves."

"That's not much to go on."

"Nothing at all. But even though I didn't see him, scarcely even heard him breathe, I know who it was. I know, I know."

The old man said all of this in an almost inaudible voice. Chance weighed the knife in his hand, looked at the gray outstretched figure, at this tired old man, at the hands lying beside the frail body like faded flowers beside a corpse. Then he caught Barlach's eyes. They were fixed on him, calm, inscrutable and clear. Chance put the knife back on the desk.

"You have to get away to Grindelwald tomorrow. You're ill. Or would you rather not go after all? Maybe mountain air is not what you need. It's winter up there, you know."

"I'll go anyway."

"Then you have to get some sleep now. Shall I stay and keep watch?"

"No, you go, Chance," said the inspector.

"Good night," said Chance, and went slowly out. The old man did not answer him; he seemed to be already asleep.

Chance opened the front door, went out and closed it behind him. Slowly he walked the few steps to the street and closed the open garden gate. Then he stopped and looked back toward the house. The night was still dark. Everything was lost in the darkness, even the neighboring houses. The only light streamed down from a street lamp high above—a lost star in the sinister night that was filled with sadness and the swirl of the river. Chance stood still and suddenly cursed softly to himself. He kicked open the garden gate again and strode resolutely up the path to the front door, retracing his former steps. He seized the door knob and turned. But this time the door was locked.

Barlach got up at six after a sleepless night. It was Sunday. The old man washed and put on clean clothes. Then he telephoned for a taxi, intending to breakfast on the train. He took his warm winter overcoat and went out into the gray morning light. He took no luggage with him. The sky was clear. A tipsy student staggered past, reeking of beer. He wished Barlach good morning. "John Blaser. Just flunked his M.D. prelims for the second time, poor devil," Barlach said to himself. "It's enough to drive you to drink." The taxi drove up and stopped. It was a huge American car. The driver's collar was turned up so high that his eyes were hardly visible. He opened the car door.

"The station," said Barlach, getting in. The car moved off.

"Well," said a voice at his side. "How are you this morning? Sleep well?"

Barlach looked round. At the far end of the seat was Gastmann. He was wearing a light raincoat and his arms were folded; he was also wearing brown leather gloves. He sat there sneering like an old peasant. Now the driver turned his head toward them and grinned; he had turned his coat collar down again. He was one of Gastmann's manservants. Barlach realized that he had fallen into a trap.

"Now what do you want of me?" he asked.

"You're still at my heels. Yesterday you went to see that novelist," said the man in the corner; his voice was threatening.

"It's my job."

Gastmann kept his eyes on him. "No one meddles in my affairs without coming to a bad end, Barlach."

The man at the wheel was driving as if possessed up the Aargauerstalden.

"I'm still alive, and I've always meddled in your affairs," was the inspector's calm reply.

Both were silent for a while.

The car was hurtling toward Viktoriaplatz. An old man hobbled across the street and only just managed to avoid being run over. "Watch out!" cried Barlach angrily.

"Drive faster," said Gastmann sharply, and gave the old man a mocking glance. "I love the speed of machines."

The inspector shivered. He hated being shut up in a stuffy vehicle. They raced over the bridge, passed a tram and, with the silver ribbon of the Aare far below them, sped into the town, which seemed to welcome them with open streets. The narrow roads were still empty and deserted; the sky above the town was as clear as glass.

"Take my advice and give up. It's time to admit defeat," said Gastmann, filling his pipe.

The old man looked at the dark arches of the porticos as they sped by and at the shadowy figures of two officers standing in front of Lang's bookshop.

Geissbühler and Zumsteg, he thought, and then added: I really ought to pay for that Fontane novel.

"Our game," he said at last, "yours and mine, is something neither of us can give up. We are both guilty, Gastmann; you because you proposed the wager that night in Turkey, and I because I accepted it."

They drove past the Parliament buildings.

"Do you still believe I killed Schmied?" asked the other.

"I never believed it for a moment," the old man replied. Watching unconcernedly as Gastmann lit his pipe, he went on, "I did not succeed in convicting you of the crime I know you committed; so now I shall get you convicted of a crime I know you have not committed."

Gastmann looked inquiringly at the inspector.

"That's a possibility I hadn't thought of," he said. "I'll have to watch my step."

The inspector did not answer.

"Perhaps you're more dangerous than I thought, old man," said Gastmann, reflectively, from his corner.

The car slowed down and stopped. They had reached the station.

"This is the last time I'll be talking to you, Barlach," said Gastmann. "The next time I'll kill you. That is, of course, if you survive your operation."

"You're mistaken," said Barlach, looking old and standing shivering in the morning freshness of the square. "You won't kill me. I'm the only man who knows you, and am therefore the only man who can judge you. I *have* judged you, Gastmann, and I've sentenced you to death. The sentence will be carried out today. The executioner I've chosen will come to you today. He will kill you, for in the name of God it's high time that deed were done."

Gastmann stared at the old man in amazement as Barlach turned and entered the station, his hands deep in his coat pockets. Without looking back, he vanished into the dark building, which was slowly beginning to fill with people.

"You fool!" Gastmann suddenly called after him, so loudly that several passersby turned to look at him. "You fool!" But Barlach was already out of earshot.

The day was coming up clear and hot. The sun, an immaculate orb, threw long, hard shadows that gradually shortened as it mounted higher. The town lay like a white shell, drinking in the light, sucking it into narrow streets only to spew it out again in the form of a thousand lamps when night fell. It was a monster that bore, destroyed, and buried its people in continuous cycles. The morning became brighter and brighter, a shining shield over the echoes of the church bells. Chance waited for an hour, his face pale in the sunlight reflected from the walls. He paced restlessly back and forth under the trees in front of the cathedral, looking up occasionally at the wild gargoyles that drained the roof, grotesquely grimacing masks staring into the street where the sunlight lay.

At last the great door opened. A dense stream of people, who had come to listen to a celebrated preacher, poured out. Chance quickly made out the white raincoat for which he had been waiting.

Anna came up to him. She gave him her hand and said she was glad to see him. They went up the Kesslergasse, surrounded by the swarm of churchgoers, young and old: a professor, a baker's wife in her Sunday best, two students with a girl, a dozen officials and teachers, all neat, well washed, hungry, all looking forward to their Sunday lunch. Chance and Anna reached the Kasinoplatz, crossed it and went down into the Marzili. They stopped on the bridge.

"Anna," said Chance, "today I'm going to close in on Ulrich's murderer."

"Do you know who he is?" she asked, surprised.

He looked at her. She stood facing him, pale and slim. "I think so," he said. "When I've dealt with him, will you be to me what—" he hesitated a moment and then went on, "what you were to—your deceased fiancé?"

Anna did not answer immediately. She drew her coat around her as though she were cold. A light breeze came up, disarranging her blond hair. Then she said, "Yes. Why don't we plan on it."

They shook hands and Anna walked on across the bridge. He watched her go. Her white raincoat gleamed between the beech trunks, lost itself among passersby, reappeared, and finally disappeared for good. He walked back to the station where he had left his car and drove out toward Ligerz.

It was almost noon before he got there, for he had driven slowly, stopping now and then to walk into the fields and smoke before returning to the car and driving on. At Ligerz he parked the car outside the station and climbed the steps to the church. He was calm now. The lake was deep blue, the last leaves had fallen from the vines, and the earth between them was brown and loose. But Chance neither saw nor cared. He went on, steadily, without pausing or hesitating or turning back. The path led steeply uphill, bordered by white walls, past vineyard after vineyard.

Chance climbed higher and higher, calm, slow, unhesitating, his right hand in his coat pocket. Several times lizards darted across his path, buzzards flew up, the land shimmered in the blaze of the sun as though it were summer. He went on as if driven. He soon left the vineyards behind and plunged into the woodland. It was cooler there. The white Jura rocks gleamed between the tree trunks. He climbed still higher, always at the same steady pace, and came to open country, pasture and arable land. The path rose more gently now. He walked past a rectangular cemetery, enclosed by a gray wall. The gate was wide open. Women in black were moving along the paths between the graves; an old man with a bent back stopped and watched Chance go by, his right hand still in his coat pocket.

He reached Prêles, passed the Bear Hotel, and took the road toward Lamboing. The air on the high plateau was still and lifeless. Even the most distant landmarks stood out with abnormal clarity. Only the ridge of the Chasseral was covered with snow; all else shone light brown, broken by the white walls, the red roofs, and the black ribbons of ploughed land. Chance strode on steadily. The sun shone on his back and threw his shadow forward. The path began to drop downward, and he turned toward the direction of the lumberyard so that the sun was now on his side. He went on, unthinking, unseeing, impelled by a *single* purpose, governed by a *single* passion. Somewhere a dog was barking. The little animal ran up, sniffed at him as he passed, and ran away.

Chance walked on, keeping to the right-hand side of the road, one step after the other, never hastening, never slackening his pace, heading for the house set in the brown background of the fields and surrounded by leafless poplars, which were just coming into sight.

Chance left the path and made his way across the fields. His shoes sank into the warm earth of an unplowed field. He went on till he reached the gate. The gate was open and he went through it. An American car was standing in the drive. Chance ignored it and headed straight for the front door. This, too, was open. He entered the vestibule, opened a second door and found himself in a great hall that took up the whole of the ground floor. Chance stopped. Bright light was pouring in through the windows opposite, and facing him, not five steps away, was Gastmann. At his side hovered the powerful figures of his two manservants, motionless and menacing, like two butchers. All three were wearing overcoats; trunks and suitcases were piled up close by. All was ready for instant departure.

Chance did not move.

"So it's you," said Gastmann. He looked with faint surprise at the policeman's calm, pale face and at the still-open door behind him.

Then he began to laugh. "So that's what the old man meant! Not bad, not bad at all!"

Gastmann's eyes were wide open and a spectral merriment shone in them.

Quietly, deliberately and without a word, one of the thugs took a gun from his pocket and fired. Chance felt the bullet strike him in the left shoulder. Then he drew his right hand from his pocket and fell to the floor. He fired three times into Gastmann's laughing face, and his laughter died away in empty infinite space.

Summoned by a telephone call from Chance, Charnel sped toward the house from Lamboing, Clenin from Twann, and the riot squad from Biel. They found Chance bleeding profusely near three dead bodies. The shootout must have been short, yet each of the three men who now lay dead had found time to fire, and a second bullet had struck Chance in the left forearm. Each man had used a revolver, and one of the manservants was still clutching his weapon in his hand.

Chance was in no state to follow what happened after Charnel's arrival. He fainted twice while the doctor from Neuveville was dressing his wounds, but the injuries proved to be not serious. Villagers, farmers, workmen, women, came to watch. The courtyard was soon crowded and the police set up a barricade. Nevertheless, one girl managed to force her way into the great hall and threw herself screaming onto Gastmann's body. It was the waitress, Charnel's fiancée. He looked on, red with fury. Then they made a way through the crowd in the courtyard and carried Chance to a car.

"There they are—all three," said Lutz next morning, with a gesture toward the bodies, but there was no exultation in his voice; it sounded sad and tired.

Von Schwendi nodded, dismayed. He had driven over to Biel with Lutz on behalf of his client. The two men were in the room where the bodies lay, and despite their overcoats they were shivering. A diagonal beam of light fell through the little barred window. Lutz's eyes were red and tired. He had spent the whole night reading Gastmann's diaries, which were writen in an almost illegible shorthand.

Lutz buried his hands deeper into his pockets. He resumed his conversation in an almost soft tone: "We surround ourselves with guards of all sorts, policemen, soldiers, and public opinion for protection from men like these, and what good does it do?" He grimaced, his eyes bulging, and forced a hollow, thin laugh that reechoed in the cold, bare room. "A fool at the head of a world power, Councillor, and we're lost already; a Gastmann in a community and our cordons are pierced, our patrol units circumvented."

Von Schwendi realized that it would be best to bring the examining magistrate back down to earth, but he didn't quite know how. "Our countries have been exploited downright shamelessly by all sorts of people," he finally replied. "It's embarrassing, absolutely embarrassing."

"No one even had the slightest idea," Lutz tried to comfort the colonel.

"And what about Schmied?" returned the councillor, happy that he fell upon the appropriate topic.

"We found a briefcase of Schmied's in Gastmann's house. It contained information about Gastmann's career and conjectures about his crimes. Schmied was out to get Gastmann and he was doing it as a private individual. It was a mistake for which he paid with his life, for we have proof that Gastmann was responsible for Schmied's murder. Schmied had to have been killed with the same pistol that one of the servants was holding when Chance shot him. The examination of the weapon has confirmed this. Gastmann's motive for killing him is also clear: Gastmann feared that Schmied was ready to expose him. Schmied should have taken us into his confidence, but he was young and ambitious."

Just then Barlach came into the morgue. At the sight of him, the look of melancholy again came over Lutz's face and he buried his hands in his pockets again.

"Well, Inspector," he said, shifting his weight from one foot to the other, "I'm glad to see you here. You've wasted no time in getting back from your leave, and the councillor and I got here as quickly as we could, too. The bodies are on display.

"We've quarrelled a lot in the past, Barlach. I was always for a smoothly operating department with all the frills, including the most modern weapons like the bomb, while you, Inspector, were more in favor of the human element, of a kind of rural gendarmerie composed of artless grandfathers. Let's bury the hatchet. We were both wrong. Chance has very unscientifically proven us wrong with his revolver. I don't really care how he did it. We can take his word that it was self-defense, we have to believe him and there's no reason not to. The end justified the means; the men he shot deserved a thousand deaths, as the locals say. If we had proceeded scientifically, we would now be nosing around in foreign affairs. It looks as if I'll have to promote Chance, while you and I stand around with egg on our faces. The Schmied case is closed."

Lutz lowered his eyes, puzzled by the inspector's enigmatic silence. He seemed to shrink into himself as he suddenly became again the meticulous, correct police officer. He cleared his throat and, suddenly becoming aware of von Schwendi's embarrassment, blushed. Then, accompanied by the colonel, he slowly went out into the gloom of the same corridor, leaving Barlach alone.

The bodies lay on stretchers and were covered with black sheets. The plaster was peeling from the bare gray walls. Barlach went up to the middle stretcher and uncovered the body. It was Gastmann. Barlach stood over him, leaning slightly forward, holding the black sheet in his left hand. He looked down in silence at the waxen face of the corpse, at the still gayish expression on the lips, but the eye sockets were deeper than ever, and there was no longer anything terrible lurking in their depths. Thus they faced each other for the last time, the hunter and the hunted, which now lay dead at his feet. Barlach knew that his own life, too, was just about played out. Once more his mind sped back through the years; once more he retraced the mysterious paths of the labyrinth that was the lives of both men. There was nothing left between them now but the infinitude of death, a judge whose verdict is silence. Barlach stood there, slightly bowed, and the dim light of the morgue fell on his face and hands and played over the corpse, the same for both, created for both, reconciling both of them. The silence of death fell on the old man, crept into him, but it did not bring him the peace it had brought the other. The dead are always right. Barlach slowly covered Gastmann's face. He had seen him for the last time; from now on his enemy belonged to the grave. For years Barlach had been obsessed by one single thought—to destroy the man now lying at his feet in this bare, gray room, sprinkled with the falling plaster as with fine, sparse snow. Nothing was left to the old man now but wearily to cover the face, and humbly beg for forgetfulness, the one mercy that can soothe a heart consumed by raging fire.

That same evening, at eight o'clock sharp, Chance arrived at Barlach's house in Altenberg. He had received an urgent invitation to be there at that hour. To his surprise he was admitted by a young woman domestic in a white apron, and when he entered the hall he could hear from the kitchen the spitting of roasting meat and the clatter of plates and dishes. The maid helped him out of his overcoat, for his left arm was in a sling, but this had not hindered him from driving over. The maid opened the door to the dining room, and Chance stopped spellbound on the threshold. The table was formally laid for two people. Lighted candles shone in the candlesticks and Barlach was seated in an easy chair at one end of the table, his face ruddy in the quiet candle glow, the picture of unruffled calm.

"Sit down, Walter," the old man called to his guest, pointing to a second chair drawn up to the table. Chance sat down, totally stupefied.

"I didn't know I was coming to dinner," he said at last.

"We have to celebrate your triumph," the old man answered quietly, and pushed the candlesticks a little to one side so that they could look each other full in the face. Then he clapped his hands. The door opened, and a stout but attractive woman brought in a platter overflowing with sardines, crayfish, and salads of tomato, pickles and peas. Mountains of eggs and mayonnaise garnished cold meats, cold chicken, and salmon. The old man helped himself to everything. Chance watched the man with the jumpy stomach pile his plate high and was so astonished that he took nothing but a little potato salad.

"What shall we drink?" asked Barlach. "Ligerzer?"

"Ligerzer is excellent," returned Chance as though in a dream.

The maid came and filled their glasses. Barlach began to eat, helped himself to bread, and avidly devoured the salmon, sardines, crayfish, cold meats, salads, and mayonnaise. He clapped his hands and called for more. Chance, benumbed, had not yet finished his potato salad. Barlach was already on his third glass of wine.

"Now the patés and the red Neuenburger," he called out.

The plates were changed. Barlach was served with three patés of goose liver, pork, and truffles.

"You're a sick man, Inspector," began Chance hesitantly.

"Not today, Chance, not today. I'm celebrating. I've cornered Schmied's murderer at last."

He emptied his second glass of red wine and began on his third paté, never pausing, greedily consuming the good things of this world, crunching them between his jaws like a demon intent on satisfying an insatiable hunger. His figure threw a grotesque and enormous shadow on the wall behind him. The vigorous movements of his arms, the rise and fall of his head resembled the dance of some triumphant Negro chieftain. With a feeling of horror, Chance watched the sinister drama that the terminally ill man was enacting for him. He sat there unmoving, eating nothing nor drinking even a sip of wine from his glass.

Barlach called for veal cutlets, rice, pommes frites and green salad, and champagne to go with it. Chance trembled.

"You've been putting on an act," he hissed. "You're not sick!"

For a while the inspector did not answer. At first he laughed, and then devoted all his attention to the salad, enjoying each leaf separately. Chance did not dare disturb the gruesome old man with a second question.

"Yes, Chance," said Barlach at last, and there was a wild gleam in his eyes. "I've been pretending. I was never ill at all." He crammed a chunk of roast veal into his mouth, and went on eating, unpausing, insatiable.

It suddenly dawned upon Chance that he had fallen into an insidious trap that had just closed tight behind him. He broke out in a cold sweat. Panic seized him with overpowering arms. The realization of his position came too late; there was no escape.

"So you know, Inspector?" he said in a whisper.

"Yes, Chance, I know," said Barlach, firmly and calmly, without raising his voice; it was as though he were indifferent to the topic. "You murdered Schmied." He reached for his glass of champagne and emptied it at one draught.

"I always thought you knew." Chance's voice was almost inaudible.

The old man's expression did not change. He seemed to be interested in nothing but his food. He mercilessly heaped his plate with a second helping of rice, poured gravy over it, and placed a veal cutlet on top. Chance tried to save himself, to defend himself against this devilish gourmand.

"The bullet that killed Schmied was fired from the servant's revolver," he stated defiantly, but there was a note of apprehension in his voice.

Barlach's narrowed eyes flashed with contempt. "Nonsense, Chance. You know perfectly well that it was *your* gun the servant was holding in his hand when he was found. You put it there yourself after you shot him. But for Gastmann's criminal record your story would certainly have been investigated and easily disproved."

"You'll never be able to prove it against me," was Chance's desperate attempt to save the situation.

The old man sat back in his chair, no longer frail and sick, but strong and powerful, the picture of superhuman superiority, a tiger playing with its prey. He finished the rest of the champagne in the bottle, and the maid, who had been running in and out the whole time, brought the cheese. He garnished it with radishes, pickled gherkins, and spring onions. He went on eating, as though he were tasting for the last time the good things earth has to offer.

"Haven't you realized, Chance," he went on at last, "that you betrayed yourself long ago? It was your revolver. The bullet that killed Gastmann's hound and saved my life came from the same gun that killed Schmied. Yours, Chance. You yourself provided all the proof I needed. You sealed your fate when you saved my life."

"When I saved your life! So that's why I couldn't find the body of the dog," answered Chance mechanically. "Did you know that Gastmann owned a bloodhound?"

"Certainly. Before we set out I took the precaution of protecting my arm with bandages."

"Then you laid a trap for me there, too," the murderer said without any emotion.

"There, too. But you provided the first proof when you took

the Ins road to Ligerz on that Friday, and treated me to the farce about the 'Blue Charon.' On that Wednesday Schmied took the road through Zollikofen, and I know it because he stopped at the garage in Lyss."

"How could you know that?" asked Chance.

"Simply by telephoning. Whoever drove through Ins and Erlach that night was the murderer—you, Chance. You came from Grindelwald. The Pension Eiger in Grindelwald has a blue Mercedes for hire. You'd been watching Schmied for weeks, observed every step he took; you were jealous of his abilities, his success, his education, even his girl. You knew that he was after Gastmann; you even knew when he visited him, but you didn't know why. Then by chance the briefcase on his desk containing the documents fell into your hands. You determined to take over the Gastmann case and to kill Schmied, so that for once in your life you would have a success yourself. You were right in believing it would be easy to pin a murder on Gastmann. When you saw the blue Mercedes in Grindelwald you knew what to do. You rented the car for Wednesday night. I went to Grindelwald to confirm that fact. The rest is quite simple; you drove through Ligerz to Schernelz and left the car in the woods by the Twann River; you took a shortcut through the wood by following the gorge, which brought you to the Twann-Lamboing road. You waited by the cliffs for Schmied. He was surprised to see you and stopped. He opened the door, and you killed him. You told me the story yourself. And now you've got what you wanted—his success, his job, his car, and his girl."

Chance listened to this pitiless chess player who had him in check and who now finished his gruesome meal. The candles were burning less steadily; their light flickered over the faces of the two men, and the shadows darkened. A deadly silence reigned in this nocturnal hell; the serving women had disappeared. The old man sat motionless, hardly seeming to breathe; the flickering light crossed his face in waves, a red fire that broke against the ice of his brow and his soul.

"You played a cat-and-mouse game with me," said Chance slowly.

"I played a game with you," returned Barlach with a chilling earnestness. "There was nothing else I could do. You killed Schmied and I had to get you for it."

"In order to kill Gastmann," added Chance, suddenly realizing the whole truth.

"You've got it. I've spent half my life trying to corner Gastmann, and Schmied was my last hope. I used every trick in the trade to catch him—a noble animal after a raging wild beast. But then you came, Chance, with your petty felonious ambition, and destroyed my only chance. So I took *you*—the murderer—and transformed you into my worst weapon. That part was easy, for you were driven on by the desperation of the criminal who has to throw his guilt on somebody else. I made my goal your goal."

"I've been through hell," said Chance.

"We've both been through hell," the old man continued with a dreadful calmness. "Von Schwendi's intervention provided the final straw and drove you to extremes—in some way you had to establish Gastmann's guilt. Any deviation from the trail that led toward Gastmann might lead back to you. Schmied's briefcase was the only thing that could help you. You knew it had been in my possession, but you did not know that Gastmann had taken it from me. That's why you attacked me here on Saturday night. The fact that I went to Grindelwald also alarmed you."

"You knew it was I who attacked you?" asked Chance, his voice lacking all expression.

"I knew it right from the start. Every move I made was made with the intention of driving you to desperation. And when you couldn't bear it any longer you went to Lamboing to force a decision with Gastmann, one way or another."

"One of Gastmann's thugs was the first to shoot," said Chance.

"I'd already told Gastmann that morning that I was sending someone to kill him."

An icy shiver ran through Chance and he reeled in his chair. "You set us on each other like dogs."

"Beast against beast," came the pitiless reply from the other chair.

"You appointed yourself the judge and me the executioner," hissed Chance.

"Precisely."

"And I, who only did your will whether I wanted to or not, am a criminal fit only to be hunted down!"

Chance got up, steadying himself on the table with his uninjured right hand. All the candles but one had gone out. Chance's burning eyes tried to make out the outlines of the old man's figure in the gloom, but all he could see was an unreal, black shadow. He made an awkward, groping movement toward his hip pocket.

"Forget it," he heard the old man say. "That won't help you. Lutz knows you're here and the two women are still in the house."

"No, it won't help," returned Chance softly.

"The Schmied case is settled," Barlach announced through the darkness of the room. "I'll keep your secret. But go! Anywhere! I never want to see you again! It's enough that I judged *one* man. Now get out of here!"

Chance went out slowly with lowered head, quickly merging into the blackness of the night. The door closed behind him, and a little later a car drove off from outside the house. As it did so, the last candle flared up and went out, throwing its final garish flicker across the face of the old man who sat silent with his eyes closed.

Barlach spent the night in his armchair, without leaving it even once. The tremendous vitality that had risen within him earlier in the evening had subsided and now threatened to die out completely. He had staked his all in one last, audacious dare, and he had lied to Chance in only one respect.

Early next morning, as dawn was breaking, Lutz came storming into the room to report breathlessly that Chance had been found dead—that a train had run into his car at the crossing between Ligerz and Twann. Lutz found the inspector mortally ill. With an effort the old man asked him to remind Hungertobel that it was Tuesday, and he was ready for the operation.

Then the old man sat and stared out of the window into the clear morning. "One more year," Lutz heard him say. "Just one more year."

Translated by Cyrus Brooks
and adapted by Susan H. Ray

PROBLEMS
OF THE
THEATER

If we consider how art is practiced these days, we cannot help but notice a conspicuous drive toward purity. The artist strives toward the purely poetic, the purely lyrical, the purely epic, the purely dramatic. The painter ardently seeks to create the pure painting, the musician pure music; and someone even told me that pure radio represents the synthesis between Dionysus and Logos. What is even more remarkable for our time, which is not otherwise renowned for its purity, is that each and everyone believes he has found his own unique and therefore the only purity. Each vestal of the arts has, if you will, her own kind of chastity. Likewise, too numerous to count are all the theories of the theater, of what is pure theater, pure tragedy, pure comedy. There are so many modern theories of the drama, what with each playwright keeping three or four at hand, that for this reason, if for no other, I am a bit embarrassed to come along now with my own theories concerning the problems of the theater.

Having said this, I would ask you not to look upon me as the spokesman of some specific movement in the theater or of a certain dramatic technique, nor to believe that I knock at your door as the traveling salesman of one of the philosophies current on our stages today, whether as existentialist, nihilist, expressionist, or ironist, or any other label put on the compote dished up by literary criticism. For me, the stage is not a battlefield for theories, philosophies and manifestos, but rather an instrument whose possibilities I seek to know by playing with it. Of course, there are people in my plays who hold to some belief or philosophy—a lot of blockheads would make for a dull piece—but my plays are not for what the characters have to say: what is said is there because my plays deal with people, and thinking and believing and philosophizing are all, to some extent at least, a part of human nature. The problems I face as playwright are practical, working problems, ones that surface not before, but during the writing. To be quite accurate about it, these problems usually come up after the writing is done, arising out of a certain curiosity to know how I did it. So what I would like to talk about now are these problems, even though I risk disappointing the general longing for something profound and creating the impression that an amateur is talking. I haven't the faintest notion of how else I should go about it, of how not to talk about art like an amateur. Consequently I speak only to those who fall asleep when listening to Heidegger.

What I am concerned with are empirical rules, the possibilities of the theater. But since we live in an age when literary scholarship and criticism flourish, I cannot completely resist the temptation of casting a few side glances at some of the theories of the art and practice of the theater. The artist indeed has no need of scholarship. Scholarship derives its laws from what already exists; otherwise it would not be scholarship. But the laws thus established have no value for the artist, even when they are true. The artist cannot accept a law he has not discovered for himself. If he cannot find such a law, even scholarship cannot help him with one it has established; and when the artist does find one, then it does not matter whether scholarship discovered it or not. But scholarship, thus denied, stands behind the artist like a threatening ogre, ready to leap forth whenever the artist wants to talk about art. And so it is here. To talk about problems of the theater is to enter into competition with literary scholarship. I undertake this challenge with some misgivings. Literary scholarship looks on the theater as an object; for the dramatist it is never something purely objective, something separate from him. He participates in it. It is true that the playwright's activity turns drama into something objective (that is exactly his job), but he then destroys the object he has thus created, forgets it, rejects it, scorns it, overestimates it, all in order to make room for something new. Scholarship sees only the result; the process, which led to this result, is what the playwright cannot forget. What he says has to be taken with a grain of salt. What he thinks about his art changes constantly as he creates it; his thoughts are always subject to his mood and the moment. The only thing that really counts for him is what he is doing at a given moment;

for its sake he can betray what he did just a little while ago. Perhaps a writer should not talk about his art, but once he starts, it is not altogether a waste of time to listen to him. Literary scholars who do not have the faintest idea of the difficulties of writing and of the hidden rocks that force the stream of art into frequently unsuspected channels run the danger of merely asserting and stupidly proclaiming laws that do not exist.

There is probably no doubt that the unities of time, place, and action that Aristotle—as was long supposed—derived from Greek tragedy were considered the ideal of dramatic action. From a logical and hence also aesthetic point of view, this thesis is incontestable, so incontestable in fact that the question arises if it does not set up the framework once and for all within which every dramatist must work. Aristotle's three unities demand the greatest precision, the greatest economy, and the greatest simplicity in the handling of the dramatic material. When it comes right down to it, the unities of time, place, and action ought to be dictates put to the dramatist by literary scholarship, and the only reason scholarship does not hold the artist to them is that Aristotle's unities have not been obeyed by anyone for ages. Nor can they be obeyed, for reasons that best illustrate the relationship of the art of writing plays to the theories about that art.

In order to exist at all, the unities of time, place, and action in essence presuppose Greek tragedy. Aristotle's unities do not make Greek tragedy possible; rather, Greek tragedy makes his unities possible. No matter how abstract an aesthetic law may appear to be, the work of art from which it was derived is still contained in that law. If I want to set about writing a dramatic action that is to unfold and run its course in the same place within two hours, for instance, then this action must have a history behind it, and that history will have to be the more extensive the fewer the number of stage characters there are at my disposal. This is simply an experience of how the theater actually works, an empirical rule. What I mean by history here is the story that took place before the stage action commenced, a story that alone makes the action on the stage possible. Thus the history behind Hamlet, of course, is the murder of his father; the drama lies in the exposure of that murder. As a rule, too, the stage action is much shorter in time than the event depicted; it often starts out right in the middle of the event, sometimes even toward the end of it. Before Sophocles' tragedy could begin, Oedipus had to have killed his father and married his mother, activities that take a little time. The stage action must compress an event to the same degree in which it fulfils the demands of Aristotle's unities. Thus the background history of the action becomes that much more important the closer a playwright adheres to these three unities.

It is, of course, possible to invent a history and hence a dramatic action that would seem particularly favorable for keeping to Aristotle's unities. But this brings into force the rule that the more invented a story is or the more unknown it is to the audience, the more careful must be its exposition, the unfolding of the background. Greek tragedy was possible only because it did not have to invent its historical background; it already possessed one. The spectators knew the myths with which each drama dealt; and because these myths were public, available to all, part of religion, they made the feats of the Greek tragedians possible, feats that have never been attained since: namely their abbreviations, their straightforwardness, their stichomythia and choruses, and hence also Aristotle's unities. The audience knew what the play was all about; its curiosity was not focused on the story so much as on its treatment. Since Aristotle's unities presupposed the general appreciation of the subject matter—a genial exception in more recent times is Kleist's *The Broken Pitcher*—as well as a religious theater based on myths, as soon as that theater lost its religious and mythical significance, the Aristotelian unities had to be reinterpreted or discarded. An audience facing an unknown story will pay more attention to the story than to its treatment, and by necessity then such a play has to be richer in detail and circumstances that one with a familiar story line. The feats of one playwright are not the feats of another. Each art exploits the chances offered by its time, and it is hard to imagine a time without chances. Like every other form of art, drama creates its own world, but not every world can be created in the same fashion. This is the natural limitation of every aesthetic rule, no matter how self-evident such a rule may be. And yet, this does not mean that Aristotle's unities are obsolete; what was once a rule has now become an exception, a case that may occur again at any time. The one-act play still obeys these unities, even though under different conditions. Instead of the past history, the situation now dominates the plot, and the unities are thus once again possible.

But what is true for Aristotle's theory of drama—namely its dependence upon a certain world and hence its validity relative to that world—is also true of every other theory of drama. Brecht is consistent only when he incorporates into his dramaturgy that *Weltanschauung*, the communist philosophy, to which he—so he maintains—is committed; but in doing so he often cuts off his own nose. Sometimes his plays say the very opposite of what they claim they say, but this misunderstanding cannot always be blamed on the capitalistic audience. Often it is simply a case where Brecht, the poet, gets the better of Brecht, the dramatic theorist, a thoroughly legitimate situation that becomes ominous only were it never to happen again.

Let's speak plainly here. My introducing the audience as a factor may have seemed strange to many. But just as it is impossible to have theater without spectators, it is also senseless to consider and treat a play as if it were a kind of ode, divided into parts and delivered in a vacuum. A piece written for the theater becomes living theater when it is played, when it can be seen, heard, felt, and thus directly experienced. This immediacy is one of the most important aspects of the theater, a fact that is often overlooked in those sacred halls where a play by Hofmannsthal counts for more than one by Nestroy, and a Richard Strauss opera for more than one by Offenbach. A play is an event; it is something that happens. In the theater everything must be transformed into something immediate, something visible, something that appeals to the senses, with the addendum—which is obviously justified today—that not everything can be translated into something immediate and corporeal. Kafka, for example, really does not belong on the stage. The bread he offers provides no nourishment; it remains undigested in the iron stomachs of the theater-going public and the regular subscribers. As luck would have it, though, many think of the heaviness they feel not as a stomachache, but as the heaviness of soul that Kafka's true works emanate, so that by error all is put right in the end.

The immediacy sought by every play, the spectacle into which it would be transformed, presupposes the audience, the theater, the stage. Hence we would also do well to examine the theaters for which we have to write today. We all know these money-losing enterprises. Like so many other institutions today, they can only be justified on an idealistic basis: in reality, not at all. The architecture of our theaters, their seating arrangements, and their stages evolved from the court theater, or, to be more precise, never got beyond it. For this reason alone, our so-called contemporary theater is not really contemporary. In contrast to the primitive Shakespearean stage, in contrast to this "scaffold"—where, to quote Goethe, "one saw but little, but where everything had a meaning"—the court theater made every effort to satisfy a craving for naturalness, even though this only resulted in much greater unnaturalness. No longer was the audience satisfied to imagine the royal chamber behind the "green curtain"; every attempt was made to show the chamber. Characteristic of such theater is its tendency to separate audience and stage, by means both of the curtain and of having the spectators sit in the dark facing a well-lit stage. This latter innovation was perhaps the most treacherous of all, for it alone made possible the solemn atmosphere in which our theaters suffocate. The stage became a peep show. Better lighting was constantly invented, then a revolving stage, and I've heard that they have even invented a revolving house! The courts went, but the court theater stayed on. And then, of course, our own time has discovered its own form of theater, the movies. But no matter how much we may emphasize the differences, and no matter how important it may be to emphasize them, it must still be pointed out that film grew out of the theater and that it can at last achieve what the court theater with all its machinery, revolving stages, and other effects only dreamed of doing: it can simulate reality.

The cinema, then, is nothing more nor less than the democratic form of the court theater. It intensifies our sense of intimacy immeasurably, so much so that the films easily risk becoming *the* genuine pornographic art that forces the spectator into being a "voyeur," and the popularity of film stars can only be explained by the fact that those who see them on the screen also come to feel that they have slept with them as well; that is how well these stars are photographed. A closeup in itself is an obscenity.

Just what, then, is our present-day theater? If film can be considered the modern form of the old theater, what is the theater? There is no use in pretending that the theater today is anything much more than a museum in which the art treasures of former golden ages of the drama are put on exhibition. There is no way of changing that. It is only too natural at a time like ours—a time which, always looking toward the past, seems to possess everything but a present. In Goethe's time the ancients were rarely performed, Schiller occasionally, but mostly Kotzebue and whoever else they may have been. It is worthwhile to point out that film robs the theater of its Kotzebues and Birch-Pfeiffers, and it is hard to imagine what sort of plays would have to be put on today if there were no films and if all the scriptwriters wrote stage plays.

If contemporary theater is to a large extent a museum, then this has a definite effect on the actors it employs. They have become civil servants, usually even entitled to their pensions, permitted to act in the theater when not kept busy making films. The members of this once-despised estate have long since settled down as solid citizens—a human gain, an artistic loss. Today actors fit into the order of professional rank somewhere between physicians and small industrialists, surpassed within the realm of art only by Nobel prizewinners, pianists, and conductors. Some actors are visiting professors of sorts, or independent scholars, who take their turn appearing in the museums or arranging exhibitions. The management, of course, takes this into account when it increasingly arranges its playbill with an eye to its guest stars: what play should we put on when this or that authority in this or that field is available to us at such and such a date? Moreover, actors are forced to perform in many different styles, sometimes baroque, sometimes classical, today acting naturalism, tomorrow Claudel. An actor in, say, Molière's day did not have to do that. The director, too, is more important, more dominant than ever, like the conductor of an orchestra. Historical works demand, and ought to demand, proper interpretation; but directors as yet dare not be as true to the works they put on as some conductors are, quite naturally, to theirs. It frequently happens that the classics are not interpreted but executed, and the curtain falls upon a mutilated corpse. But then, where is the danger in it all? There is always the saving convention by which all classical things are accepted as perfection, as a kind of gold standard in our cultural life, with all things looked upon as gold that shine in deluxe editions of the classics. The theater-going public streams to see the classics, whether they be performed well or not; applause is assured, indeed it is the duty of the educated man. And thus the public has legitimately been relieved of the task of thinking and of passing judgments other than those learned by rote in school.

Yet there is a good side to the many styles the present-day theater has to master, although it may at first glance appear rather negative. Every great age of the theater was possible because of the discovery of a unique form of theater, of a particular style, which determined the way plays were written. This is easily demonstrable in the English or Spanish theater, or the Vienna National Theater, the most remarkable phenomenon in the German-speaking theater. This is the only way one can explain the astounding number of plays written by Lope de Vega. A play was no problem for him stylistically. But to the same degree that a uniform style of theater does not exist today, indeed can no longer exist, writing for the theater now has a problem and is thus more difficult. Contemporary theater, therefore, is two things at once: on the one hand it is a museum, while on the other an experimental field where each play confronts the author with new challenges, new questions of style. Today style is no longer a common property, but something highly private, an individual decision. We have no style, only styles, to describe the situation in art today in a nutshell. For contemporary art is a series of experiments, nothing more nor less, just like all of our modern world.

If there are only styles, then it follows that we have only theories of the art and the practice of the theater, but no longer one dramaturgy. We now have Brecht's and Eliot's, Claudel's and that of Frisch or of Hochwälder: each individual has his own ideas. Nevertheless, one single theory of drama is still conceivable, one that would cover all particular instances, much in the same way that we have worked out a geometry that embraces all dimensions. Aristotle's theory of drama would be only one of many possible theories in this dramaturgy. It would have to be a new *poetics,* which would examine the possibilities not of a certain stage, but of *the* stage, a dramaturgy of the experiment itself.

Finally, what can we say about the audience without which, as we have said before, no theater is possible? The audience has become anonymous, just "the paying public," a matter far worse than is at first apparent. The modern author no longer knows his public, unless he writes for some village stage or some drama festival, neither of which is much fun. A playwright has to imagine his audience; but in truth the audience is he himself—and this is a danger that can neither be altered nor circumvented. All the dubious, well-worn, politically misused notions that attach themselves to the concepts of a "people" and a "society," to say nothing of a "community," have necessarily crept into the theater as well. What points is an author to make? How is he to find his subjects, what solutions should he reach? All these are questions for which we may perhaps find an answer once we have gained a clearer notion as to what possibilities still exist in the theater today.

In undertaking to write a play I must first make clear to myself just where it is to take place. At first glance that does not seem much of a problem. A play takes place in London or Berlin, in the mountains, in a hospital, or on a battlefield, wherever the action demands. But it does not work out quite that way. A play, after all, takes place upon a stage, which in turn must represent London, the mountains, or a battlefield. This distinction need not, but can be made. It depends entirely upon how much the author takes the stage into account, how strongly he wants to create the illusion without which no theater can exist, and whether he wants it smeared on thickly like gobs of paint heaped upon a canvas, or transparent, diaphanous, and fragile. A playwright can be deadly serious about the place: Madrid, the Rütli, the Russian steppe— or he can think of it as just a stage, as the world, or as his world.

How the stage is to represent a given place is, of course, the task of the stage designer. Since designing scenes is a form of painting, the developments that have taken place in painting have not failed to touch the theater. But the theater can really abstract neither man nor language, which is in itself both abstract and concrete; and scenery, no matter how abstract it would pretend to be, must still represent something concrete to make sense, and for both these reasons abstraction in scenic design has essentially failed.

This is why the "green curtain" behind which the spectators have to imagine the royal chamber had to be reinstituted. The fact was recalled that the dramatic place and the stage were not one and the same, no matter how elaborate, how convincing the stage setting might be. The fact is, the place has to be created by the play. One word: we are in Venice; another, in the Tower of London. The imagination of the audience needs but little support. Scenery is to suggest, point out, intensify, but not describe the place. Once more it has become transparent, dematerialized. Even the place of the drama to be shown on the stage can be freed from reality.

Two fairly recent plays that most clearly illustrate the possibility referred to as dematerializing the scenery and the dramatic place are Wilder's *Our Town* and *The Skin of Our Teeth*. The dematerializing of the stage in *Our Town* can be described as follows: the stage is nearly empty; only a few objects needed for rehearsals stand about—some chairs, tables, ladders, and so on; and out of these everyday objects the place is created, the dramatic place, the town, and this is all done through the word, the play, which wakens the imagination of the spectators. In his other play Wilder, that great fanatic of the theater, also dematerializes the dramatic place: where the Antrobus family really lives, in what age and what stage of civilization, is never wholly clear; now it is the ice age, now a world war. This sort of experiment may be met quite often in modern drama; thus we don't know where the strange Count Wasteland lives in Frisch's play *Graf Öderland,* no one knows where to wait for Godot, and in *The Marriage of Mr. Mississippi (Die Ehe des Herrn Mississippi)* I expressed the indefiniteness of the locale (in order to give the play its spirit of wit, of comedy) by having one window of a room look out upon a northern landscape with a Gothic cathedral and an apple tree, while the other window of the same room opens on a southern scene with an ancient ruin, a touch of the Mediterranean, and a cypress. The really decisive point in all this is that, to quote Max Frisch, the playwright is composing *with* the stage, a possibility that has always intrigued me and that is one of the reasons, if not the main one, why I write plays. But then—and I am thinking of the comedies of Aristophanes and the comic plays of Nestroy— plays have always been written not only *for,* but *with* the stage.

Let us turn from these incidental problems to more basic ones. What are the particular problems that I—to cite an author whom I know at least partially, though not fully—have had to face? In *The Blind Man (Der Blinde)* I wanted to juxtapose the word against the dramatic place, to turn the word against the scene. The blind duke believes he is living in his well-preserved castle, whereas he is really living in a ruin; he thinks he is humbling himself before Wallenstein, but sinks to his knees before a Negro. The dramatic place is one and the same, but by means of the pretense carried on before the blind man, it plays a dual role: the place seen by the audience and the place in which the blind man fancies himself to be. So also, when in my comedy *An Angel Comes to Babylon (Ein Engel kommt nach Babylon)* I chose for my dramatic locale the city in which the Tower was built, essentially I had to solve two problems. In the first place the stage had to express the fact that there were two places of action in this comedy, heaven and the city of Babylon; heaven as the secret point of origin of the action, and Babylon as the locale where that action ran its course.

Well, I suppose heaven could have been simply represented by a dark background to suggest its infinity, but since what I most wanted to convey in my comedy was the idea that heaven was not something infinite, but something incomprehensible and altogether different, I asked for the stage background, the heaven above the city of Babylon, to be occupied entirely by the Great Nebula in Andromeda, just as we might see it through the telescope of Mount Palomar. What I hoped to achieve with this was that heaven, the incomprehensible and inscrutable, would take on form—gain, as it were, its own stage presence. In this way heaven's rapprochement with the earth was also brought out, reiterating the coming together of the two that is expressed in the action through the angel's visiting Babylon. Thus, too, a world was constructed in which the result of the action, namely the building of the Tower of Babylon, became possible.

In the second place I had to think of how to make the stage represent Babylon, the place in which the action unfolds. What I found challenging about Babylon was its modernity, its Cyclopean big-city character, its New York look with skyscrapers and slums, and by having the first two acts take place along the banks of the Euphrates I wished to hint at Paris. Babylon, in brief, stands for the metropolis. It is a Babylon of the imagination, having a few typically Babylonian features, but in a modernized parodied version, with its modernities—for instance the convenience of electric streetlights. Of course, the execution of the scenery, the building of the stage itself, is a job for the stage designer, but the playwright must always decide himself just what kind of stage he wants.

I love a colorful stage setting, a colorful theater, like the stage of Theo Otto, to mention an admirable example. I have little use for a theater that uses black curtains as was the fashion once upon a time, or for the tendency to glory in threadbare poverty, which some stage designers seem to aim for. Of course, the most important element in the theater is the word; but note: after the word there are many other things that also rightfully belong to the theater, even a certain wantonness. Thus, when someone asked me quite thoughtfully with respect to my play *Mississippi,* where one of the characters enters through a grandfather clock, whether or not I thought a four-dimensional theater was possible, I could only remark that I had not been thinking of Einstein when I did it. It is just that in my daily life it would give me great pleasure if I could join a gathering and astonish those present by entering the room through a grandfather clock or by floating in through a window. Surely, no one should deny us playwrights the opportunity to satisfy such desires now and then at least on the stage, where such whims can be fulfilled. The old argument as to which came first, the chicken or the egg, can be transformed in art into the question of whether one should present the egg or the chicken, the world as potential or as rich harvest. Artists might very well be divided then into those favoring the egg and those favoring the chicken. The argument continues today. Alfred Polgar once said to me that it was odd that while in contemporary Anglo-Saxon drama everything came out in the dialogue, there was always much too much happening on the stage in my plays and that he, Polgar, would sometimes like to see a simple Dürrenmatt play. Behind this truth, however, lies my refusal to say that the egg came before the chicken, and my personal prejudice of preferring the chicken to the egg. It happens to be my passion, not always a happy one perhaps, to want to put on the stage the richness, the manifold diversity of the world. As a result my theater is frequently open to many interpretations and appears to confuse some. Misunderstandings also creep in, as when someone looks around desperately in the chicken coop of my plays, hoping to find the egg of Columbus, which I stubbornly refuse to lay.

A play is not only bound to a place, but to a time as well. Just as the stage represents a place, so it also represents a time, the time *during* which the action takes place as well as the time *in* which it occurs. If Aristotle had really demanded the unity of time, place, and action, he would have limited the duration of a tragedy to the time it took for the action to be carried out (a feat the Greek tragedians nearly achieved), and thus, of course, everything would have to be concentrated upon that action. Time would pass "naturally," one thing coming after the other without breaks. But this does not always have to be the case. In general the actions on the stage do follow one another; but in Nestroy's magical farce, *Death on the Wedding Day* (*Der Tod am Hochzeitstag*), to cite an example, two acts take place simultaneously and the illusion of simultaneity is skillfully achieved by having the action of the second act form the background noise for the first, and the action of the first act the background noise for the second. Other examples of how time is used as a theatrical device could be easily recalled. Time can be shortened, stretched, intensified, arrested, repeated; like Joshua, the dramatist can call to his heaven's orbits, "Theater-Sun, stand thou still upon Gibeon! And thou, Theater-Moon, in the valley of Ajalon!"

It may be noted further that the unities ascribed to Aristotle were not wholly kept in Greek tragedy either. The action is interrupted by the choruses, which means that the choruses distribute time. When the chorus interrupts the action—as far as time is concerned (to elucidate the obvious like an amateur)—it achieves the very same thing the curtain does today. The curtain cuts up and spreads out the time of an action. I have nothing against such an honorable device. The good thing about a curtain is that it so clearly defines an act, that it clears the table, so to speak. Moreover, it is psychologically often extremely necessary to give the exhausted and frightened audience a rest. But a new way of binding language and time has evolved in our day.

If I cite Wilder's *Our Town* once again, I do so because I assume that this fine play is widely known. You may recall that in it different characters turn toward the audience and talk of the worries and needs of their small town. In this way Wilder is able to dispense with the curtain. The curtain has been replaced by the direct address to the audience. The epic element of description has been added to the drama. For this reason, of course, this form of theater has been called the epic theater.

Yet when looked at quite closely, Shakespeare's plays or Goethe's *Götz von Berlichingen* are in a certain sense epic theater, too, only in a different, less obvious manner. Since Shakespeare's histories often extend over a considerable period of time, this time span is divided into different actions, different episodes, each of which is treated dramatically. *Henry IV, Part I,* consists of nineteen such episodes, while by the end of the fourth act of *Götz* there are already no less than forty-one tableaux. I stopped counting after that. If one looks at the way the overall action has been built up, then, with respect to time, it is quite close to the epic, like a film that is run too slowly, so that the individual shots can be seen. The condensation of everything into a certain time has been given up in favor of an episodic form of drama.

Thus, when an author in some of our modern plays turns toward the audience, he attempts to give the play a greater continuity than is otherwise possible in an episodic form. The void between the acts is to be filled; the time gap is to be bridged, not by a pause, but by words, by a description of what has happened in the meantime, or by having some new character introduce himself. In other words, the expositions are handled in an epic manner, not the actions to which these expositions lead. This represents an advance of the word in the theater, the attempt of the word to reconquer territory lost a long time ago. Let us emphasize that it is but an attempt; for all too often the direct address to the audience is used today to explain the play, an undertaking that makes no sense whatever. If the audience is moved by the play, it will not need prodding by explanations; if the audience is not moved, all the prodding in the world will not help.

In contrast to the epic, however, which can describe human beings as they are, the drama unavoidably limits and therefore stylizes them. This limitation is inherent in the art form itself. The human being of the drama is, after all, a talking individual, and speech is his limitation. The action only serves to force this human being on the stage to talk in a certain way. The action is the crucible in which the human being is melted into words, must become words. This, of course, means that I, as the playwright, have to get the people in my drama into situations that force them to speak. If I merely show two people sitting together and drinking coffee while they talk about the weather, politics, or the latest fashions, then I provide neither a dramatic situation nor dramatic dialogue, no matter how clever their talk. Some other ingredient must be added to their conversation, something to add pique, drama, double meaning. If the audience, for instance, knows that there is some poison in one of the coffee cups, or perhaps even in both, so that the conversation is really one between two poisoners, then this artistic device makes this coffee klatsch a dramatic situation, out of which and on the basis of which dramatic dialogue can develop. Without the addition of some special tension or special condition, there can be no dramatic dialogue.

Just as dialogue has to develop out of a situation, so it must also lead into a situation, that is to say, of course, a new situation. Dramatic dialogue effects some action, some suffering, some new situation, out of which in turn new dialogue can again develop, and so on and so forth.

A human being, however, is more than just a talking head. The fact that a man also thinks, or at least should think, that he feels, yes, more than anything *feels,* and that he does not always wish to tell others what he is thinking or feeling, has led to the use of another artistic device, the monologue. It is true, of course, that a person standing on a stage and carrying on a conversation with himself out loud is not exactly natural; and the same thing can be said, only more so, of an operatic aria. But the monologue (like the aria) proves that an artistic trick, which really ought to be avoided, can achieve an unexpected effect, to which—and rightly so—the public succumbs time and again; so much so that Hamlet's monologue, "To be or not to be," or Faust's, are probably the most beloved and most famous passages in the theater.

But just because it sounds like a monologue does not mean it is a monologue. The purpose of dialogue is not only to lead a human being to a point where he must act or suffer; at times it also leads into a major speech, to the explanation of his personal point of view. Many people have lost an appreciation for rhetoric ever since, as Hilpert maintains, some actor who was not sure of his lines discovered naturalism. That is unfortunate. A speech can win its way across the footlights more effectively than any other artistic device. Yet many critics no longer know what to make of a speech either. An author who dares a speech today will suffer the same fate as the peasant Dicaeopolis: he will have to lay his head on the executioner's block. Except that instead of the Acharnians of Aristophanes, it will be the majority of critics who descend upon the author—the most normal thing in the world. Nobody is more anxious to bash someone's brains out than those who have none of their own.

Moreover, the drama has always contained some narrative elements; epic drama was not the first to introduce this. The background of an action, for instance, has always had to be related, or an event announced in the form of a messenger's report. But narration on the stage is not without its dangers, for it does not live in the same manner, is not tangible the way an action taking place on the stage is. Many attempts have been made to overcome this, such as by dramatizing the messenger, by letting him appear at a crucial moment, or by making him a blockhead from whom the report can only be extracted with great difficulties. Yet certain elements of rhetoric must still be present if narration is to succeed on the stage. Stage narratives cannot exist without some exaggeration. Observe, for instance, how Shakespeare elaborates on Plutarch's description of Cleopatra's barge. This exaggeration is not just a characteristic of the baroque style, but a means of launching Cleopatra's barge upon the stage, of making it visible there. But while the speech of the theater cannot exist without exaggeration, it is important to know when to exaggerate, and, above all, how.

Furthermore, just as stage characters can suffer a certain fate, so also can their language. The angel that came to Babylon, for example, grows more and more enthusiastic about the earth's beauty from act to act, and hence his language must parallel this rising enthusiasm until it grows into a veritable hymn. In the same comedy the beggar Akki relates his life in a series of *makamat,* passages of a rich and stately prose interspersed with rhymes that come from the Arabic. In this way I try to convey the Arabic character of this personage, his joy in inventing stories and in duelling and playing with words, without at the same time wandering off into another form, such as the chanson. Akki's *makamat* are nothing less than the most extreme potential offered by his language, and therefore they intensify his being. Through the *makamat* Akki has become pure language, and this is just what an author must always strive for, that there are moments in his plays in which the characters he has created with the written word become living language and nothing less.

A danger lurks here, too, of course. Language can be seductive. The joy of being able all of a sudden to write, of possessing language—as it came over me, for instance, while I was writing *The Blind Man*—can overwhelm the author, can make him escape from his subject into language. To keep close to the subject is itself a great art, achieved only by masterful control of the impetus to talk. Dialogue, like playing on words, can also lead an author into byways, take him unawares away from his subject. Yet ideas flash into his mind again and again—ideas that he ought not resist, even if they threaten to disrupt his carefully laid plans. For in addition to being on guard against these tempting flashes, a writer must also have the courage to follow some of them.

These elements and problems of place, time, and action, which are all, of course, interwoven and are but hinted at here, belong to the basic material, to the artistic devices and tools of the craft of the drama. But let me make it clear that I make war upon the notion of "the craft of the drama." The very idea that anyone who makes a sufficiently diligent and steadfast endeavor to achieve something in that art will succeed in the end, or even that this craft can be learned, is a notion we thought discarded long ago. Yet it is still frequently met with in critical articles about the art of playwriting. This art is supposed to be a sound and solid, respectable and well-mannered affair. Thus, too, the relationship between a playwright and his art is considered by some to be like a marriage in which everything is quite legal and blessed with the sacraments of aesthetics. This is probably the reason why critics often refer to the theater, much more than to any other form of art, as a craft which, depending on the particular case, has been more or less mastered. If we investigate closely what the critics really mean by "the craft of the drama," then it becomes obvious that it is little else than the sum of their prejudices. There is no craft of the theater; there is only the mastery of the material through language and the stage or, to be more exact, it is an overpowering of the material, for any creative writing is a kind of warfare with its victories, defeats, and indecisive battles. Perfect plays do not exist except as a fiction of aesthetics, which, as in films, is the only place perfect heroes may be found. No playwright has ever yet left this battle without his wounds; each one has his Achilles' heel, and the playwright's antagonist, his material, never fights fairly. It is cunning stuff, often not to be drawn out of its lair, and it employs the most secret and lowest of tricks. This forces the playwright to fight back with every permissible and even nonpermissible means, no matter what the wise exhortations, rules, and adages of the masters of this craft and their most honored trade may say. Best foot forward won't get an author anywhere in the drama, not even his foot in the doorway. The difficulties in writing drama lie where no one suspects them: frequently in the problem of how to have two people say hello, or the difficulty in writing the opening sentence. What is sometimes considered to be the craft of the drama can be easily learned in half an hour. But how difficult it is to divide a given body of material into five acts, and how few subjects there are that can be divided that way, how nearly impossible it is to write in iambic pentameter any more—those things are hardly ever suspected by the hack writers, who can always divide any subject into five acts, and who have always written and still do write with facility in iambic pentameter. They really do pick their material and their language in the way some critics think they do. They are not so much amateurs when they talk about art as when they tailor art to their talk. No matter what the material is like, they always fashion the same dressing gown to be sure the audience will not catch cold and that it will sleep comfortably. There is nothing more idiotic than the opinion that only a genius does not have to obey those rules prescribed for writers of talent. In that case I should like to be counted among the geniuses. What I really want to emphasize strongly is that the art of writing a play does not necessarily start out with the planning of a certain child, or how a eunuch thinks love is made; rather, it starts out with the lovemaking, of which the eunuch is incapable. Though really the difficulties, pains, and also fortunes of writing do not lie within the realm of things we mean to talk about or even can talk about. We can only talk about the craft of the drama, a craft that exists only when one *talks* of drama, but not when one writes plays. The craft of the drama is an optical illusion. To talk about plays, about art, is a much more utopian undertaking than is ever appreciated by those who do it most.

Employing this (really nonexistent) craft, let us try and give shape to a certain body of material. Usually there is a central point of reference, the hero. In theories of the drama a distinction is made between a tragic hero, the hero of tragedy, and a comic hero, the hero of comedy. The qualities a tragic hero must possess are well known. He must be capable of rousing our sympathy. His guilt and his innocence, his virtues and his vices must be mixed in the most pleasant and yet exact manner, and administered in doses according to well-defined rules. If, for example, I make my tragic hero an evil man, then I must endow him with a portion of intellect equal to his malevolence. As a result of this rule, the most sympathetic stage character in German literature has turned out to be the devil, and he has remained so. The only thing that has changed is the social position of the character who awakens our sympathy.

In Greek tragedy and in Shakespeare the hero is a member of the highest class in society, the nobility. The audience sees a suffering, acting, raving hero who occupies a social position far higher that its own. This state of affairs still continues to impress audiences today.

Then when Lessing and Schiller introduced the bourgeois drama, the audience saw itself as the suffering hero on the stage. But the evolution of the hero continued. Büchner's Woyzeck is a primitive proletarian who represents far less, socially speaking, than the average spectator. But it is precisely in this extreme form of human existence, in this last, most miserable form, that the audience can also see the human being, indeed itself.

And finally we might mention Pirandello, who was the first, as far as I know, to render the hero, the character on the stage, in a dematerialized and transparent form, just as Wilder did the dramatic place. The audience watching this sort of presentation attends, as it were, its own dissection, its own psychoanalysis, and the stage becomes man's internal milieu, the inner space of the world.

Of course, the theater has never dealt solely with kings and generals; in comedy the hero has always been the peasant, the beggar, the ordinary citizen—but this was always in comedy. Nowhere in Shakespeare do we find a comic king; in his day a ruler could appear as a bloody monster but never as a fool. In Shakespeare the courtiers, the artisans, the working people are comic. Hence, in the evolution of the tragic hero, we see a trend toward comedy. The same can be seen in the case of the fool who becomes more and more of a tragic figure. This fact is by no means without significance. The hero of a play not only propels an action forward, he not only suffers a certain fate, but he also represents a world. Therefore we have to ask ourselves how we should present our own precarious world and with what sort of heroes. We have to ask ourselves how the mirrors that catch and reflect this world should be ground and set.

Can our present-day world, to put it more concretely, be represented by Schiller's dramatic art? Some writers claim it can be, since Schiller still holds audiences in his grip. To be sure, in art everything is possible when the art is right. But the question is if an art valid for its time could possibly be so even for our day. Art can never be repeated. If it were repeatable, it would be foolish not just to write according to the rules of Schiller.

Schiller wrote as he did because the world in which he lived could still be mirrored in the world his writing created, a world he could build as an historian. But just barely. For was not Napoleon perhaps the last hero in the old sense? The world today as it appears to us can hardly be encompassed in the form of the historical drama as Schiller wrote it, for the simple reason that we no longer have any tragic heroes, but only vast tragedies staged by world butchers and produced by slaughtering machines. Hitler and Stalin cannot be made into Wallensteins. Their power was so enormous that they themselves were no more than incidental, corporeal, and easily replaceable expressions of this power; and the misfortune associated with the former and to a considerable extent also with the latter is too vast, too complex, too horrible, too mechanical, and usually simply too devoid of all sense. Wallenstein's power can still be envisioned; power as we know it today can only be seen in its smallest part for, like an iceberg, the largest part is submerged in anonymity and abstraction. Schiller's drama presupposes a world that the eye can take in, that takes for granted genuine actions of state, just as Greek tragedy did. For only what the eye can take in can be made visible in art. The modern state, however, cannot be envisioned, for it has become anonymous and bureaucratic; and not only in Moscow and Washington, but even in Berne as well. Actions of state today have become post-hoc satiric dramas that follow the tragedies previously executed in secret. There are no true representatives, and the tragic heroes are nameless. Any small-time crook, petty government official, or policeman better represents our world than a senator or president. Today art can only embrace the victims, if it can reach men at all; it can no longer come close to the mighty. Creon's secretaries close Antigone's case. The state has lost its physical reality, and just as physics can now cope with the world only in mathematical formulas, so the state can only be expressed in statistics. Power today becomes visible, material, only when it explodes as in the atom bomb, in this marvelous mushroom that rises and spreads immaculate as the sun and in which mass murder and beauty have become one. The atom bomb can no longer be reproduced artistically, since it is mass produced. In its face all man's art that would recreate it must fail, since it is itself a creation of man. Two mirrors that reflect one another remain empty.

But the task of art, in so far as art can have a task at all, and hence also the task of drama today, is to create something concrete, something that has form. This can be accomplished best by comedy. Tragedy, the strictest genre in art, presupposes a formed world. Comedy—insofar as it is not just satire of a particular society, as in Molière—supposes an unformed world, a world being made and turned upside down, a world about to fold like ours. Tragedy overcomes distance; it can make myths originating in times immemorial seem like the present to the Athenians. But comedy creates distance; the attempt of the Athenians to gain a foothold in Sicily is translated by comedy into the birds undertaking to create their own empire before which the gods and men will have to capitulate. How comedy works can be seen in the most primitive kind of joke, in the dirty story, which, though it is of very dubious value, I mention only because it is the best illustration of what I mean by creating distance. The subject of the dirty story is the purely sexual, which, because it is purely sexual, is formless and without objective distance, but if it wants to take on a form, it becomes the dirty joke. This type of joke, therefore, is a kind of original comedy, a transposition of the sexual to the level of the comical. This is the only way, in a society where the Masters and Johnsons are in vogue, to talk in an accepted way about the purely sexual. In the dirty story it becomes clear that the comical exists in forming what is formless, in creating order out of chaos—which brings us to the next point.

The means by which comedy creates distance is the conceit. Tragedy is without conceit. This is why there are few tragedies whose subjects were invented. By this I do not mean to imply that the ancient tragedians lacked inventive ideas, as is sometimes the case today, but that the marvel of their art was that they had no need of these inventions, of conceits. That makes all the difference. Aristophanes, on the other hand, lived by conceits. The stuff of his plays is not myths but inventions, which take place not in the past but the present. They drop into their world like bombshells, which, by creating huge craters, transform the present into the comic and at the same time into the visible. This, of course, does not mean that drama today can only be comical. Tragedy and comedy are but formal concepts, dramatic attitudes, figments of the aesthetic imagination, which can embrace one and the same thing. Only the conditions under which each is created are different, and these conditions have their basis only in small part in art.

Tragedy presupposes guilt, despair, moderation, lucidity, vision, a sense of responsibility. In the Punch-and-Judy show of our century, in this backsliding of the white race, there are neither guilty nor responsible individuals any more. No one could do anything about it, and no one wanted to. Indeed, things happen without anyone in particular being responsible for them. Everything is dragged along and everyone gets caught somewhere in the sweep of events. We are all collectively guilty, collectively bogged down in the sins of our fathers and of our forefathers. We are the children of our forebears. That is our misfortune, but not our guilt:

guilt today can exist only as a personal achievement, as a religious act. Comedy is the only thing that can still reach us. Our world has led to the grotesque as well as to the atom bomb, and so it is a world like that of Hieronymus Bosch whose apocalyptic paintings are also grotesque. And yet, the grotesque is only a way of expressing in a tangible manner, of making us perceive physically the paradoxical; it is the form of the unformed, the visage of a faceless world. And just as our thinking today seems to be unable to do without the concept of the paradox, so also art and our world, which still exist only because the atom bomb exists: out of fear of the bomb.

But the tragic is still possible even if pure tragedy is not. We can achieve the tragic out of comedy, we can bring it forth as a frightening moment, as an abyss that opens suddenly. As a matter of fact, many of Shakespeare's tragedies are really comedies out of which the tragic arises.

After all this the conclusion might easily be drawn that comedy is the expression of despair, but this conclusion is not inevitable. Of course, whoever perceives the senselessness, the hopelessness of this world might well despair, but this despair is not a result of this world, but rather an answer given by an individual to this world. Another answer would be not to despair; it might be an individual's decision to endure this world in which we frequently live like Gulliver among the giants. He also achieves distance, he also steps back a pace or two who takes measure of his opponent, who prepares himself to fight his opponent or to escape him. It is still possible to portray man as a courageous being.

This then is one of my principal concerns. The blind man, Romulus, Übelohe, Akki, are all men of courage. The lost world-order is restored within them; the universal escapes my grasp. I refuse to find the universal in a doctrine; I take it for the chaos it is. The world (and thus the stage that represents this world) is for me something monstrous, a riddle of misfortunes that has to be accepted but before which there can be no capitulation. The world is far bigger than any man, and thus necessarily takes on threatening characteristics. If one could but stand outside the world, it would no longer be so threatening. But I have neither the right nor the ability to be an outsider to this world. To provide solace in poetry is frequently all too cheap an escape; it is probably more honest to retain one's human point of view. Brecht's thesis that the world is an accident, which he developed in his *Street Scene,* where he shows how this accident happened, may yield—as in fact it did—some magnificent theater, but he did it by concealing most of the evidence! Brecht's thinking is inexorable, because there are many things he inexorably refused to think about.

And lastly it is through the conceit, through comedy, that the anonymous audience first becomes possible as an audience at all, first becomes a reality not only to be counted on, but to be taken into account as well. The conceit easily transforms the crowd of theatergoers into a mass that can be attacked, deceived, outsmarted into listening to things it would otherwise not so readily listen to. Comedy is a mousetrap in which the public is easily caught and in which it will get caught over and over again. Tragedy, on the other hand, is predicated on a community, a kind of community whose existence in our day is frequently an embarrassing fiction. Nothing is more ludicrous, for instance, than to sit and watch the mystery plays of the Anthroposophists when one is not a participant.

Granting all this, there is still one more question to be asked: is it permissible to go from a generality to a particular form of art, to do what I just did when I went from my assertion that the world is formless to the possibility that writing comedies can still be done today? I doubt that this is permissible. Art is something personal, and something personal should never be explained with generalities. The value of a work of art does not depend on whether more or less good reasons for its existence can be found. Hence I have also tried to avoid certain problems, as, for example, the argument, quite current today, as to whether plays ought to be written in verse or in prose. My own answer lies simply in writing prose, without any intention of thereby deciding the issue. A man has to choose his own path, after all, and why should one way always be worse than another? As far as my concepts of comedy are concerned, I believe that here, too, personal reasons are more important than more general ones that are always open to argument. What logic in matters of art could not be refuted! One talks best about art when one talks of one's own art. The art one chooses is an expression of freedom without which no art can exist, and at the same time an expression of necessity without which art cannot exist either. The artist always represents his world and himself. If at one time philosophy taught men to derive the particular from the general, then—unlike Schiller, who started out believing in general conclusions—I cannot construct a play as he did when I doubt that the particular can ever be reached from the general. But my doubt is mine and only mine, and not the doubt and problems of a Catholic, for example, for whom drama holds possibilities non-Catholics do not share. This is so even if, on the other hand, a Catholic who takes his religion seriously is denied those possibilities that other men possess.

The danger inherent in this thesis lies in the fact that there are always those artists who, for the sake of finding some generalities to believe in, accept conversion, taking a step that is all the more remarkable for the sad fact that it really will not help them. The difficulties experienced by a Protestant in writing a drama are exactly the same difficulties he has with his faith. Thus it is my way to mistrust what is ordinarily called the construction of the drama, and to arrive at my plays from the particular, the sudden idea or conceit, rather than from some general concept or plan. Speaking for myself, I need to write off into the blue, as I like to put it to give critics a catchword to hang onto. They use it often enough, too, without really understanding what I mean by it.

But these matters are my own concerns and hence it is not necessary to invoke the whole world and to pretend that what are my concerns are the concerns of art in general (lest I be like the village judge Adam in Kleist's play *The Broken Pitcher,* who goes back to the devil to explain the origin of a wig that is, in fact, his own). As in everything and everywhere, and not just in the field of art, the rule is: no excuses, please!

Nevertheless the fact remains (always keeping in mind, of course, the reservations just made) that we now stand in a different relationship to what we have called our "material." Our unformed, amorphous present is characterized by being surrounded by figures and forms that reduce our time to a mere result—even less, to a mere transitional state—and that give excessive weight to the past as something finished and to the future as something possible. This applies equally well to politics. Related to art it means that the artist is surrounded by all sorts of opinions about art and by demands on him that are based not upon his capacities, but upon the historical past and present forms. He is surrounded therefore by materials that are no longer materials—that is, possibilities— but by materials that have already taken on shape—that is, some definitive form. Caesar is no longer pure subject matter for us; he has become the Caesar whom scholarship has made the object of its researches. And so it happened that scholars, having thrown themselves with increasing energy not only upon nature but also upon intellectual life and upon art—establishing in the process intellectual history, literary scholarship, philology, and goodness knows what else—have created a body of factual information that cannot be ignored (for there can be no conscious naiveté that could ignore the results of scholarship). In this way, however, scholars have deprived the artist of materials by doing what was really the artist's task. The mastery of Richard Feller's *History of Berne,* for instance, precludes the possibility of writing a historical drama about the city of Berne; the history of Berne was thus given shape before some literary artist could do it. True, it is a scholastic form (and not a mythical one, which would leave the path open for a tragedian), a form that severely limits the field for the artist, leaving to art only psychology, which, of course, has also become a science. To rewrite such a history in a creative literary manner would now be a tautology, a repetition by means that are not suitable or fitting, a mere illustration of scholarly insights; in short, it would be the very thing science often claims literature to be. It was still possible for Shakespeare tò base his Caesar upon Plutarch, for the Roman was not an historian in our sense of the word but a storyteller, the author of biographical sketches. Had Shakespeare read Mommsen he could not have written his Caesar, because he would of necessity have lost the supremacy over his materials. And this holds true in all things, even for the myths of the Greeks, which—since we no longer live them but only study, evaluate, and investigate them, recognizing them to be mere myths and as such destroying them—have become mummies; and these, dripping with philosophical and theological trappings, are all too often substituted for the living thing.

This is why the artist must reduce the subjects he finds and runs into everywhere if he wants to turn them once more into real materials, always hoping that he will succeed. He parodies his materials, which means he consciously contrasts them with what they have actually become. By this means, by this act of parody, the artist regains his freedom and hence his material; and thus material is no longer found but invented. For every parody presupposes a conceit and an invention. The dramaturgy of available materials is thus being replaced by the dramaturgy of invented materials. In laughter man's freedom becomes manifest, in crying his necessity. Our task today is to demonstrate freedom. The tyrants of this planet are not moved by the works of the poets. They yawn at a poet's lamentations. For them heroic epics are silly fairy tales and religious poetry puts them to sleep. Tyrants fear only one thing: a poet's mockery. For this reason, then, parody has crept into all literary genres, into the novel, the drama, into lyric poetry. Much of painting, even of music, has been conquered by parody, and the grotesque has followed overnight, as it were, and often well camouflaged, on the heels of parody: all of a sudden the grotesque is simply there.

But our time, up to every imaginable trick there is, can handle all that and nothing can intimidate it: the public has been educated to see in art something solemn, hallowed, and passionate. The comic is considered inferior, dubious, unseemly; it is accepted only when it makes people feel as bestially happy as a bunch of pigs. But the very moment people recognize the comic to be dangerous—an art that exposes, demands, moralizes—it is dropped like a hot potato, for art may be everything it wants to be so long as it remains comfortable.

We writers are often reproached with the idea that our art is nihilistic. Today, of course, there does exist a nihilistic art, but not every art that seems nihilistic is so. True nihilistic art does not appear to be nihilistic at all; it is usually considered to be especially humane and supremely worthy of being read by our more mature young people. A man must be a pretty bungling sort of nihilist to be recognized as such by the world at large. People call nihilistic what is merely uncomfortable. People are now saying that the artist is supposed to create, not to talk; to give shape to things, not to preach. Certainly. But it becomes more and more difficult to create "purely" or however people imagine the creative mind should work. Mankind today is like a reckless driver racing ever faster, ever more heedlessly along the highway. And he does not like it when the frightened passengers shout: "Watch out," and "There's a stop sign," "Slow down," or "Don't kill that child!" Moreover, the driver hates it when someone asks who is paying for the car or who's providing the gas and oil for this mad journey, to say nothing of what happens when he is asked to show his driver's license. After all, unpleasant facts might then come to light. Maybe the car was stolen from some relative, the gas and oil squeezed from the passengers themselves, and it was really not gas and oil at all but the blood and sweat of us all; most likely he wouldn't even have a driver's license and it might even turn out that this was his first time behind the wheel. Of course, it would be embarrassing if such personal questions were to be asked. The driver would much prefer the passengers to praise the beauty of the countryside through which they are traveling, the silver of the river, and the brilliant reflection of the ice-capped mountains in the distance; he would even prefer to have amusing stories whispered into his ear. Today's author, however, can no longer confine himself with good conscience to whispering pleasant stories and praising the beautiful landscape. Unfortunate, too, is the fact that he cannot get out of his mad race in order to write the pure poetry demanded of him by all the nonpoets. Fear, worry, and above all anger force him to speak.

How very nice it would be if we could end now on this emphatic note. It would be a conclusion that could be considered at least partially safe in a field that is not wholly impossible. But in all honesty we must ask ourselves at this point if any of this makes any sense today, if it would not be better if we were to practice silence. I have tried to show that the theater today is, in the best sense of the word to be sure, in part a museum, and in part a field of experimentation. I have also tried to show here and there what these experiments are. The question is, is the theater capable of fulfilling this, its latter destiny? Not only has the writing of plays become more difficult today, but also the rehearsing and performing of these plays is harder. The very lack of time results at best in only a decent attempt, a first probing, a slight advance in what may be the right direction. A play that is to be more than a merely conventional piece, that is really to be an experiment, can no longer be worked out at the typewriter. Giraudoux's fortune was that he had Jouvet. Unhappily this happens only once or twice. The repertory theater of Germany is less and less able to experiment. A new play must be got rid of as quickly as possible. The museum's treasures weigh too heavily in the scales. The theater—our whole culture—lives on the interest of the well-invested intellect, to which nothing can happen any more and for which no royalties need be paid. Assured of having a Goethe, Schiller, or Sophocles at hand, the theaters are willing now and then to put on a modern piece—but preferably only for a premiere performance. This duty is discharged heroically, and sighs of relief are breathed all around when the next Shakespearean play is performed. There is nothing we can do about it, except perhaps to clear the stages completely. Make room for the classics! The world of the museum is growing and bursts with its treasures. The cultures of the cave dwellers have not yet been investigated to the nth degree.

The custodians of the future may concern themselves with our art when our turn comes around. It does not make much difference then if something new is added, if something new is written. The demands made of the artist by aesthetics increase from day to day. What is wanted is the perfection that is read into the classics. And let the artist be even suspected of having taken one step backwards, of having made a mistake—just watch how quickly he is dropped. Thus a climate is being created in which literature can only be studied but no longer made.

How does the artist exist in a world of educated and literate people? This question oppresses me, and I know no answer. Perhaps the writer can best exist by writing detective stories, by creating art where it is least expected. Literature has to become so light that it will weigh nothing upon the scale of today's literary criticism; only in this way will it regain its true worth.

Translated by Gerhard Nellhaus
and adapted by Susan H. Ray

Note: This version of *Problems of the Theater* was prepared for publication from the manuscript of a lecture delivered by Friedrich Dürrenmatt in the autumn of 1954 and the spring of 1955 in several cities of Switzerland and West Germany.

A MONSTER LECTURE ON JUSTICE AND LAW

Together With a Helvetian Interlude
(*A Brief Discourse
On the Dramaturgy of Politics*)

Contents

Note: This lecture was in part given before the *studium generale* of Johannes Gutenberg University, Mainz, and was in part expanded later on the basis of discussions with the students, but there proved to be no reason for not retaining the lecture format.

Ladies and Gentlemen,

In all honesty, I think I am lost. Two Swiss gentlemen who busy themselves as professors of law at the University of Mainz misled me, a certain patriotism took me still further astray, and so it happened that I agreed to lecture on the subject of justice and law.

Patriotism blinds men. In their blindness, the Swiss lawyers assumed that I, as a Swiss writer of comedies, had something to do with justice and law; and in my own blindness I assumed that I would be able to speak on a topic with which I have nothing to do. The error of the two lawyers is understandable and is to be ascribed to patriotism only to the extent that patriotism lured them into the very thoughtlessness that is its essence and so hindered their discovering the error. The error arose from the fact that dramatists use all possible and impossible manner of crimes— murder, skulduggery, adultery, etc., etc.—for their subject matter, which fact may easily give rise to the mistaken opinion that it is justice and law that concern the dramatist.

In reality the dramatist is as little occupied with these matters as the criminal is; like the criminal, the dramatist is quite content with providing lawyers material for their rumination and classification. Whether it was a real Mr. X or a fictive Mr. Oedipus who slew his father and slept with his mother does not interest the lawyer worried about the theory of law. His only interest is the case itself—whether actual or fictional is a matter of indifference. And for the practicing lawyer the question is of interest only so far as he can expect a fee from Mr. X but not from Mr. Oedipus. To demand that the dramatist offer jurisprudence rather than subject matter is unjust; one does not, after all, demand that the criminal have an intimate knowledge of the problems of justice and law. He has both the right and the freedom to commit his offense in complete naiveté—with the exception of those criminals whose crime is possible only on the basis of their knowledge of the law, among whose numbers dramatists, in contradistinction to lawyers, are not generally counted.

My own error, however, even allowing for the mitigating circumstance of patriotism, is more complicated. There is on the one hand the influence exerted by a certain inferiority complex arising from the fact that after five years of philosophy and without a degree to my name I switched my major to comedy; on the other hand there is the influence of delusions of grandeur, without which no dramatist can write his plays. My feelings of inferiority in the presence of academicians lure me into trying for once to show academicians what an academician really is, and my delusions of grandeur seduce me into doing just that. I would therefore define the situation in which I find myself as follows: in dramaturgical terms, much like what would occur should Rudi Dutschke suddenly have to run the government.

But let us not anticipate ourselves. In tactical terms, my job is to be comedically academic; that is, as a comedist whose basic material is the story, I have to tell my tale in such a complicated fashion that you, as academicians, will feel you are attending an academic lecture. I shall therefore base my lecture concerning justice and law on two stories from the Arabian Nights. I shall tell them from memory—not with great precision, nor scientifically, nor newly translated from the Arabic with learned commentary, but simply told anew.

The First Story

Muhammad the Prophet is sitting atop a hill in a desert region. At the foot of the hill is a well. A rider approaches. While the rider is watering his horse, a money pouch attached to the saddle falls off. The rider departs without noticing the loss of his money pouch. A second rider approaches, finds the money pouch, and rides off with it. A third rider approaches, and he waters his horse at the well. In the meantime the first rider has noticed the loss of his money pouch and returns. He assumes the third rider has stolen his money; a fight enuses. The first rider kills the third rider, is taken aback when he finds no money pouch, and dashes off. The Prophet up on the hill is in great despair. "Allah," he cries out, "the world is unjust. A thief escapes punishment, and an innocent man is slain." Allah, silent on most occasions, answers: "You fool! What do you understand of my justice! The first rider had stolen the lost money from the second rider's father. The second rider merely took what was properly his. The third rider had raped the wife of the first rider. By slaying the third rider, the first revenged his wife." Then Allah falls silent again. The Prophet, having heard the voice of Allah, praises his justice.

Ladies and gentlemen, the story I have just told is an ideal story, a positive story. It includes an observer, a course of events that is observed, an interpreter who provides the observer with a perfect interpretation of the events observed; and an amoral story proves to be a moral one.

Now of course it is not a matter of indifference *who* it is who does the observing. There is no "pure" observer; an observer observes, interprets, or acts according to his nature. The observer in our story is the Prophet, and what he observes is an instance of injustice. The desire, however, to remain nothing but an observer in this case requires a certain inhuman hardness of heart, for even a slight attack of human kindness would have caused the Prophet to call out to the first rider that he had lost his money pouch, with the result that the second rider would not have stolen it and the third rider's life would have been spared; but that would also have meant that the machinery of cosmic justice, momentarily flummoxed, would have ground to a halt and therefore that Allah would have been allowed no demonstration of its workings, hindered therein by one small human gesture so understandable to us all. Just one grain of humanity, and we would have forfeited tons of divine preeminence. Or, had the observer atop the hill been himself a criminal, he would have stolen the first rider's money pouch before the second ever arrived and so have given still another twist to the story and its standards of justice. The second rider would have had absolutely no opportunity to steal and thus obtain his rights; and to the unpunished theft committed against the father of the second rider, we would have to add the unpunished theft committed by our criminal observer. Moreover, the second column on the account books of cosmic justice is threatened with an even worse imbalance, for as far as the death of the third rider goes, a just punishment for his rape of the first rider's wife is suddenly thrown into question by the shift in timing that could now occur. Because the second rider found absolutely nothing to steal at the well, he would have had no reason to depart posthaste. This being the case, the first rider upon his return would have found two riders at the well, the second who still lingered there and the third who had since arrived. The first rider would have then accused either one of the two or both of them together of theft. Were he to accuse only one of the two other riders, he would have accused the second rider, since he had arrived at the well before the third. Acting on whatever accusations he might have made, the first rider would have to do battle with either both the others or the second rider.

In the first variant, with two against one, the death of the first rider is probable; in the second variant either the first slays the second, or the second the first. In either of these variants, the rape goes unpunished, and in each variant justice is imperfect. Either the first rider is punished with death for the theft he has committed against the father of the second, despite which the second rider's property is not restored; or the second loses not only his property but his life as well—though on the whole the first rider has the poorest statistical chance of survival. Here too: a considerable increase in cosmic injustice—another instance in which it is impossible for Allah to prove cosmic justice. This time tons of divine preeminence are annihilated by the grubby thievery of an observer. Thus we see that should an observer interfere in any way whatever in an event he observes, both the event and its results are altered. Other results are achieved; indeed, many other results are imaginable, not just as regards the riders, but as regards the justice and injustice of the world and so the very structure of the cosmos.

Equally apparent here are the fragility and exclusivity of poetic parables. They attempt to say something special about this world, for there is no need of poetic parables that say something about the world's self-evidencies. But an event that says something special about the world is too special not to be especially invented for the occasion. To the coincidence that at this isolated well three riders meet who, without knowing of each other's existence, are all so tightly bound up in one another's fate, is added the coincidence that they are observed by the Prophet—and the still stranger coincidence that Allah speaks. The incredibility of this story is what lends it its usefulness. We ought, in fact, to ask ourselves whether a poetic parable proves anything, or if it merely demonstrates what can only be proven by means of logic, or, ultimately, if the poetic parable may not simply demonstrate something that cannot be proven but only surmised—and does it by means of poetic license.

Let us not be discouraged by such considerations; let us be bolder still and replace our Prophet with a scientist, with a phenomenologist, let us say, who studies human behavior at isolated wells and who, on principle, does not intervene in events in order not to falsify his results. And if our scientist conducts himself as the Prophet did, the question arises whether he will interpret what he observes in the same way and whether, should the scientist share the Prophet's interpretation of the event as unjust, he too will be enlightened by Allah. Now Allah, when he does speak, does not customarily speak with scientists—precisely because they are scientists and not prophets. It is equally probable, however, that the scientist's opinion of the event will be different from that of the Prophet. The coincidental nature of the event would not of itself upset the scientist. Coincidence is for him a matter of low statistical probabilities; nevertheless it remains a possibility. If it occurs, then it simply has occurred. The events at the well seem perfectly natural to the scientist. Each rider behaves on the basis of his character. Whoever finds a money pouch beside an isolated well and has neither the moral nor the financial wherewithal to disdain it, will take it; whoever thinks he has discovered a thief in a desert region, is himself hot-tempered, and is endowed with the requisite physical strength, will punish the alleged thief by slaying him forthwith.

What the scientist rejects, however, is the conclusion the Prophet draws concerning cosmic injustice. First, the scientist is most cautious about employing terms such as justice and injustice, since they are scientifically slightly suspect, being terms more appropriate to political or moral or even religious matters. At most, he

will characterize the events at the isolated well as a breach of law—
one which, however, is to be disregarded when the well is located
in a nation so underdeveloped that its law is the law of the strong-
est. To the scientist it seems dubious to apply notions of legality
under such protolegal conditions. Secondly—and this is his principal objection—even if he were to employ justice and injustice as
useful fictions that are, after all, maintained by human society, the
Prophet's conclusion will seem to him premature and therefore
logically impossible, since, given a global population of three billion, it is inadmissible to draw a conclusion about the moral state
of the entire population of the planet on the basis of the moral
state of three riders. We would have to investigate the moral state
of thousands of people at isolated wells in order to dare a cautious
conclusion about the probable moral state of the aggregate. Thirdly
and finally—and this is the second principal objection—the cultural level and social environment of the three riders he has observed seem to the scientist to be atypical for a world that is constantly reaching for the pill because it suffers from overpopulation
and to have nothing in common with the cultural level of the
masses of humanity who are more or less civilized and, to the
extent that they are civilized, rush about in overcrowded streets,
and ruled by megalogovernments, live in megalopolises, and work
in megalofactories. In short, the scientist questions the validity of
our model—it is too specific for anything more general to be predicated on it.

Our Prophet will therefore have to permit us to fit his model to
our world, and our task will be so to modify his model that it will
be valid not only for the citizen of a bourgeois country but also
for the citizen of a socialist country. At first glance, it would seem
impossible to fulfill such a demand; in actual fact, we need only
perform a very simple manipulation. In order to ascertain what
this manipulation is, we must consider what factor or factors are
characteristic of the worlds of both the bourgeois and the socialist
citizen. Let us view the events at the well with classically bourgeois eyes. For the classic bourgeois the three riders have acted in
a perfectly understandable, albeit illegal manner. That one person
should attack another, that wars rage among human beings, that
every person will try to have his own way and to increase his own

wealth and power at the expense of another—the classic bourgeois accepts these things as quite natural; he is a realist. *Homo homini lupus.* In order, however, to prevent mankind's egocentric traits from leading to pandemic war, each wolf has bound itself to certain rules over against the other wolves—or, more precisely, a game has been established among the wolves. If, however, any game is to be possible among wolves, security must be guaranteed to two elements: the players and the booty that is the game's reward. If a player has no guaranteed security, he may be attacked at any time by another wolf who has grown tired of the game; if the booty has no guaranteed security, the wolf will turn instinctively to the hunt, since the game cannot deliver the booty.

To transpose now from the vulpine to the bourgeois world: the individual citizen and his property are secured in such a fashion that one citizen can prevail over another only when he obeys the rules of the game, and one citizen can come into the possession of another citizen's property likewise only when he obeys the rules of the game. First, however, the relationships among citizens and the relationships between citizens and the things that constitute their possessions must be transformed into game relationships; this is done by converting the things possessed into chips. This is why the classic bourgeois is bound to money and capital: money is represented by chips, and the capital a citizen has at his disposal (either by inheriting or earning it) is the sum of chips available for play. For precisely this reason, the classic bourgeois sees nothing evil in the task that the money he stakes performs for him. This task is a property inherent in the chips in the same way that certain permissible moves are inherent in each of the figures on a chessboard. The profits that the citizen realizes by staking his chips are the booty he wins in the game, a booty which, thanks to the rules, he may secure against loss. The more differentiated the originally simple rules of the game become, the more complicated the game becomes; the more complicated the game is, the more comprehensive; the more comprehensive it is, the more frequently it is the turn of the players whose clever playing has brought them more playable chips than the others have; the more unequally the chips are distributed among the players, the more pressing the question becomes as to who is really controlling the game. To be sure, it is in the interest of all players to obey the rules, but the complexity of the game on the one hand entices more sophisticated players to cheat—something the less sophisticated notice too late—and on the other hand tempts players with the fewest chips to become free wolves once more, to rob the players loaded with chips and so to get ahead in the game by unsportsmanlike conduct.

The game itself necessitates an umpire, not only that he may supervise it, but also that he may introduce the chips into the game. For chips represent things; things can be produced; therefore chips must be produced as well. It is self-evident that the primary production of such chips can be permitted to no one but the umpire. The players themselves can be permitted only a kind of secondary production of chips, in the form of stocks and bonds for instance, with which they may also play. An umpire must be paid as well. Thus every player has to contribute several chips for the umpire's compensation, with the result that the salaried umpire soon starts playing the game himself and, since everyone is paying him, becomes its most powerful player. At this stage of the game it is no longer possible to discern whether the umpire exists for the sake of the players or the players for the sake of the umpire. The umpire is the bourgeois state.

If, then, we want to modernize our old model, we must introduce the power of the state into it. This can be done very easily: we order a policeman out to the isolated well—but with one necessary restriction. We are forced to add it because we will not always be dealing with three riders only. If we place our policeman at the well so that he is visible to all three, our revised model is much too ideal. In daily life, we certainly do not have a policeman standing next to us watching every move we make in the game. The police are there, of course, to prevent cheating or other serious infractions of the rules, but the effects of such prevention can hardly be calculated. They may be significant or trivial, we do not know; but even a casual glance at the world and its dealings gives rise to the suspicion that there must be an immense amount of cheating the police do not catch people at. The quantifiable portion of police work is represented by the set of persons who have violated the rules and are found out—i.e., by the set of clumsy criminals arrested by the police. The effect of police work is visible only after the fact. It consists in the punishment of the apprehended offender, who can either be fined a sum of money—payable in chips—or be removed from the game and kept out of play for a period of time. This means that unreliable players are, under certain conditions, brought to a place where they may no longer participate in the game. They are put in prison. Therefore, the restriction we impose on our policeman so that he fits our model of classic bourgeois reality can only take the form of his hiding himself near the isolated well.

The citizen of the socialist country, however, will interpret the incident at the well in yet another fashion—presuming said citizen is a socialist, since of course there are citizens of socialist countries who are not socialists but who are required to be socialists. The spontaneously socialist citizen, then, like the Prophet finds the course of events unjust, but for a different reason: it is not the world that is unjust, but the structure of society. The injustice of the structure lies in the money pouch that the first rider owns, lies in the possession of that money pouch; the world can be put in order only by abolishing property. Now property is not abolished by having it belong to no one; property that belongs to no one is an absurdity. It can only be abolished by having it belong to everyone—only then is the abolition meaningful.

It is here that the socialist runs into difficulty. If his criticism is directed against property, then it is also directed against the game the wolves have set up, against the great "Wolf Game" of bourgeois society. The socialist points out that this game includes certain amoral moves, that it exploits the player low on chips and favors the player loaded with them, that in the course of play various classes of players emerge and become established, and, finally, that the umpire is unfair, since his primary function is to safeguard the booty gained from immoral moves. Whoever wants to abolish the great bourgeois Wolf Game, however, must suggest another game, for the bourgeois Wolf Game did not arise out of an instinctual sense of play among wolves, but out of very specific economic difficulties that a barter economy could no longer master. Human beings have a demiurgic ability constantly to produce new objects, to harness the forces of nature to serve them, and even to remold nature itself. This ability has made the human environment so complex and inconstruable, has resulted in such a tangled web' of modes of production and products, that people have only been able to make sense of it by contriving a system of order: the simulated playing board called the Wolf Game, onto which objects and events can be transposed. Since it is no longer possible to abandon this abstract system of relationships among people and between people and the things they produce, the socialist, by destroying the Wolf Game, runs the risk of leading mankind back to a state in which people simply cannot survive. There is no way back from the necessity of abstraction.

When a socialist comes to power, he must *nolens volens* take over the old system of abstract relationships and suggest a new game that can be played on the old playing board. For this he needs a different point of departure and new rules. He must reprogram the wolves into lambs. The classic bourgeois believes man to be an intelligent wolf; the socialist believes him to be an intelligent lamb. *Homo homini agnus.* From personal experience and on the basis of religious reminiscences, the bourgeois considers man guilty per se; the socialist declares him innocent per se and only made guilty by the Wolf Game of bourgeois society, which the socialist now counters with the "Good Shepherd Game" of a socialist society.

This game was originally conceived as a game played by lambs among lambs. Just as in the Great Wolf Game, the personal security of each player is guaranteed, but the booty now belongs to everyone, so that chips produced by the production of goods all go into one communal kitty. The more goods produced, the greater the number of chips for each player. But as ideal as this game of lambs may appear to be, it is equally difficult to implement. The inevitable consequence is that only a portion of the lambs, though quite the larger portion, may remain lambs, while the other portion has to play at being wolves—or, in classically bourgeois terms, a portion of the wolves must play the role of lambs, while another portion of wolves must remain wolves. The wolves are charged with administering the lambs' booty and defending it against outside wolves—for as long as outside wolves may exist. If one day there should be no more outside wolves, those lambs who play at being wolves may also become lambs again, particularly since the lambs who have been allowed to remain lambs, once they can no longer be lured away by outside wolves, will want to remain lambs for good and administer their own affairs. The wolves of the Good Shepherd Game are thus temporary wolves, humanist wolves, good shepherds. Just as the players of the Wolf Game are divided into players low on chips and players loaded with chips, the players of the Good Shepherd Game are divided into the watchers and the watched.

The formal advantage of the Good Shepherd Game lies in its needing no special umpire, since wolves can assume this role. Its disadvantage lies, firstly, in the fact that the lambs who must remain lambs dream of becoming wolves and must therefore be watched that much more closely, so closely that the main task of the wolves as regards the lambs is to prevent them from becoming wolves; and, secondly, in the fact that the lambs who are permitted to play at being wolves are determined to remain wolves and thus often tear each other to pieces in order to establish themselves as real wolves for good and all.

To put it another way: in the Good Shepherd Game, just as in the Wolf Game, the players soon have only the umpire (here, the established class of wolves) as their opponent and are therefore at an equally hopeless disadvantage. At this stage of the Good Shepherd Game, both games have converged to such an extent that the umpires differ hardly at all, especially since they both begin to adopt one another's rules. Suddenly, moves taken from the Good Shepherd Game are allowed in the Wolf Game, and the Good Shepherd Game permits rules used in the Wolf Game. In both games the state has grown too powerful. Applied to our model, this means: we can employ the revised version for both games, since the Wolf Game and the Good Shepherd Game do not illustrate bourgeois and socialist theory but, rather, bourgeois and socialist reality. The social order built by the socialist is likewise adequately symbolized by a policeman hidden near the isolated well.

Let us return to our hill and seat ourselves again next to the Prophet; let us hide our policeman near the isolated well; let us also have our three riders trot up—twice, once as bourgeois, once as socialist riders. The results are perplexing. Now it is true that a money pouch—or, better, let us say a wallet stuffed full of large bills (after all, in our civilized world a money pouch contains only loose change)—is also a temptation for a policeman. Police salaries are often quite modest. A policeman can either resist or succumb to temptation. Should the policeman in our case succumb to temptation, he may either take off with the stuffed wallet or remain in hiding near the well with the stolen wallet until such time as one of the three riders is slain at the well. Then the policeman will arrest the murderer. If the man he arrests is the first rider, the malfeasant policeman, desiring to camouflage his own theft, must also accuse him of having fabricated the loss of his wallet, in hopes perhaps of swindling his insurance company—but it is not these possibilities that perplex us. Let us, therefore, simply assume that the policeman would resist temptation—and in general we can rely on his doing so.

There is another matter that puzzles us even more, for the question arises: who, in a civilized land, would arrive at an isolated well on horseback while carrying a wallet crammed with money? The poorer citizens of a capitalist nation or the unpropertied citizens of a people's democracy out gathering wood—should that be permitted—would arrive on foot, ditto Boy Scouts or *komsomols* tramping about in desert regions on maneuvers; moreover, they have no wallets and if they do have them, they contain no such large sums. Athletes, too, arrive on foot when training for a marathon—but do they carry wallets along for training purposes? Persons out riding for sport? Here as well, the wallet disturbs us. If we want to comply with the conditions required by our model, then only one possibility remains open. If previously these were average riders at a place and time when the customary means of transport was the horse, so now the riders must belong to exclusive social circles, for in these days of the train, car, and airplane only very important people come to isolated wells on horseback, while carrying wallets stuffed with money—i.e., fabulously wealthy capitalists or exceedingly powerful members of the Party who begin their day with a morning's constitutional ride. Thus our Prophet sees himself confronted, all at one time, by what may be a prominent banker, a major industrialist, and an important politician, if this is a capitalist land; or by a field marshal and two members of the politburo, if socialist. In theory, it is quite possible that a major industrialist might rob a prominent banker of his wallet and the banker then murder an important politician, or that one member of the politburo might pilfer the wallet of a field marshal and the field marshal then slay a second member of the politburo. But what would the policeman do? As the policeman of the bourgeoisie, he would in all probability arrest the industrialist and the banker, since his sense of justice would be enhanced just that much more by the sensation such measures would cause. The peoples' policeman, however, would probably not interfere. He would not dare.

But these are idle speculations, for to our great surprise, no bloodbathed Shakespearean tragedy results. It is improbable that in such exclusive society anyone would steal a sum of money that could find room in a wallet, since in such circles the much larger sums required are customarily purloined and plundered in quite different, perfectly legal, and much more effective ways; and it is even more improbable that anyone would commit murder for such a ridiculous sum; for in these circles people are accustomed to using other, but no less effective means of dealing with their enemies. We need only insert the names. It is unlikely that Siemens would steal Abs's wallet and that Abs would murder Strauss, or that Brezhnev would take Zhukov's wallet and that Zhukov would kill Kosygin. These gentlemen have no need of such measures. Nothing would happen at the isolated well, and the Prophet, who, as is the wont of prophets, is a bit naive and who has been rendered more helpless still by our having transported him to our own century, would cry out: "Allah, the world is just at last!" But scarcely would the Prophet have offered this opinion, when he would recoil before Allah's mighty voice. "You fool," Allah would thunder, "what you hail as human justice is in truth human injustice, for these three riders need neither steal nor murder. Since they hold the reins of power, they are allowed to commit and go unpunished for far more shameful wrongs than a simpleton like you could ever imagine." Allah would, however—and here we must amend our story—utter these words only in a bourgeois society; he would hold his peace in a socialist one, where his freedom of speech is severely restricted.

That is the tale of the Prophet and the three riders. In whatever way we modify it, the Prophet always comes to the conclusion— must come to it—that the world is unjust, even if in the last version it is Allah himself who has to explain this to him. Prophets, as we all know, are radical in their judgments. But we are also painfully aware—and for many people it is real physical pain— that such radical judgments carry a certain truth within them. The world is a mess, and because it is a mess it is unjust. This statement seems so patently true that we accept its truth without much reflection. But in actual fact, it is a problematical statement, because justice itself is problematical. Justice is an idea that presupposes a society of human beings. One person all alone on an island can deal justly with his or her goats, but that is all. Though a given idea may be thinkable, the question remains whether it can be realized, whether a just human society, for example, can be constructed in the same way as a machine can.

With exact concepts for a basis, a human being can construct other things about which he or she then has exact concepts. Using such exact concepts, a person develops exact systems and structures for the compass of human thought and its environment: numbers, seconds, the meter, money, scientific instruments, machines, etc. Only man himself cannot be transformed into exact concepts. The concept "man" is a double one. Its usage is both universal and particular. There are, of course, many concepts that express both universality and particularity. The concept "number" can mean a given number and all numbers, the concept "dog" a particular dog or all dogs. But neither the concept "number" nor the concept "dog" posits concepts, nor is there behind the concept that we have of number and dog a creature "number" or a creature "dog" that posits concepts. Only man posits concepts about himself. The problematic nature of thought starts to unfold only where thinking takes place.

In his particular concept of himself, man sets himself apart from other men; in his universal concept he places himself in the ranks of other men. In his particular concept of himself, he holds fast to his identity in order not to dissolve into the universal concept; in his universal concept he yields up this identity in order to become a function of the universal concept. In his particular concept of himself, man sees himself as something unique, weighed down by a particular fate, fully aware that he must die, and often losing himself in the subconscious region that reason illumines only partially: he sees himself as a particular individual. If the particular concept of man is an existential concept, then the universal concept is a logical one. The existential concept is immediately obvious to each individual; in a sense, everyone possesses it unconsciously. One's logical concept of oneself, however, is arrived at indirectly. It must be deduced. It is by it that a person conceives of himself or herself as an individual human being among other human beings, and with it comes a person's awareness of the problems inherent in being one human being among others. Because man, in thinking about himself, forms two concepts that do not coincide, he becomes a paradox. The particular concept that he has of himself is not included in the universal concept he has of himself. Man excludes himself as an individual from his universal concept of himself.

If, therefore, we wish to construct a just social order, there are, on the basis of the human material at our disposal, two possible modes of construction. We can proceed from the particular concept of man, from the individual, or from the universal concept of man, from human society. We must choose. But before we choose, we must be quite sure about what this justice is that we want to realize in our ordering of society. Just as man, however, is posited on two concepts, so he also possesses two ideas of justice. Individual justice consists in the right of each individual to be himself. This is the particular concept of justice that each man carries with him, the existential notion of justice. In contrast, societal justice consists in the freedom guaranteed to each individual, something that is first possible only if society limits the freedom of each individual. It is this latter idea that we call justice; it is the universal concept of justice, a logical idea.

Freedom and justice form the two basic notions with which politics operates, and a political policy is successful at handling the affairs of men to the extent that it takes both ideas into account. If a political policy ignores one of the two, that policy is cast into doubt. Without freedom, politics is inhumane, and without justice equally so. Nevertheless the relationship between freedom and justice is problematic. It is a commonplace to define politics as the art of the possible; but if we examine the matter more closely, it proves to be the art of the impossible. Freedom and justice only apparently qualify one another. The existential idea of freedom belongs on a different plane from that of the logical idea of justice.

An existential idea is an emotional given, a logical idea must be thought out. It is possible to think of a world of absolute freedom and of a world of absolute justice. These two worlds would not coincide; they would, rather, contradict one another. Both, of course, would be a hell—the world of absolute freedom a jungle where every man would be hunted down like a wild animal, the world of absolute justice a prison where every man would be tortured to death. The impossible art of politics consists in reconciling the emotional idea of freedom with the noetic idea of justice. That is only possible on a moral level, not on a logical one. To put it another way: politics can never be a pure science.

For simplicity's sake, we can equate the Wolf Game with the attempt to construct a just social order on the basis of the individual and the Good Shepherd Game with such an attempt on the basis of universal concepts. If I consider the Wolf Game a just game, I understand its justice to consist in the security guaranteed each player and his booty—to the extent that he obeys the rules. Provision is made for the freedom of each individual by rules that allow him to play cleverly but not dishonestly. Justice and freedom in the Wolf Game, therefore, coincide only for players loaded with chips or for those who have hopes of playing cleverly enough to be loaded with chips in the future. For those players low on chips, however, who have given up hope of becoming loaded with them or for those who do not know how to play cleverly, freedom and justice do not coincide in the Wolf Game. These players are free, to be sure; but they are not in a position to use their freedom, so that to them such freedom seems a bondage and the justice of the game an injustice. They tend to place their hopes in the Good Shepherd Game, or they begin to play with a disregard for the rules. The judicious player therefore demands that the umpire conduct the game more fairly or that he make the game more just for more players. More justice is achieved by having the umpire demand higher taxes on the booty of players loaded with chips; the extension of justice to more players is effected by taking care that the players loaded with chips, plus those who hope to be so, constitute the majority. If the latter proves impossible, the players loaded with chips form the minority. In order to insure that the

Wolf Game can continue, they must then resort to providing the umpire themselves.

In such a case, the freedom and justice of the Wolf Game become illusory: the players low on chips are dependent on those loaded with them. Justice and freedom prove useful only to those who profit from them; morality becomes the privilege of players loaded with chips. If, however, the umpire becomes omnipotent by using the higher taxes the players loaded with chips must pay him in such a way that he equalizes the game and makes all the players dependent on him, then the Wolf Game itself becomes illusory—it is a disguised Good Shepherd Game. Because the Wolf Game is continually running into such difficulties, it is forced to employ the idea of a just and free social order—which it had originally intended to realize but which has led to an unjust and unfree order—as an argument for holding fast to an unjust social order. The Wolf Game becomes ideological. A social order first needs an ideology when something has gone wrong with it.

The Good Shepherd Game runs into similar difficulties. It is confronted with a distribution problem. This problem at first seems to be of a purely technical nature, but it proves difficult nonetheless. It is not a matter of indifference to the individual player whether the booty that he wins by playing belongs to him or to everyone, because the booty is itself the inducement for playing in the first place. If the booty belongs to everyone, the game becomes dull, the intensity of play slackens, the players begin to lose interest in the game. The player's very sense of himself as a player suffers, since it is a natural tendency to consider booty as one's personal property. The player has a moral right to his booty; this moral right is a part of his freedom. The distribution of booty that is now declared to be communal property cannot, therefore, take place without the use of force: it must not only be distributed, it must be collected as well.

Whoever demands that people play the Good Shepherd Game must, for tactical reasons, turn to those players of the Wolf Game who are low on chips and depend on other players for their booty. To these dependent players low on chips, it will seem much more just for their booty to be part of the communal booty rather than part of the booty of another individual or group of individuals. I can acquire booty in many different ways. Perhaps I produce a product and demand chips for this product, or as a player loaded with chips perhaps I lend another player some of them and then demand back more than I lent. Producers and buyers, creditors and debtors make up systems of players that can be enlarged in many ways. For instance, one player, along with others, produces a product, which is then transformed by still other players into a product, and so on until the end product is tossed directly into the game by the end player. The booty of the many different players who participated in different stages of production of the end product is payed out by the end player, who gains his booty by selling the end product. Thus the greater the number of players involved in a given system, the less their individual booty. Since these players are dependent not only on the system in which they play but also on the end player who plays with the system as a unified whole, they are dependent and, therefore, unfree players: they are workers. Because the products of present-day technology can only be produced by complicated and often mammoth systems of players (industries), the unfree player has become the rule, the free end player (entrepreneur) the exception. We live in a world of workers. In the place of free end players, moreover, there generally appear groups of players loaded with chips who have a shared interest in the end-product booty of a system of players.

In the same way that dependent players are meshed into systems, the individual systems are meshed into still larger systems; likewise, the players and the groups of players loaded with chips are meshed into a network that makes a fiction of the freedom of the individual player. Everything is conditioned by and woven into everything else. Therefore, if it is suggested that the free individual player be done away with, that the players' system of the Wolf Game be transformed into the unified players' system of the Good Shepherd Game, such a demand has in part already been met, for the Wolf Game has in fact become a game played mainly among the different systems of players. Thus, in many respects the Wolf Game represents an evolutionary development that leads to a tempered Good Shepherd Game; meanwhile, the Good Shepherd Game, if it wants to develop further, finds itself in a crisis. Although it truly attempts to assure booty for all, it must retain the various systems by which products can be produced—so that in this game, too, an unfree player remains an unfree player. He is free only to the extent that there are no free players at all any more. Since the Good Sheperd Game must retain the various systems of players, it is confronted with the choice either of drawing nearer to the Wolf Game by erecting some form or other of free players' systems or of coordinating its various systems into one unified system. Should it follow the second course, however, it would finally melt into one gigantic molecule inside which even the minutest error in planning might impede the Good Shepherd Game, or even cripple it completely.

Although the Good Shepherd Game is unable to free the unfree player, it must nevertheless give him the feeling that he is free: the Good Shepherd Game cannot do without an ideology either. Here the inevitable question arises why it is that people in power—whether they rule as wolves over wolves or as wolves over sheep—have any need at all of an ideology in order to exercise that power, and why people who strive to gain power must base it on ideology. In other words: why does Brezhnev run around as a communist and Strauss as a Christian—that is, playing roles in which no one ought actually to accept them and in which nevertheless the whole damned world does accept them—instead of showing themselves for what they are: men who hold power? Ideologies are the cosmetics of power, but why must power use makeup? On the one hand, political ideologies are philosophies dedicated to perpetuating or transforming political circumstances. Politics is played out on the field of power, philosophy on the field of intellect. An ideology is an attempt to influence power structures by the application of some philosophy or other. Since, however, power is stronger than intellect and is transformed by it only very gradually and indirectly, and since it is the dream of mankind that it might be vice versa, power is always more powerful the more intellectual it pretends to be. Brezhnev the communist and Strauss the Christian are representatives of intellectual principles. Ideologies are excuses for remaining in power or pretexts for achieving it. But power can only be upheld or gained by using the instrumentalities of power: i.e., force. Ideologies, therefore, not only justify power, they also glorify force, and afterwards handle the victims much as a funeral parlor would, putting to rights what they have put on the rack. But on the other hand, the impulse to justify force with ideology cannot be explained on purely aesthetic terms. True, whoever wades around in blood gladly pulls on a pair of boots. But there must be yet another reason why man, who makes all nature the object of his thinking, acts so unobjectively when the object is himself and his concerns. The reason does not lie solely in man's social organization; it lies in man himself.

Ladies and gentlemen, when at the start of my lecture I announced that the lecture would be derived from two tales from the Arabian Nights, I did so, among other reasons, in order to keep you in suspense about when the second tale might finally begin, thereby employing in my exposition the same narrative device that keeps the Arabian Nights moving along at full tilt. The narrative device consists in developing a second story out of the first, a third out of the second, and so on, each beginning before the other has come to its end; it was used for the very good reason that it enabled Shahrazad to hang on for a thousand and one nights. Had King Shahryar lost his appetite for one more story for just one night—let us say on the third or the seven hundred and twelfth—Shahrazad would have been minus her head the next morning; that Shahrazad was not beheaded after the thousand-and-first night was in all probability merely the result of the king's having grown used to her—she had, after all, borne him three sons in the meantime.

Now, I would not want to assert that I find myself in the same position as Shahrazad, though I am speaking before an assemblage of students; but my task is to give a lecture on "Justice and Law" and not to write an essay on the topic. The essay form allows for annotation; it can always be reread; and, besides, annotations lend that certain touch of sagacity. A lecture can be annotated only with difficulty; its effect must be immediate and direct. Its ideas, should it have any, must be instantly clear, or the speaker allows them to remain in such darkness that no one understands them: this latter is called giving a profound lecture. Since I am at pains, however, to give an intelligible one, I have seen no way to avoid providing some annotations to several of my ideas that were not immediately self-evident, since a lecture containing nothing but self-evidencies would itself be so self-evident that there would be no need to give it. In order, however, to insert my annotations, I have turned to the narrative device of the Arabian Nights and boxed tales inside other tales. Thus I inserted the tale of the Wolf Game and the Good Shepherd Game into the tale of the Prophet at the isolated well; and not only that: I also added a tale that did not even sound like a tale, but like a piece of philosophy. I told an abstract tale, the one, you recall, about how man forms two concepts of himself, one particular and existential, the other universal and logical. Where before I proceeded with poetic license, I now proceed with philosophical license, though at the same time I choose to leave open the question of whether poetic license may not result in philosophy or philosophical license may not result in poetry. The truth is, I have only been concerned with using an intellectual construct to give the ideas of freedom and justice a specific meaning, about which meanings discussion can then take place within the context of my intellectual construct. But just as we varied the story of the Prophet at the isolated well, so too the abstract story about the two concepts that man has of himself can be varied. Just as my stories about the Great Wolf Game and the Good Shepherd Game served to illustrate two different socioeconomic orders, the variations on this abstract story about man can serve to set up two socioemotional orders, the one founded on an existential basis, the other assembled from logic.

Man is inclined to broaden the existential, particular concept he has of himself, while narrowing the logical, universal concept he deduces about himself. If an individual were not so inclined, he would confront the rest of mankind as an isolated, asocial creature—a position generally assumed only by criminals. Man broadens his *I* to a *We* with whom he then identifies himself, and he reduces humanity as a whole, to which he also belongs, to the *Others*, with whom he does not identify himself. On the contrary, he is capable of transforming the *Others*, if he hates them, into the *Enemy*. He sets up emotional realities: the more intimate *We* and the more general *Us*, the more intimate *Enemy* and the more general *Others*. To the *We* belong spouse, family, friends, and so on; to *Us* belong one's own tribe, countrymen, race, and so on.

Included in the concept of the *Others* are the stranger, the other tribe, the people of other countries and other races—everyone, that is, who under certain circumstances can become the *Enemy*, the enemy tribe, the enemies who are citizens of other countries, the enemy race. Once this supposition has been accepted, politics puts ideology to work and with its help transforms social institutions, whose appropriate functions are actually those of technical administration and umpirage, into emotional realities with which the individual can identify himself. That is why man is forever being taken in by politics. The emotional side of politics is just as powerful as its economic side: the state becomes the native soil, the fatherland.

To apply all this to the Great Wolf Game: the individual wolf instinctively makes a *We* of his pack; at its head stands the lead wolf, who represents not only the pack as a whole, but also the individual wolf who can identify himself with his leader. The individual lead wolves, if they choose to cooperate, lead a collective pack, an *Us,* with which both the lead wolves and other individual wolves identify themselves. If this *Us* is led jointly by the lead wolves, the result is a vulpine democracy; if the individual wolves are ruled over by a head wolf or by a clique of lead wolves, a vulpine dictatorship is the outcome. For the average individual wolf, the extended pack, quite apart from its organization, represents a superhuman figure—or, to stick with our metaphor, a supervulpine one—with which he identifies himself. The more powerful this superwolf is, the more powerful the individual wolf feels himself to be. To transfer all this back to the world of men: the state becomes the fatherland, for which one kills and is willing to be killed, happy even as the death blow falls.

Nevertheless, the state has a weak point once it passes itself off as the emotional reality called fatherland. The individual wolf identifies himself with it purely emotionally. Should that emotion be lacking, the superwolf once again becomes a mere institution, an umpire whose calls are either more or less fair and whom individual wolves, caught up as they are in the Wolf Game, at times criticize, at times curse. What player ever accepts an umpire's ruling without contradiction? All this puts the superwolf in great danger; his ideology is no longer believed; what was once an *Us* becomes the *Others*, yes, even the *Enemy*. The superwolf's problem is peace. During a time of peace, he must prove how necessary he is; but during times of danger, usually brought on by crisis or war, emotions are set loose that transform the state back into a fatherland.

War, however, is never in serious danger of degenerating into real peace. In the Wolf Game the state of war predominates. During peacetime as well, the superwolves fight each other, while the lead wolves claw at one another and, economically speaking, maul the individual wolves. To this must be added the human inclination, even in peacetime, to construct both a *We* with which the individual wolf gladly identifies himself and an *Enemy* by which he feels threatened. One such *We* is the international jet set, whose ideological function within the Wolf Game is to demonstrate just how far an individual wolf can go once he is loaded with chips. He can allow himself what the vulpine player low on chips can never allow himself: everything. Each jet-setter is proof that the Wolf Game offers the chance to win and win big. This also explains why their society is international; it is the great intimate *We* for all wolves who are somewhat low on chips. Reinforced by an immense industry dedicated to illusion (the press, the movies), these wolves dream dreams much like those dreamed by an untalented chess player sure that he will one day be world champion. In addition to this intimate *We*, there is also a more general *Us* that wolves can be proud of and that transforms their state into a fatherland. The Germans, for instance, talk about "our soccer team," "our Goethe," "our Schiller" (they even have two of these), and we Swiss stand behind "our watch industry," believe in "our Pestalozzi," honor "our Gottfried Keller." This *We* and this *Us* stand opposed to the *Others* and the *Enemy*. For the Wolf Game players the *Enemy* was originally the Good Shepherd Game players, just as for the Good Shepherd Game players the *Enemy* was the Wolf Game players. But in times of peace, the *Enemy* is not the same as in war: in war the *Enemy* develops out of the category of the *Others*, in peace out of the *Us*. Just as for Allah and Satan the *Enemy* is neither Satan nor Allah but, rather, the atheist who believes in neither of them, so in both of these games it is the intellectuals who are the *Enemy*. Both forms of society as they now exist are mere systems of organized power; each has proven such a traitor to the ideology to which it holds fast that rebellions against either of them can only be in the right—which is not to say that the rebels always do the right thing.

HELVETIAN INTERLUDE

In the Wolf Game, the emotional realities of *We, Us,* the *Others,* and the *Enemy* are the building blocks of the fatherland, to which ideology then lends a particular political meaning. And so, ladies and gentlemen, since I speak to you as a Swiss citizen, we shall as a matter of courtesy proceed to discuss Switzerland, examining it as our example of Wolf Game politics and of the contradictions in which such politics become entangled. Every nation has an ideology that is the result of its economic, international, historical, and emotional structure. Switzerland's ideology consists in Switzerland's pretense of passivity. Switzerland is a superwolf that, by proclaiming its neutrality, declares itself a superlamb. In other words: Switzerland is a superwolf that announces it harbors no aggressive intentions toward other superwolves. The effect, moreover, is amazing. Not even the superwolf Hitler made a meal of the Swiss superwolf in lamb's clothing. Switzerland, however, is faced with a dilemma on account of its playing the ideological lamb; since every Swiss citizen is a wolf like every other wolf, Switzerland is necessarily defined as a nation of wolves guarded over by a superlamb. Such a notion is quite obviously an impossibility; it issues in the notion of "intellectual national defense," a most remarkable phenomenon, for if there is one thing that cannot be defended intellectually, it is the nation. A nation, it is true, has more to do with the intellect than many people may think. As an institution it must be administered, an activity which, contrary to the opinion of many civil servants, demands use of the intellect. And if a nation does not wish its continued existence to be meaningless, two intellectual faculties must remain active: the ability to stabilize and preserve and the ability to plan ahead. But its existence needs no rationale as such; if it founders and sinks, then it simply no longer exists—and has no need of any further reasonings either. Whoever attempts to defend it intellectually must either be afraid or have a bad conscience. Both are true of Switzerland. It has a bad conscience because it pretends to be a lamb, and so it plays on the humanitarian feelings of the wolves and tries to be useful to them by maintaining an all-night apothecary, the Red Cross. It is afraid because in reality it is a wolf after all, and such a small one that it constantly fears it will be eaten alive by the other wolves. And so it instinctively bares its teeth. Having little trust in its own bite, however, it soon goes back once more to cultivating "intellectual national defense." Intellectual national defense is the thread on an endless screw.

To be sure, only if the international situation became very serious for a nation would it actually be compelled to employ its intellectual national defense. But since intellectual national defense, like every other national defense, requires drilling and training if it is to function in an emergency, the international situation is always very serious for Switzerland. Not that such a view is so very false, but neither can it be denied that Switzerland is one of those nations which, in order to defend itself intellectually, lives from the Cold War. A very serious international situation, however, is not alone sufficient reason for a nation to defend itself intellectually; the nation must itself be worthy of defense. Thus the question arises: what qualities does the Swiss citizen possess that make Switzerland worth defending? If the Swiss citizen has no such special qualities, the country can go ahead and merge its economy with that of southern Germany and its hotels with those in Tirol; likewise, the basis of our major banks and munitions factories is more economic than intellectual. Therefore, as a consequence of its intellectual national defense, Switzerland must be declared an extraordinary superwolf created by divine fiat, a metaphysical entity, a shrine. And in the same moment, the nation is placed beyond the reach of the Swiss citizen. If he wants, then, to defend his nation intellectually, he must himself be worthy of that distant shrine. He must be an especially noble wolf, a noble wolf whose qualities evolve out of the premises of the Wolf Game: he must be free, obedient, capitalistic, social-minded; a democrat, a federalist, a believer, an anti-intellectual, a man ready to defend his country. These qualities demand more precise definition.

Free and obedient. Like other Wolf Games, the Swiss version is based on individualism and the ideal of freedom, though at the same time this freedom has been restricted to allow the game to function. The individual must be both free and obedient. This dichotomy in particular leads to the creation of the superwolf known as the state, which has all the freedoms that the individual wolf caught up in the game no longer has, though he still assumes he does. For instance, the fact that the Swiss citizen views Switzerland as an independent nation leads him to believe that he himself is free. For him, as a committed Wolf Game player, freedom and independence are identical. The independence of a nation, however, does not necessarily result in the freedom of its citizens. Independence is probably a precondition for freedom as long as there are other superwolves around, but never more than a precondition. Independence makes freedom possible, but does not guarantee it. Intellectual national defense, however, holds fast to the equation, Independence = Freedom. If it did not, the Swiss citizen would begin to ponder his own personal freedom—and become a suspect citizen. For he could then no longer simply accept the equation, Freedom = Obedience, which intellectual national defense derives from the first equation, since its tactic, you see, is to sacrifice the freedom of the Swiss citizen to maintain the independence of Switzerland. This means that the real Switzerland is wiped out to make room for the ideological Switzerland, or, to stay with our metaphor: the Swiss citizen is required to be a wolf in lamb's clothing if he wants to be a loyal Helvetian.

Capitalist and social-minded. Though a wolf may don lamb's clothing, he remains a wolf; and the only game he believes in is the Wolf Game, because only it can give the individual wolf who has had to disguise himself as a lamb the assurance that he is a wolf despite it all. One problem, however, remains unsolved: players low on chips are dependent on players loaded with them, and this reinforces the inclination of the players low on chips to introduce the Good Shepherd Game, i.e., not to remain mere wolves in disguise, but to become real lambs. We have already demonstrated the impossibility of a pure Wolf Game. Just as there is a revisionist socialism, so there is a revisionist capitalism that must pretend it is social-minded in order to give its nations' basic capitalist structure an excuse for remaining capitalist. It simultaneously offers the Good Shepherd Game players an excuse to howl with the wolves. All in all, it is a tendency that is aesthetically compatible with intellectual national defense: a socialist Switzerland sounds bad, a social-minded Switzerland sounds progressive.

A democrat and a federalist. Democracy is one of the great political ideas of mankind. One finds rudiments of it in Switzerland—though it is an imperfect democracy that disenfranchises its women. Democracy is the attempt to allow the greatest number of persons to share power within a given power structure: the majority rules over the minority. But the more complex a nation is, the more complicated the implementation of democracy is. Switzerland, which still retains some possibilities for direct democracy, is no exception. A nation must not only be governed, it must also be administered. Decisions must not only be made, they must also be implemented. Political policy has two components: the politicians who decide on it and the civil servants who carry it out. The more complex the total political apparatus of a nation becomes, the more politicians there are who become civil servants and vice versa. Our present-day parliament consists primarily of civil servants and functionaries, a trend that is further reinforced by the tendency of both the Wolf Game and the Good Shepherd Game to weave, braid, and knot society into one vast, dark power structure. In reality, the parliament represents no one but itself; it represents the people only ideologically. The structure of modern society, in which everyone is in one way or another employed by someone else, works against democracy. Everyone has grown used to being supervised. Democracy, however, presupposes a critical eye keeping a close watch on things. But a parliament made up entirely of civil servants and functionaries is soon tempted to dictate what people should be like. Teenage hairstyles caused Zurich's chief of police to lose his temper before the television cameras; so, too, our politicians demand a standardized intellectual haircut: intellectual national defense. We are to be obedient democrats. Intellectual national defense would have us believe that a democracy that no longer functions is a functioning democracy. Its effect on federalism is much the same. The nation's intellectual defenders are partial to calling their nation their native soil, to sentimentalizing it: the Swiss citizen defends not his nation, but his valley.

A believer and an anti-intellectual. Intellectual national defense, strictly interpreted, presupposes an emotional reality that in fact does not "exist in and of itself." A nation is not an emotional, but rather a constructed reality, not unlike a work of art. It has a function: to facilitate man's communal existence. A function must be open to critical review. It presupposes critique, for if it does not function then its theoretical premises must be reexamined. In such a case, the differentiation between destructive and constructive criticism is as absurd as that between positive and negative art. Either a critique is correct, and thus justified, or it is incorrect, and so no critique at all. But a thing that can be critically examined cannot be believed in. For those people who demand that we believe in a function, any criticism is not criticism but unbelief. Whoever criticizes is a communist or a nihilist, depending on the political climate. But whoever believes in his fatherland and cannot see through it as an emotional reality avails himself of whatever other belief he may hold, especially his belief in humanism or Christianity. He acts as if there were such a thing as a humanist, or even a Christian Switzerland. At this point, Swiss intellectual national defense reveals itself to be a state religion, for if there is one thing that can be neither humanist nor Christian, it is a state, whether it title itself native soil or fatherland. Only people can be Christian or humane, not institutions.

Ready to defend his country. Here intellectual national defense proves what a comedy it is. Though the Swiss citizen is a wolf in lamb's clothing, he must nevertheless continually make it clear to other wolves that he is a wolf after all. This is the reason why any wolf in lamb's clothing who asserts that he is a lamb is punished, even if it should turn out that he is truly a lamb and not a wolf. The Swiss citizen is supposed to believe in the ideology he is fed, not to take it seriously. It is not by chance that those who busy themselves with Switzerland's intellectual national defense also demand atomic weapons along with the intellect. Good old Helvetia would then be left standing in a rather embarrassing situation, the dreadful weapon in hand, but blinded by the specks of intellect she had strewn in her own eyes.

END OF THE HELVETIAN INTERLUDE

Ladies and gentlemen, at this point a parenthetical personal comment is necessary. It troubles me not in the least to be Swiss, just as I would not be troubled by having to be French, German, Italian, or whatever. I am even Swiss with something of a passion. I like living in Switzerland. I like to speak Swiss German. I love the Swiss and love forever wrangling with them. I find it difficult to imagine working anywhere else. I know that I am bound to Switzerland for emotional reasons, but I also know that Switzerland is only a nation and nothing more, that its constitution, its social and economic structure, and the people who comprise it exhibit certain defects. And finally, I know that many of the things for which other nations admire us simply are not true, for instance that people who speak different languages live so well together there—they do not live together, they live alongside one another. To say a person cannot manage without emotions is not to say he can also manage without thinking.

I love Switzerland and I also think objectively about it. There are, of course, good things to say about it: it is one of the smaller nations, and I consider small nations a much happier political invention than large ones—if only because small munitions depots are less dangerous than large ones in the event of an explosion. I am not ashamed either of having taken no part in the war or of having been spared by it. I am grateful that I did not have to be a hero, since I do not know whether I could have been one; and I am conscious of the fact that I owe this good fortune more to the smallness of my country than to any fear Hitler might have had of it, since a functioning Switzerland was more useful to Greater Germany than a conquered one. As for the rest, I am an obedient citizen wherever obedience to the state is appropriate; I obey its laws, I pay my taxes, and my dealings with my fellow citizens and my handling of my automobile are all as correct as possible. It is true that I no longer serve in the national militia. I owe this bit of luck, however, not to any free decision of my own—I subjected myself to no voluntary martyrdom; I owe it solely to my body, which in payment plays other tricks on me. On the contrary, just as I have nothing against the Swiss nation, so I have nothing against the Swiss militia. It is a popular element in Swiss national life and therefore an important political instrument, a bit of folklore, a fraternity that binds the Swiss together—and yet for precisely that reason, Switzerland could afford to do what it does not do: make provision for its conscientious objectors. Those who exhibit sufficient laziness or cunning can dodge military service anyway. The man who openly refuses to serve shows courage. Why then should he be the one who is forced into military service, particularly since he asks to perform civilian service that is no less demanding?

I consider an army superfluous for small nations on purely tactical grounds. The small nation is not out to win a war, but to survive it. Denmark did not defend itself in World War II; and I consider the Swiss no better than the Danes, just as I consider the Danes no better than the Swiss. For small nations, what is decisive is internal resistance, not the deployment of troops. Even Czechoslovakia still has a chance, I think. It is in the nature of small nations that they can be submerged and yet are able to reemerge again and again. Therefore, when I trace the concept of fascism back to Switzerland's attempt at intellectual national defense, I do so not to offend Switzerland nor to characterize it as a fascist nation—just as I do not see a fascist in each of our intellectual national defenders. What I am concerned to do is to define fascism politically, to remove the nimbus that says we are dealing with something demonic. You slide into fascism, you are not snatched away by it as if by Satan. Whoever feels possessed by Satan all too easily sees himself guiltless once Satan has been driven out again. I point my finger at prefascist elements in Switzerland and not at those in Germany not because I want to exculpate the Germans, but because I do not wish to absolve either the Germans or the Swiss; for fascism arises out of the Wolf Game, out of the individualistic concept that man has of himself, out of the idea of freedom.

Fascism can be explained only on the basis of this paradox. Its dangerousness lies in the quite ordinary emotions of its politics. Only emotional realities make fascism possible; and these emotional realities become total realities. The *We* becomes the absolute fatherland, the *Us* the master race with which each individual belonging to the *Us* can identify. The *Others* become the absolute *Enemy:* the Jews, Bolsheviks, subhumans, etc. The freedom of the individual is sacrificed to the independence of the fatherland. The equation, Freedom = Independence, is given an absolute status. There is no other freedom than that of the fatherland. The individual's natural conflict with the state is decided in the state's favor. Fascism is the Wolf Game played to its conclusion; it is checkmate. All the individual wolves are sacrificed to the super-wolf, to the state. That is why Switzerland shows fascist traits as well; in the attempt to defend itself intellectually, Switzerland becomes a total, emotional concept, one that eliminates the very people it actually intends to defend.

Yet another example is found in the ideology of the ideologues of separatism. The "Jurassic people" is itself an emotional construct. There are people living in the Jura region, and some of them speak French and some German, but there is no special people to whom the Jura region belongs—which does not preclude me from considering a separate Jura canton to be unnecessary, but which simply means that it is a matter of complete indifference to me whether I find myself in the canton of Bern or in the canton of Jura. It is not by chance that every form of fascism is linked to a "blood and soil" literature. Things emotional must also be cultic. Just as nowadays we speak of the difference between hot art, where the appeal is more to the emotions, and cold art, which is addressed to reason, so we can also speak of hot and cold politics. Fascism, as an emotional entity, leads to hot politics. It entices the individual to identify himself with an emotional reality; moreover, all his emotions are set loose, both the positive and the negative ones: love, trust, loyalty, hate, aggression—feelings that once joined with pure, emotional, hot politics become destructive, even suicidal.

Before I address myself to the ideology of the Good Shepherd Game, let me set one matter straight: if I have spoken of wolves and lambs in this lecture, it is not because I have anything against wolves and lambs. On the contrary, I consider it an honor that we humans may compare ourselves to wolves and lambs. It is not easy to discuss the Good Shepherd Game, to which we now turn, because it represents an ideology that has been piled so high with a second and even a third ideology that what we are dealing with is in fact an ideological complex. Within this complex, the belief in any one of the several different ideological tracks that may be followed leads to battles over the faith much like those that Christianity has fought and still fights. Whereas the various forms of the Wolf Game are differentiated into power blocs, the various forms of the Good Shepherd Game become questions of faith; and battles over the faith are customarily even more pitiless than battles for power. The Good Shepherd Game originally proceeded from a universal, logical definition of man. Its point of departure is not man as he is, but as he ought to be: a reasonable lamb, not a ravenous wolf. The Good Shepherd Game is a fiction. Arguing from universal premises, it conceives man to be a reasonable creature, an idea that certainly honors man, but does not correspond to him—any more than does the Wolf Game fiction that man, viewed existentially, is a reasonable wolf.

The Good Shepherd Game, however, leads to a difficulty unknown in the other game. Even the most unreasonable wolf can base his emotional realities on an existential foundation. These realities are, it is true, like man himself, unreasonable, but they arise instinctively. It appears impossible, however, to move from a universal, logical premise to an existential *We* and *Us*, to emotional realities with which the existential *I* is able to identify itself. And although man defined in universal terms lives his life under the primacy of justice, nevertheless the dichotomy inherent in the two concepts that man posits about himself forces him to construct emotional realities as well. It is for this reason that the Good Shepherd Game is forced to form an existential, logical concept, a particular universal. That genius Karl Marx came up with the concept of classes. Mankind is divided into two classes: one that exploits and another that is exploited. The exploiting class represents mankind, interpreted individualistically, as a free but unjust society of wolves; the exploited class represents mankind, interpreted universally, as unfree and unjustly treated, while the reason for this exploitation lies in the exploiting class. Because the exploited class appears to be, so to speak, a passive entity, it becomes—if not an intimate *We*—at least a general *Us* with which all unfree and unjustly treated men are able to identify. The Marxist dialectic is thus a dialectic between two concepts, the existential and the logical, that man posits about himself. Its political form is the class struggle, by means of which the exploiting class becomes the *Enemy*. The goal of the class struggle is the classless society.

Even this dialectic, however, is problematic. The Good Shepherd Game must demand of every player that he see it as the only just game. This demand can be accepted by the individual in three ways: he can reason his way to it by insight, he can comprehend it by hope, or he is finally doomed to it by force. The acceptance occurs by insight when the individual realizes that his fate is dependent on the fate of all men; by hope, when the individual is unable to change his situation by himself; by force, when a power external to him uses violent means to set up the Good Shepherd Game. People have tried to legitimate this dubious alliance—insight and hope joining with power in order to change the world—in the demand for a dictatorship of the proletariat, which suggests that the hope of the masses for a change in their situation and the insight that such a change is necessary have to be allied with force, since it alone can make such a change possible.

The proposal to establish a dictatorship of the proletariat serves the tactical function of establishing the communist party, an organization that equates the existential with the logical concept of man. This party can be compared only with the church. The equation of the existential and logical concepts of man, like the equation of God and man in Christ, is a dogma that cannot be proved, but only believed—and from it all other dogmas follow. If by dogma we understand a formal construct built of logical and existential or logical and theological concepts (in which, to be sure, truth may be embodied), then Marxism is not science but dogmatics. Communist politics are politics that have become "theology," the most striking characteristics of which are its cultic forms and its constantly repeated confessions, these latter in formulas that are unintelligible to the noncommunist and whose intent is to preserve purity of doctrine. Such a dogma has the advantage, however, of reducing the general, logical concept of the exploited class, the *Us* construct, to a more intimate, logical *We:* to the party, which battles on to victory for the exploited class. At the same time, the dogma differentiates between the more general *Others*—that is, those members of the exploited class who do not know that they are exploited—and the construct of the more intimate *Enemy,* who are supposed to be represented by wealthy capitalists. Supposed to be.

Like every other church, however, the communist church is a construction of its own dogmas; which is to say, it is a paradox, a manmade vessel into which the most contradictory streams of belief may flow. As a dogmatic construct, it runs the danger of assimilating every emotional reality; and, in fact, communism has reappropriated such notions as state, fatherland, nationality, even race, etc. As in the Wolf Game, the actual *Enemy* is not the capitalist, who has become the *Other* with whom coexistence is possible, but the heretical communist. The communist also demands of his noble lambs qualities very similar to those that intellectual national defense demands of the noble wolves of Switzerland. The noble lamb is likewise required to see his own freedom in the independence of his fatherland, to be obedient and socialist, to be a democrat, a federalist, a believer, an anti-intellectual, and a man ready to defend his country—and, ultimately, in his own way a capitalist, since he has to believe that Marxist economic policies will enable him to achieve a higher standard of living than is possible in capitalism. The Marxist does not have to *be* better, but to *live* better than the capitalist—a reproach made most caustically by the Marxist Konrad Farner.

Contemporary communism is therefore in many ways a logically disguised fascism, a fascist state with a socialist structure. It is national communism, which actually ought to be called national socialism, had not Hitler usurped the term—and how it is that we have come to such a pass is told in the intellectual history of recent decades. The present course of world events is the sad proof of the impossibility of appealing solely to man's reason. People want emotional, hot politics to warm their hands by.

Having rung the changes on the economic and emotional structures of the modern world, we are confronted by some rather grave conclusions. Unable to free themselves from emotions, both the Wolf Game and the Good Shepherd Game require ideologies in order to rule over mankind. The ideas of freedom and justice—in whose name injustice is done—are therefore merely the ideologies used by the social systems with which we are familiar: the Wolf Game is more inclined to use freedom as its excuse, the Good Shepherd Game more inclined to use justice. To apply this to the issue of what a just social order is: because of the emotions inherent in them, social orders are in and of themselves a botched job, not only in terms of justice but also of freedom. Or to put it another way: social orders are the unjust and unfree orders that we must establish if we are to have any order at all, since, owing to the contradiction of human nature, we are incapable of purely reasonable politics. Or to put it even more nastily: there is no just social order because if man seeks justice, he is perfectly justified in finding every social order unjust, and if he seeks freedom, he is equally justified in finding every social order unfree.

There appears to be only one logical possibility. Since we have proven that in both games one institution emerges as the big winner, with the result that man ends up subjected to the rule of other men who manage this institution, we have no choice but to separate the existential concept of man, which cannot be ruled, from the logical concept, which is determinable, and to rule the determinable part with a computer. A computer is an artificial human brain. It is a machine. What an animal accomplishes by means of an evolution that has lasted for millions of years—whereby a reptile, let us say, has developed its bones over the course of time into those of a land, water, and air reptile—man accomplishes, thanks to the machine, in a much more thorough fashion than the reptile ever can. We speed along in cars, fly in planes and rockets, swim in ships. Man is incapable of life without technology. The more perfectly we build our machines, the more capable they are of performing all our chores, including that of ruling over us. Man can be ruled objectively, it would appear, only by machines; he has no choice but to entrust himself to them. Only by complete automation can he free himself from the struggle for existence; machines alone can make him free. Through them, man becomes the complete consumer, the consumer who does not need to work for what he consumes.

What is important to such a person? Works of art? Will we see a mammoth growth in the number of amateur painters? Will there still be politics, or will politics become a farce? A ceremony? Solemn protest marches demonstrating against a computer's irrevocable decisions, the point of which is clear only to computers? Will new sects arise, new religions, because man, assured of material goods, will only be interested in metaphysics? Will blood-drenched religious wars sweep across the face of a world managed by computers? Will the clean-shaven exterminate the bearded, or the bearded the clean-shaven? Will soccer become so crucial for human life that fans of the various teams will hack one another to pieces? Will a new priesthood be formed to rule over men, will the handful of technicians who service the computers seize command of the earth? Under the rule of computers, will mankind unleash a revolution against the machines; will man once again become a Lake Dweller? Are we entering the realm of total freedom where everything is possible: the sublime, the absurd, the humane, the horrible—the survival and the doom of the human race? While mankind tumbles toward its Last Judgment, man must put up with himself. An evolution in this direction puts all else in doubt. Is this the only way open to us? Have we no choice; have we boarded a train that is now moving so fast we cannot jump off? Are we describing the future or the present? Has not modern society long since created a civilized wilderness to which man reacts as if he were a Neanderthal? Man does not comprehend the natural forces that control him; he uses telephones, radios, televisions, stereos, electricity, medicines, computers, planes and cars, etc., without truly understanding them. To him, the scientists and technicians who do understand something about them seem to be medicine men possessing secret knowledge with which they rule the world.

Modern man has fallen victim to the barbarism of his civilization. He has settled himself in this wilderness like a primitive farmer tilling his plot. He sits in an office or works in a factory. He earns his bread by whatever means of livelihood his wilderness civilization offers him, but without understanding the whole, often without even understanding the ultimate effects of his own occupation. In contrast to him, a race of men has arisen who use this wilderness civilization as nomads would, who ride motorcycles instead of horses, who do not live in the culture but wander through it from one place of work to another, from one ramshackle house to another. Rockers are the first people who in their own way have freed themselves from modern civilization, who no longer ask about its meaning, for whom it no longer seems a prison but nature itself. Their protest is aimed at those people who, though they truly believe they live in a prison, never cry out against it. Rockers are a shock to the philistines who, having accepted their fate as immutable, surrender themselves to it.

But let us turn once again to our story, to the Prophet, to the three riders, to Allah. We have not forgotten that in his first answer Allah proved the justice of his world. To be honest, he had it easy, given the wide scope of his view; but later, as things got more difficult, he unfortunately fell silent—and it was in just such puzzling circumstances that we had hoped for his answer. Perhaps he was silent on purpose. He sees us as an exact, not as a paradoxical concept. It may be that from his vantage point we offer a sight just as astonishing as that offered to him by the Andromeda nebula two million light-years away. It may be that from Allah's point of view the catastrophes of man's world— the famines, wars, extermination camps—do have meaning. We do not know. Allah is silent about it all. He does not wish to give us cheap consolation; for we do not stand outside of ourselves, and as observers we are mixed up in what we observe, incapable of total interpretation. He does not wish to console us at all. For Allah establishes his justice by establishing our injustice; his first and his second answers are not contradictory. Through our injustice, the world is justly unjust, and the world could only become justly just if we ourselves were just. From the viewpoint of the absolute, from Allah's viewpoint—whether we believe in him or simply posit him— the justice of this world is dependent on human behavior. The world is what man makes of it. Allah in his justice simply judges it. *Mene, mene, tekel upharsin.* The Allah of our story is pitiless; he is not the gracious God whom our love of comfort would so like to believe in, the God whose job is to practice mercy and keep both eyes closed when we make a mess of things. For the Allah of our story, there is no way to change human society without first changing human beings.

Ladies and gentlemen, I think dramaturgically. This means that, as a dramatist, I begin my thinking process by transforming man's social reality into theater, and then, using this transformed reality, I think matters through. I contemplate the world by playing it out as drama. The result of this process is not a new reality, but a comedic vision in which reality rediscovers itself in analyzed form, or more precisely, in which the audience rediscovers itself in analyzed form. This analysis is governed by imagination, by the experiment of thought, by the enjoyment of the game; thus it is not rigorously scientific, but frivolous about many things—and useful for exactly that reason. The Wolf Game and the Good Shepherd Game are therefore not intended as some theory of liberal or

Marxist economics; they are, rather, comedic repetitions of the political structures in which we and others live. Dramaturgical thought explores reality by examining its tensions and strains. The more paradoxically reality can be presented, the more suitable it is as the stuff of theater. Dramaturgical thinking is dialectical, but not in the sense of a political ideology. Dialectical materialism, for instance, must willy-nilly give a positive twist to its system. Dialectics are suspended, and the belief in the reasonable world that is to come sets in—a lovely twist, but one not without fatal consequences. The system may not issue in paradoxes, because the system is meant to make logically positive behavior possible. Therefore, it has a moral: whoever acts in harmony with the system is revolutionary and progressive, whoever does not so act is reactionary; whoever profits from the system is a shareholder in it, whoever deviates from it is a traitor. And because the course of history must be positive, every conceivable crime committed within the system can be represented as politic, necessary and positive; the result of this mode of thinking is that it allows even the Russians to see themselves as revolutionary.

Dramaturgically dialectical thinking need not fear paradoxes; it can afford to issue in paradox—though, naturally, it cannot then also be purely dialectical. A story told as dialectics must also come to an end. Where political dialectics tries to erect a doctrine—e.g., in a chess game white will be the winner—dramaturgical dialectics represents a description of the game in which it is a matter of indifference whether white or black is the winner, whether the game results in a draw or checkmate. It is the game alone that counts, the themes of its opening, the drama of its final moves. Dramaturgical thought, applied to politics, is the attempt to get behind the rules, not behind the content. Granted, that may hardly seem exciting to many people: the rules by which *Hamlet* is constructed are simple enough, but what a play!

Yet it is this fact that might make dramaturgical thinking useful in politics. It is a corrective. It sheds a different light on political reality, illumines it with the stage spot, with the harsh light of satire. Dramaturgical thinking points to the contradiction between man's thoughts and his actions. It functions as a manual for thinking about reality playfully and critically, as a proposal for the way in which politics ought perhaps to consider reality sometimes: to look to the future without ideology and with imagination, that most prerequisite of talents. Dramaturgical thinking might prevent politics from making absolutes of its measuring rods, its goals, and its adversaries. It might. It could lead people to understand ideologies as mere working hypotheses, which might be replaced more easily by other working hypotheses should that prove necessary. This would represent only a small correction in terminology, to be sure, but prisons and forced labor camps might be less heavily populated for the sake of a working hypothesis than for that of an ideology. In the same way, the word *fatherland* would be replaced with the word *management:* who would think it sweet to die for the management! (Though I grant that in our retrograde epoch, face to face with the superpowers, there are certain constellations that give the word fatherland new meaning.)

Politics could function more critically and more freely in many ways. At present it all too often functions ideologically, and thus inflexibly—or simply cynically. We need only think of Vietnam. For ideologues, there are only the guilty and the innocent. Either the Americans are guilty and the Russians and Chinese innocent, or the Americans are innocent and the Russians and Chinese guilty, or the Americans and Russians are guilty but the Chinese are innocent. It is just the opposite for the dramaturge, to whom the ideological struggle among the three superpowers possibly seems to be a monstrous shadowboxing match, with both North and South Vietnam as its victims. The dramaturgical imagination can only presume that, should peace ever be achieved, the Americans would fear an alliance of Russians and Chinese, the Russians would fear an alliance of Chinese and Americans, while the Chinese would fear an alliance of Americans and Russians. Ideological thinking depicts such struggle as necessary; dramaturgical thinking seeks the real reasons for it—and they lie not only in economics and power politics, but also in the emotions. Such thinking does not try to justify political policies, but to see through them.

All of which is lovely and worth wishing for. But wishing is not political action. He who seeks paradoxes will end up as a paradox himself—and that not simply because the comedist must all of a sudden hope to be taken seriously. As a dramatist, I can only de-

304 · *Friedrich Dürrenmatt*

pict politics when I think dramaturgically; as a political person, which like every other thinking person I also am, I must act politically. That seems to be a contradiction. It is a contradiction. As a dramatist, I present the world as problematical; as a political creature, I am part of the problematical world and so am myself problematical. As a dramatist, I may legitimately use murder and manslaughter as the dramatic means to set a plot going or put an end to it; as a political creature, I stand in horror of murder and manslaughter. I hold on principle that war is a crime, along with many other things that many people do not consider crimes. I have nothing against social institutions that are halfway reasonable, but I refuse to declare them holy and to accept the other whopping half, with all its unreasonableness and taboos, as ordained by God. I consider halfway-reasonable social institutions to be worth reforming. I agree with Socrates that a person's greatness lies in the ability to bear whatever injustice befalls him or her; but for this such greatness is needed that I believe it is my political duty to try anything to prevent someone from landing in a situation where he or she has to summon the greatness required to bear a given injustice. I believe revolutions to be sometimes sensible, sometimes senseless. In South America, for example, I can imagine perfectly sensible revolutions; whereas in a highly industrialized nation with a giant administrative apparatus, a tightly woven economy, and a high standard of living, a revolution is probably senseless. It is senseless because it would be only an apparent revolution. The administrative apparatus would have to be taken over and rebuilt in even more outlandish form. The compromises would have to be such that, ultimately, the revolution would pay dividends not to the masses but solely to the men with the brains behind the revolution—pay them for the illusion of having carried out a revolution.

What can we do? The question remains. Protest? Certainly. Against Vietnam, against the atom bomb, against the dictators in Greece, against writers' being put on trial, against . . . the possibilities are endless. But is our protest at all sensible? Do we accomplish anything by it or are we easing our consciences with the illusion that we have accomplished something? Whoever tries to act politically acts in large measure emotionally. He acts in the belief that he is doing something sensible, even something useful.

We leap into the water to save a drowning person—if we ourselves can swim—without first analyzing whether the rescue makes
any sense. If the drowning person is a determined suicide, we shall
barely have saved him before he throws himself under the next
express train. Our act of rescue has been proven senseless—and
nevertheless we are incapable of acting any differently. We must
believe that rescuing is sensible if we are to do any rescuing at all.
An analysis of whether a drowning person may be worth our rescuing leads to his death, since our attempt at rescue—if it finally
ensues once the worth of a rescue is established—will come too
late. Our political actions often meet the same fate. In our world,
causes and effects are so entangled that we are unable to deter-
mine precisely what it is we have accomplished. The most exact
calculations also yield uncertain results. The individual does not
change reality; reality is changed by everyone. All of us are reality,
and we are always individuals. One of the difficulties of politics
lies in that dramaturgical statement of fact.

Even though my comedic meditations represent only a rough
sketch of political reality, the sketch does allow us to draw certain
conclusions about political reality—although in arriving at these
conclusions, we must take account of the extent to which political
reality is constantly changing. If we compare the planet we live
on—and depsite space travel we have no other at our disposal—if
we compare our earth, then, with a ship, I am perfectly able to
present a description of its division into several cabin classes and
to indicate the various rules and regulations affecting communal
life, such as the social necessity of wearing black tie for dinner in
first class.

This description is thrown into question, however, if the number of passengers on board changes. The class divisions and so the
description of them are only certain if the number of passengers
remains essentially stable. Should the number of passengers shrink,
or should it swell, the class divisions and any description of them
become problematical. If the first class consists of single cabins,
the second of doubles, and the third of ten-man rooms, the class
divisions become meaningless when there are only two persons
occupying each class. Each passenger then has one cabin, with
those in third class occupying the largest; and owing to the pure

boredom of the passengers, a bond is formed among them. The wearing of the socially proper black tie becomes wearisome for lack of society; why should two people harness themselves in evening dress while the other four run around with their shirt collars unbuttoned?

And if there are too many passengers on board, the system of class divisions likewise falls apart. On a normally booked ship, the governing principle for the first-class passengers is freedom. Each has his or her own cabin and is to be left as free and undisturbed as possible. Second-class passengers—and to a still greater extent third-class ones—are more largely governed by the principle of justice. But if the number of passengers increases, single cabins can no longer be permitted after a while; a stricter code of behavior for communal life must necessarily be introduced. Both the single cabin and evening dress are privileges that grow more and more offensive as the number of passengers swells. The imperative of justice, therefore, is dependent on the number of passengers—the larger that number, the less freedom there is for the individual. It diminishes to a point where, with all three classes herded together, all that is left is freedom of the mind. To apply this to our planet: the larger the population, the more crucial justice becomes and the more total is its primacy. The population explosion leads to the Good Shepherd Game, to socialism; people can no longer afford the Wolf Game. The problems posed by the Good Shepherd Game become the important ones—mankind goes into a leftward skid.

An increase in population, however, has still broader implications. Whereas up till now mankind was divided into rich and poor, powerful and weak, and it was from these polarities that politics received its impetus, another polarity becomes conspicuous as the population increases. The economic, political, and social systems that make up a nation can be regarded as a single organization. If the population grows, the organization grows as well. The result is the formation of ever-more-powerful organizations. But the more powerful, complicated, and far-reaching an organization becomes, the more it uses all its powers to maintain its balance; it grows increasingly inflexible and sees its purpose exclusively in itself; it becomes more and more difficult for the organization to examine its own usefulness and to introduce changes if it proves to lack any rationality. The organization becomes a given, an established order; in the minds of its members, it assumes a fatal inevitability.

But no human organization is capable of living only in and from itself; it is bound up with human beings, with their mortality, and so it needs fresh recruits, a posterity that can be trained as a part of the organization. But it is precisely through such training that newcomers are forced to think about the organization they will be taking over. Whoever thinks about something, examines it. Students who, because the modern world can only be mastered by thinking, must learn to think and who, because they must learn to think, cannot be hindered from thinking about politics as well, such students are the weak link in the armor of modern established order. They are in the privileged position of being able to think about the organization with which they are confronted, because they have not yet been fully incorporated into it. Their demands, however, come not only from the intellect, but also from the emotions. As young men and women they instinctively resist the given order, and as thinking men and women they resist that order whenever it is phony. That is the reason for the impact students have when the established order is a phony one—and where do we have a real one nowadays!

But this privileged position leads to an isolation of the students as well. They are not a social class like workers; they must first be trained to be a class. Their freedom consists in their not yet being what they are supposed to be. Workers have been fitted into the established order; they are accustomed to being organized, and so they know how to organize themselves. Their rights are derived from their function as a class. Students do not yet have a real function; their role as functionaries still lies before them. Their rights are based solely on the correctness of what they think. Either they are intellectuals or they are not, either they are scientists or they are not. They can legitimate themselves only by being intellectuals and scientists—only then do they take on a function, only then do they represent more than a generation gap. Their rights, therefore, are founded on the absurd fact that our society, instead of being guided by human knowledge, uses it as it would a whore. If, however, the students slip off into romanticism, into impossibilities, if they lose themselves in ideological hair-splitting the only purpose of which is to invent new adversaries who can be used for windmill jousting, if in the end they confuse necessary changes in the real world with throwing one helluva party, then they will also miss their political chance.

Tactics are important; so too is an analysis of the situation in which we find ourselves. We are not simply the prisoners and usufructuaries of a civilization that deforms everyone, digesting even its revolutionaries and anarchists; at the same time we are also members of the human race, two-thirds of which vegetates in such a lamentable condition that what I say here would be unintelligible to them. There are various paths we must pursue, various methods we need to apply. We cannot exchange our field of battle for another; everyone will have to take up his position where he stands. But we are all called upon to take the political reality with which we are confronted at its word, to judge it by what it asserts to be, to demand democracy from democracy, socialism from socialism, yes, even Christianity from Christianity—it really is getting disgusting to see what all dares run around as a Christian nowadays.

We have established that, whether we wish it or not, the world is slipping irrevocably to the left; that is the trend. And yes, there is a sort of duty to be a Marxist; but it is not a duty to parrot Marxists phrases, but to think Marxism through anew. It is indeed of Marxism that we must make our demand for freedom of the mind, a demand that is anything but harmless. Freedom of the mind is the only freedom that remains a possibility for mankind. It represents a risk, just as every freedom does. Political reality is tested and retested by each individual who exercises it. It pulls political freedom along with it and ultimately raises the question of who is at the controls of power. The chess game does not change its rules when better players take it over. A political system without an opposition is inhuman, frozen within its own institutions. Only an opposition allows politics to retain the character of a game; without it, politics is no longer politics. Marxism becomes a farce when it allows no new political freedoms to be based upon it or no free discussion of what it is that must be done—which is why the Russians intervened in Czechoslovakia: so that Marxism could remain a farce.

Konrad Farner is most certainly correct: it is not living better, but being better that is important. But in a society that affronts human dignity, most people *are* already better than the life they live, since they live so miserably. Therefore, Konrad Farner's demand is valid only for a society where human dignity is preserved. Only then does the commandment "Be better rather than live better" take on meaning. Turning back to the tale from the Arabian Nights, I have but one political, humane thing to say: my highest respects to the Prophet. He is right. He has convinced us, just as all great men do. The world is unjust, and we have tried to draw conclusions from that fact. Nevertheless, I would have called out to the first rider: "Hey, you've lost your money pouch!" Without a doubt, justice is something grand, something unattainable—and yet, with a simple turn of the hand, it is a very obvious matter of everyday deeds. Which is, of course, no consolation. But the hope remains that as the human race develops, slipping ever closer to calamity, it will be forced to use reason. Our curse is that perhaps we have damned little time left.

And with that, ladies and gentlemen, I would gladly close my lecture if I could; that I do not close has nothing to do with a desire to live by Goethe's maxim: "It is because you cannot close that you are great." But I am speaking not only before students, but before jurists as well. My topic is not merely justice, but the law, and therefore, strictly construed, I have come no further than the verge of the first half of my lecture. Now I could cry out, as does the homicidal rapist in Musil's *Man Without Qualities,* "My rights are my law," and, with that not ungenial definition, forgo all further discussion. But that, too, would not be right; even jurists have a right to their rights. I am, moreover, somewhat embarrassed in their presence. I feel like the physicist who is constantly talking to electricians about electricity without ever mentioning, at least onece in a while, all the lovely uses that electricians make of electricity—first-rate street lighting and excellent electric motors, electric ranges and steam irons. Or, to use a negative example, I feel like the chemist who discourses at length and in breadth before a group of distillers about the chemical composition of alcohol without once uttering a word about the deleterious effects whiskey has upon human society.

I will therefore take most speedy flight in a second story, which, owing to the late hour, takes place at night and which, moreover, can be so easily interpreted by jurist and nonjurist alike that it needs no further commentary on my part. My story deals with the usefulness of the law, especially when it is administered by the higher social classes, though it is also an instructive tale for the lower social classes, since it warns them most emphatically not to let their restive instincts run their natural course. You may think it strange that I thus conclude with a story instead of with a moral; but, firstly, my story has a moral and, secondly, I can appeal to no less an authority than Aristotle, since it is said he illustrated his principal philosophical work—unfortunately now lost to mankind—with unusal stories, making it still more incumbent upon me, seeing that I am no philosopher, at least to emulate that great thinker in that much.

The Second Story

The Caliph Harun al-Rashid and his Grand Vizier were hard pressed by the Christians, in that the Christians, who knew how to whip themselves into a battlefield frenzy by partaking of alcoholic beverages before battle, had a slight advantage over them. The Caliph and his Grand Vizier decided to use scientific means to get at the root of the matter, and the holy Imam, a great scholar of the Koran, granted them permission to drink several captured bottles of Châteauneuf-du-Pape for research purposes. After they had drilled themselves thoroughly in Christian battle tactics, having drunk three bottles of Châteauneuf-du-Pape, they began—neither knew just why—to speak of women. The Grand Vizier owned a beautiful slave girl, whom the Caliph demanded he give him as a present. The Grand Vizier swore by the beard of the Prophet that he would not give his slave away. The Caliph declared his readiness to buy the slave girl; the Grand Vizier, strangely stubborn, which was quite out of character for him, swore by the beard of the Prophet that he would not sell her. After two more bottles of Châteauneuf-du-Pape, the Caliph likewise swore by the beard of the Prophet that the slave girl would be his personal property that very night.

No sooner had he uttered his oath, than they both stared at one another in alarm—each had sworn by the beard of the Prophet the opposite of what the other had sworn. They summoned the holy Imam, who entered weaving and reeling, for he too had been allowed to take along a few bottles of Châteauneuf-du-Pape for research purposes. The Caliph and the Grand Vizier explained their dilemma to the holy man.

The Imam yawned. "Great Caliph," he said, "the problem is easily solved. The Grand Vizier shall sell you one-half of his slave girl and give you the other half, and thus he will not have broken his oath; for what he swore by the beard of the Prophet was neither to sell nor give away the entire slave."

The Imam was rewarded with a hundred pieces of gold and he went home. The Caliph and the Grand Vizier drank another bottle of Châteauneuf-du-Pape, and the slave girl was led in. She was so beautiful that the Caliph swore, unfortunately once again by the beard of the Prophet, that he would sleep with her that very night.

The Grand Vizier turned pale, uncorked another bottle of Châteauneuf-du-Pape in the name of science, and mumbled thickly, "O mighty Caliph, you have sworn a new impossible oath by the beard of the Prophet, for the girl is still a virgin; and by the law of the Koran, you may first sleep with her only after rites lasting several days." The dismayed Caliph summoned the Imam. The holy lawyer, awakened now the second time, listened to the tale of woe.

"Great Caliph," he said, "easy as ABC. Call a male slave." The slave was called and stood quivering at attention before the Caliph. "Give the girl to be this slave's wife," commanded the Imam. The Caliph obeyed. "Now the slave shall express his desire," the holy man continued, "to be allowed to divorce this girl. You shall perform the divorce, and according to the law of the Koran, you may sleep with a divorced woman any time you wish."

But the girl was so beautiful that the slave refused to divorce her. The Caliph offered him money, ten pieces of gold; in vain, the slave remained obstinate.

The great Imam shook his head. "Great Caliph," he yawned sadly, "how meager is your knowledge; nothing can impede the law of the Koran. There are still two possibilities. Hang the slave and bed his widow whenever you please, for the widow of a hanged man is without honor."

"And the second possibility?" asked the Caliph.

"Free the slave girl," the Imam calmly commanded.

"She is a free woman," said the Caliph.

"You see," the Imam asserted, "now you can divorce her from the slave against his will, since she is a free woman and he a slave; and the marriage between a free man and a slave woman or between a slave and a free woman can be dissolved at any time—there is no telling what would become of our social order otherwise. And now I am finally going to get some sleep."

The great lawyer was paid a thousand pieces of gold; he bade them good night and departed. The Grand Vizier had fallen asleep by now and was borne out of the palace; the slave was hanged anyway; and the Caliph Harun al-Rashid was left alone with his beautiful, freed slave girl and the last bottle of Châteauneuf-du-Pape.

Ladies and gentlemen, I thank you for your attention.

Afterword

This lecture was not intended as a complete survey of the political realities of this world, but only as a rough outline of several of its laws. Just as in Kepler's laws only a limited aspect of the universe is rendered visible, so, too, in my lecture only a limited and one-sided aspect of politics has been illuminated—and even that not in its entirety. What is going on in China nowadays, for example, if it were to be dramaturgically characterized, would probably demand a dramaturgy all its own—just as Chinese theater itself does.

Translated by John E. Woods

ACKNOWLEDGMENTS

We gratefully acknowledge permission to reprint the following material:

The Visit. Copyright © 1956 by Peter Schifferli Verlag AG "Die Arche," Zurich, Switzerland. English version © 1962 by Jonathan Cape Limited, London, England. Translated from the German by Patrick Bowles. Reprinted by permission of Grove Press, Inc.

Romulus the Great. Translated from the German by Gerhard Nellhaus. Copyright © 1957 by Peter Schifferli Verlag AG "Die Arche," Zurich, Switzerland. English version © 1964 by Jonathan Cape Limited, London, England. Reprinted by permission of Grove Press, Inc.

Problems of the Theater. Translated from the German by Gerhard Nellhaus. Copyright © 1958 by Gerhard Nellhaus. Reprinted by permission of Grove Press, Inc. Original German version (*Theaterprobleme*) © 1955 by Peter Schifferli, Verlags AG "Die Arche," Zurich.

21 Points from *The Physicists.* Translated from the German by James Kirkup. Original German version by Friedrich Dürrenmatt copyright © 1962 by Peter Schifferli Verlag AG "Die Arche," Zurich, Switzerland. Copyright © 1964 by James Kirkup for the English translation.

Der Richter und sein Henker © 1952 Benziger Verlag Zurich. The Cyrus Brooks translation of this work, *The Judge and His Hangman,* was published by Warner Books/New York as END OF THE GAME. Copyright © 1955 by Harper & Bros. Reprinted by arrangement with Warner Books.

"Monstervortrag über Gerechtigkeit und Recht nebst einem helvetischen Zwischenspiel," © 1969 by Peter Schifferli, Verlags AG "Die Arche," Zurich.